T0146999

AN
ODD
COUPLE:

Francis Bacon and Rudolf Steiner

AN ODD COUPLE:

Francis Bacon and Rudolf Steiner

KEITH FRANCIS

AN ODD COUPLE: FRANCIS BACON AND RUDOLF STEINER

iUniverse books may be ordered through booksellers or by contacting:

iUniverse
1663 Liberty Drive
Bloomington, IN 47403
www.iuniverse.com
1-800-Authors (1-800-288-4677)

ISBN: 978-1-5320-5861-5 (sc)
ISBN: 978-1-5320-5862-2 (e)

Print information available on the last page.

iUniverse rev. date: 10/29/2018

What is the ultimate truth about ourselves? Various answers suggest themselves...
But there is one elementary inescapable answer. We are that which asks the
question. Whatever else there may be in our nature, responsibility towards
truth is one of its attributes.

(Sir Arthur Eddington: *New Pathways in Science.*[1])

Contents

Author's Note

As a physicist and historian of science, I had taken a professional interest in Francis Bacon long before I first encountered Rudolf Steiner and joined the Anthroposophical Society. The present study started life as an effort to correct what seemed to me to be a deeply mistaken view of Bacon's life and work prevalent within the anthroposophical community. After many rewritings and reorganizations, it has retained its original purpose, while in some respects developing into a kind of test case; Steiner regarded Bacon as a key figure in the development of Western European civilization, and spoke of him and his antecedents so negatively, so frequently and at such considerable length, that any conclusions about this aspect of the Steinerian world view have a strong tendency to color one's responses to the whole anthroposophical endeavor.

*   *   *

Memories from seventy years ago tell me that the education of an English schoolboy, growing up in the aftermath of the Second World War, did not encourage a wide or deep appreciation of world history. It seemed that the past could be divided into very convenient, easily defined eras. We had the classical period, the Dark Ages, the Middle Ages, the Renaissance and—well, we weren't quite sure when (or whether) the Renaissance ended or what came next. Later on some of us began to wonder whether it had happened at all. Being thoroughgoing monarchists we felt that Oliver Cromwell[2] was a deplorable character—a view in which we turned out to have been justified—and developed a strong tendency to regard the seventeenth century as an unfortunate event that should not have been held. As far as the eighteenth century is concerned, it seemed that the Age of Enlightenment involved far too many foreigners to be of any great interest, and American history was utterly absent from our curriculum. The industrial revolution, however, seemed to be a peculiarly British affair and we tut-tutted quite a bit about the naughtiness of some of our more recent ancestors, while taking a certain pride in the Factory Acts that curtailed their noxious activities to some extent.

The Greeks were foreigners too, but the Romans had actually invaded England, and we read Caesar, Ovid and Virgil in our Latin classes; so history really began for us with Julius Caesar, and ended soon after the time (1850) when Lord Palmerston sent a squadron of the British Navy to blockade Piraeus[3]. We learned a certain amount about Disraeli and Gladstone, but the Boer War of the 1890's was a bit too recent to have made it into our textbooks. The world east of Baghdad and west of the Scilly Isles might just as well not have existed for all that we learned about it in our history lessons.

I mention all this because the following study may give the impression that I am still unaware of the existence of any lands other than Europe and Asia Minor. My youthful impression that philosophy, logic, political science, natural history, physics, drama, art and music were all invented by ancient Greeks, imbibed by Roman and Arabian sages, and transmitted to Western European savants while the rest of the world slept, has long since been radically modified, and I have grown out of the schoolboy notion that whatever global dominance the peoples of Europe have enjoyed in the past six centuries has been due to any innate superiority.[4] The story of the past three thousand years of civilization, as understood by many Europeans of my generation, picks up its trail in the ancient Middle East, Greece and Rome and passes into Western Europe without visiting any of the other great civilizations of the world. It contains elements that really are specific to the civilizations surrounding the Mediterranean Sea, but that is not to say that developments of equally crucial importance were not happening in other parts of the world.

It is of some interest that my teachers could paint the history of the world in great generalized swaths up to the beginning of the seventeenth century without going into the degree of messy detail that seemed necessary in later periods. It may be true, as some say, that the world has become smaller, but in another sense it has become much larger since the days when I sat in Mr. Shipley's lessons and *memorized* the Seven Causes of the French Revolution. Ignorance is a great aid to simplicity, brevity and conviction, but there is not as much excuse for it as there used to be.

Introduction

The lives of Francis Bacon (1561-1626) and Rudolf Steiner (1861-1925), devoted as they were to providing new ways of understanding the world and improving the human condition, were so full of incident, accomplishment and intrigue that it is a wonder that they have not been the subjects of best-selling historical novels, movies and grand operas. Just as remarkable as the characters themselves is the clash that took place between them across a gap of three centuries, which is the subject of this study.

The following paragraphs are intended to give a starting point for readers who are not familiar with Steiner and Bacon.

Francis Bacon—legal adviser to Queen Elizabeth I, and disgraced Lord Chancellor under King James I—devoted the latter part of his life to the creation of a new path to an earthly redemption and a new relationship to God and nature. The *Instauratio Magna*, his heroic, unfinished, possibly foolhardy and, in any case, ill-fated attempt at the complete reorganization and redirection of scientific method and knowledge, was to have consisted of an introduction and six large volumes. In 1620, when he published only the introduction, an incomplete version of the *Novum Organum,* and preliminaries for his *Natural History,* he explained his decision to do so with the remark, "I number my days and would have it saved." At the time he was a mere lad of fifty-nine, and might well have lived another twenty or thirty years if it hadn't been for an unfortunate episode with a frozen chicken. I, at a considerably more advanced age, have the same feeling about my project.

Rudolf Steiner, the son of a station-master in a rural area that used to be Austrian but is now part of Croatia, achieved intellectual maturity at such an early age that by the time he was twenty one he had been invited to become the editor of Goethe's scientific writings for a complete edition of the master's works. As he reports in his autobiography, however, something of crucial importance had happened thirteen years earlier, when he became convinced that the reality of the spiritual world was just as certain as that of the physical. His combination of spiritual penetration and scientific knowledge made a tremendous impression on the people around him, many of whom became committed followers, and led eventually to the foundation of the Anthroposophical Society. "Anthroposophy" suggests "human wisdom" or "knowledge of the human being", but Steiner often referred to his work as "spiritual science."

"Spiritual penetration" means different things to different people. To Steiner and his followers it meant, and still means, something more than the ability to tune in to the currents of experience that go beyond the purely physical. Committed anthroposophists believe that that which is "occult" or hidden to ordinary mortals was open and visible to Steiner, that his descriptions of the evolution of the world and the hierarchies of angelic beings who did the work are very much like eye-witness reports, and that his views of human history, the social order, education, agriculture, medicine and the arts are based on knowledge inaccessible to almost everyone else. This commitment to esoteric sources immediately alienates people to whom any form of occultism is anathema. It is possible, however, even for those who maintain such an attitude, to regard Steiner's anthroposophical endeavors as phenomena worth examining, especially as they relate to the thinking of other world figures.

On non-occult matters, including the sciences, Steiner was very well-informed, as the appointment to the Goethe editorship shows, and he was evidently a compelling speaker. Late in his life, his thinking and lecturing about the nature of the ideal human society brought him under attack from proto-Nazi elements and he found that it was no longer safe for him to remain in Germany. In the 1920's he became physically frail and he died in 1925, after the successful launching of the Waldorf School Movement but before the completion of his last great project, the formation of a School for Spiritual Science.

Our putative novelist, screen-writer or librettist would find that there is plenty of fascinating material about Steiner's career as an editor, writer and lecturer, his difficulties with the Theosophical Society, the foundation and internal miseries of the Anthroposophical Society, and the building and fiery destruction of the Society's first home in Switzerland. As in the case of Mozart, rumors about his actual cause of death are still current and would provide an enigmatic end to the story.

Mozart, however, has been generally recognized as a transcendent genius, and Steiner has not. Membership in the Anthroposophical Society remains small[5], and the Society has suffered from the kinds of schism that often afflict spiritual movements. Its founder was, however, clearly a human being with very unusual powers and insights, whether or not one accepts the validity of his occult vision, and some of the offshoots of the anthroposophical movement have become visible forces in society at large.

It may not be without significance that Steiner, who was born three hundred years after Bacon, died at almost the same age, with a great project less than half finished. The correspondence is imperfect and possibly misleading, but the coincidences of their ages and the states of completion of their work are not the only similarities to be found. People with a feeling for history will not be surprised to find that while Bacon's scientific agenda is in many ways antithetical to the Goethean science developed by Steiner, there are significant parallels in their thinking about the nature of science and the state of human society in their life-times.

Steiner said a lot about Bacon, but Bacon, of course, said nothing about Steiner, except, perhaps, in some realm where his comments are inaudible to us. Unlike Steiner, I don't put words into Bacon's mouth, but I do allow him to speak from the grave to the extent of saying, in effect, "Excuse me, Dr. Steiner, I said that already."

*   *   *

One thing that most people agreed upon in my youth—and, as far as I can see, the situation hasn't changed much in the intervening seventy years—was that human nature has always been the same. The ancients wore funny clothes and were ignorant of human biology, calculus and other useful disciplines, but their thoughts, perceptions, feelings and desires were really just the same as ours. Rudolf Steiner gave a very different picture, in which the events of world history are the outward signs of an evolving human consciousness, and of struggles in the spiritual world for the control that evolution. Some knowledge of this view of the evolution of consciousness, as it plays out in certain aspects of ancient Greek, Arabian and mediaeval European history and philosophy, is necessary in order to understand Steiner's picture of Francis Bacon as the agent through whom forces active in the mediaeval Arabian world entered the stream of Western European culture. Therefore, after giving an introduction to Bacon's life, times and intentions, I give a brief and highly selective history of notions of human thinking, individuality and immortality as seen by mainstream historians and through the lens of anthroposophy. After that, there will be a description of Bacon's scientific method, as proposed in the *Novum Organum*, an introductory account of Steiner's Goethean science, and an examination of Steiner's exoteric objections to Bacon's method and his esoteric observations on the Chancellor's background and influence. Finally there will be an attempt to gather the threads and arrive at a suitable stopping place.

Part I

Bacon: Historical Perspectives

"Lastly, I would like to address one general admonition to all—that they reflect on the true ends of knowledge, and that they seek it neither for intellectual satisfaction, nor for contention, nor for superiority to others, nor for profit, fame or power, or any of these baser things; but that they direct and bring it to perfection in charity, for the benefit and use of life. For the angels fell through desire for power; men through desire for knowledge. But of love and charity there can be no excess, neither did angel or man ever run into danger thereby."

(Francis Bacon, *The Great Instauration*, Preface[6])

(i)

Turmoil: Christianity in Sixteenth Century England

The sixteenth century was a period of religious and political upheaval in much of Europe, and nowhere was the situation more chaotic than in England. Modern historians have found it difficult to sort out and explain the course of events through which England severed its ties with the Church of Rome and eventually established a reformed church of its own, so the following brief summary is anything but definitive.

Henry VIII (1492-1553), his desperate desire to provide a male heir, his divorce, his six wives, "Bloody" Mary, "Good Queen Bess", "Merrie England", and the image of Anne Boleyn walking the Bloody Tower ("with 'er 'ead tucked underneath 'er arm"[7]) became part of English folklore long ago; but the frightful tale of political and ecclesiastical intrigue, plots, rebellions and executions, which formed the background for Bacon's emergence, is still largely unknown, except to specialist historians, as are the actual characters of the successive monarchs.

In the Year of Our Lord 1509, when Henry took the throne, the Roman Catholic Church in England, besides being spiritually decadent, was exceedingly wealthy and powerful, and was responsible for a large annual contribution to the financial well-being of the Church in Rome. As a young man Henry was a devout Roman and received the title "Defender of the Faith" (*Fidei Defensor*) as a reward for writing *The Defence of the Seven Sacraments* (1521) in opposition to Martin Luther's refusal to acknowledge any sacraments other than baptism and the Eucharist. Luther's ideas had, however, gained a foothold in England and became part of the mixture of incompatibles from which Henry strong-armed the Church of England into existence.

Henry's desire to divorce his first wife, Catherine of Aragon, whom he had married in 1509, was a potent factor in the process of withdrawal from Rome. The situation was complicated by the fact that Catherine was Henry's brother's widow and that the marriage had required a special dispensation from Pope Julius II. By the mid-1520's his unfulfilled desire for a male heir, coupled with the attractions of Anne Boleyn, who had recently become a maid of honor to the Queen, had led to his unsuccessful application to Pope Clement VII for an annulment of his first marriage. Regardless of the impediments imposed by Canon Law, things might have gone differently if Clement had not been more afraid of Catherine's nephew, the Holy Roman Emperor Charles V, who had recently sacked Rome and held the Pope prisoner, than he was of the English monarch. Having thus been thwarted, Henry summoned Parliament in 1529 to deal with the matter, only to find himself thwarted again when the English ecclesiastical authorities concluded that Parliament could not empower their archbishop to defy the Pope.

Using every political and legal weapon at his disposal, Henry bullied Parliament and the clergy into submission, and obtained recognition as "the sole Protector and Supreme Head of the Church and Clergy of England", a title that gave him spiritual jurisdiction over the church. A series of Acts of Parliament, dictated by the king, stripped the church of its authority to make laws of any kind, outlawed all ecclesiastical appeals and financial contributions to the Roman church, and declared that "this realm of England is an Empire, and so hath been accepted in the world, governed by one Supreme Head and King having the dignity and royal estate of the Imperial Crown of the same unto whom... all people... be bounden and owe to bear next to God a natural and humble obedience." Just to make sure there was no misunderstanding, the Act of Supremacy of 1534 proclaimed that Henry was the "Supreme Head in Earth of the Church of England" and the Treasons Act made denial of the Royal Supremacy an offence punishable by death.

By this time, Henry, abetted by his new Archbishop, Thomas Cranmer, had married Anne in Westminster Abbey (after a honeymoon in France) and Anne had produced the future Queen Elizabeth I three months after the wedding. The Pope's response was to excommunicate the King and the Archbishop—an empty gesture, since the King and the Archbishop now had a church of their own.

If all of these goings-on seem to be of a sordidly worldly nature, we must not forget that there were also currents of deeply religious feeling that affected the course of events, even in the heart of Henry himself. Impulses for reform had already been apparent in the work of the theologian John Wycliffe (1330-1384), philosophically an extreme realist, whose teaching on universals and determinism[8] underlay his view of the Eucharist and the nature of the church. His ideas, condemned by the church, were incorporated in the Lollard[9] movement, which was effectively destroyed when the rebellion of 1415 was put down, leaving a residue of dissenters to whom Luther's ideas would appeal. English village life, however, was strongly coupled to the church calendar and its seasons and festivals, so that when Henry's reforms, carried out largely by his chief minister, Thomas Cromwell, reached the stage of abolishing Feast Days and discouraging pilgrimages, there was tremendous resentment. Cromwell's efforts to consolidate England's independence from Rome, increase the King's wealth and further break the power of the church, included the dissolution of the monasteries, abbeys and priories. These actions, often accompanied by senseless iconoclasm and wanton destruction, led to uprisings in many parts of the country, fueled both by strong religious feeling on the part of many Roman Catholics and by economic hardships among those who depended on these institutions for their livelihood.

For some time Cromwell was able to conceal the extent of these disruptions from the king, but when Henry found out what was going on he issued a proclamation, later reinforced by the Six Articles enacted by Parliament, forbidding free discussion of doctrinal matters and reaffirming many Roman Catholic beliefs and practices, including the Transubstantiation and priestly celibacy. Contrary to Cromwell's wishes, he also restricted the reading of the Bible to men and women of noble birth. "The Word of God" Henry remarked, "is disputed, rhymed, sung and jangled in every alehouse and tavern, contrary to the true meaning and doctrine of the same." In July of 1540 Cromwell was executed for reasons that are not clear but may have included failure to enforce the Six Articles and supporting certain heretics.

With the split from Rome complete and the succession secure in the person of the future Edward VI, the son and heir provided by Henry's third wife, Jane Seymour, the king appeared to be ready to leave his realm in the hands of a conservative regency council. This plan was undermined by Edward Seymour, Jane's brother and the future king's uncle, who gained control of the Privy Council and became Lord Protector in 1547 on the accession his nine-year-old nephew. The attack on "popish" practices now became much more virulent; all images, stained glass windows, shrines, roods, vestments, bells and plate were to be destroyed or sold. Priestly celibacy was no longer required, chantries were abolished and masses for the dead were prohibited. By 1550 Cranmer had produced the English Book of Common Prayer and wooden tables had replaced the customary stone altars. The idea that a priest is someone divinely ordained to speak to God on behalf of the congregation received a further blow in the shape of an ordinal providing for Protestant pastors rather than Catholic priests, and in 1552 a revised prayer book radically altered the shape of the service. Opposition to these changes was widespread and effective enough to cause the removal of Seymour as Lord Protector. When Edward VI died in July of 1553, the unpopularity of the protestant movement enabled Catherine of Aragon's daughter, the Roman Catholic Mary Tudor, to overcome efforts to have the protestant Lady Jane Grey put in his place and to take the throne herself. Many churches celebrated this event by bringing out their concealed plate, images and vestments and digging up their stone altars.

Mary did her best to repair the schism with Rome and validate her claim to the throne by causing Parliament to reverse the annulment of her father's first marriage. Nothing was easy, however. The Pope, as might be expected, insisted on settling property disputes first, and the reconciliation was delayed until late in 1554 when Cranmer was replaced by Cardinal Pole as Archbishop of Canterbury. Pole's attempt to rebuild the past and to enliven the future with scripture, education and improved moral standards among the clergy achieved only moderate success and the conciliatory impulse with which the new regime had begun was replaced by a harsh insistence on conformity. Heresy laws, brought back from mediaeval obscurity, were used in the persecution of Protestants, 283 of whom were burnt at the stake. This number included Thomas Cranmer, who, after recanting his protestant beliefs, changed his mind at the end and thrust his right hand, with which he had signed the recantation, first into the fire. When we remember "Bloody" Mary and the 283 protestant martyrs, we are apt to forget that the casualties of her father's reign had far exceeded that number, and that "Merrie England" was still the scene of religious chaos and persecution under "Good Queen Bess".

Anxious to provide an heir, Mary took the advice of the Holy Roman Emperor and married his son, Phillip II of Spain. The only offspring of this union was a great deal of trouble for Mary's successor.[10] Mary's apparent pregnancy turned out to be the onset of stomach cancer, of which she died in 1558.

The reign of the protestant Elizabeth I, like that of her half-sister Mary, began in a somewhat relaxed mood—the Queen allowed certain Roman Catholic practices, such as the use of candlesticks and crucifixes—but, with the beginning of the Puritan movement, it soon hardened into the pursuit of strict conformity. Destruction of everything considered idolatrous proceeded again at full speed and in 1559 Parliament passed an Act of Supremacy which reinstated ten Acts that Mary had repealed and made Elizabeth "Supreme Governor of the Church of England". In the same year the Act of Uniformity made Sunday attendance at an Anglican church compulsory. The Puritans were unsuccessful in their desire to abolish the Prayer Book and change the way in which the church was governed, but they did not altogether lose their influence and emerged with greater virulence in the following century. Meanwhile many of those still loyal to Rome went underground, taking their vestments and precious objects of veneration with them, secretly celebrating the Mass and hoping for the wind of change to blow again.

It seems clear that the "morbid elimination of old spirituality", to borrow a phrase from Rudolf Steiner, was rampant throughout England in the sixteenth century, and had already surfaced in Europe as a whole in the tangled relationships of church and state. The gradual loss of perception of the magic inherent in nature, ancient and good, was accompanied by a changing relationship to organized religion. Whatever remained of ancient wisdom in the practices of the church was being dissipated from within by negligent, self-serving clergy and attacked from without by those who no longer perceived the function of ecclesiastical art and ritual in connecting priest and congregation with the divine world. People who still found strength and solace in the old forms of worship, and those who were attracted to the newer anti-Catholic practices were forced equally into Elizabeth's rigid system.

It was into this atmosphere of spiritual and political turmoil that Francis Bacon was born in London in 1561. Growing up close to the

Queen's court and in the Queen's favor, he had little option about toeing the line and helping her with his legal expertise to make sure that no one crossed it; but, being a person of independent mind, he not only published his own views on the nature of Christianity and the responsibilities of the Christian, but also took the risk of counseling a greater degree of moderation than Her Majesty favored. In the midst of these apparently endless disputes his philosophical aspirations were already taking shape and the impulse to inaugurate a new scientific and religious endeavor had to coexist with the desire for a high position at court and all the luxuries that would accompany such recognition.

(ii)

Bacon: a Biographical Sketch

Bacon's family was wealthy, well-educated and well-connected. His father, Sir Nicholas Bacon, was Lord Keeper of the Seal.[11] His mother, Lady Anne Cooke, Nicholas's second wife, was the daughter of a former tutor to the royal family. She was also the sister-in-law of William Cecil, Lord Burghley, who was the most powerful statesman in Elizabethan England. Lady Anne was a student of Greek, Latin, French and Italian, and a mother who took a great deal of responsibility for the early education of her children, Anthony and Francis. It seems clear that her puritan leanings and the emphasis on work, public service and political and religious life that Bacon experienced in his home had a great deal to do with his later development.

In 1573 Anthony and Francis entered Trinity College, Cambridge, their father's *alma mater*, where the Master, John Whitgift, a future Archbishop of Canterbury, kept a personal eye on them. Most of the teaching was in Latin, and the mediaeval curriculum of the *Trivium* (grammar, rhetoric and dialectic), the *Quadrivium* (arithmetic, geometry, astronomy and music), and the three philosophies (moral, natural and metaphysical) was still in force. But the wave of humanism that swept through Europe following the rediscovery of the ancient Greek and Latin authors had radically changed the way in which these subjects were taught. Plato's complete works had been translated for the first time and Aristotle was available in fuller, more accurate form. Relieved to some extent of the weight of theological and doctrinal burdens, the scholars focused on the manifold problems of humanity. "It has been said that mediaeval thinkers philosophized on their knees, but, bolstered by the new studies, [Renaissance thinkers] dared to stand up and rise to full stature."[12] The ancients were not accepted uncritically, and Bacon was undoubtedly aware that Aristotle had been attacked for not being a Christian—some zealots regarded him as an emissary of Satan—and that the received forms of his philosophy had been severely criticized by the French philosopher Pierre de la Ramée (1515-1572). According to Bacon's secretary and first biographer, Dr. William Rawley, "he fell into the dislike of the philosophy of Aristotle; not for the worthlessness of the author, to whom he would ever ascribe all high attributes, but for the unfruitfulness of the way."

The next stage of Bacon's preparation for public service was legal training, but before entering Gray's Inn he was sent to Paris as an assistant to Sir Amyas Paulet, the ambassador to France and another strong puritan influence, and he was still there in 1579 when his father died. Bacon, the second son of a second marriage was left with practically no resources, so he returned to England and took his law degree at Gray's Inn in 1582. Twenty years old and enjoying the Queen's favor, he was already a Member of Parliament, in which capacity he continued for thirty-six years. Meanwhile his legal career flourished and he seemed to be heading for high office. In 1593, his outspoken opposition to a new tax levy landed him in Queen Elizabeth's doghouse, but by 1596 she had relented sufficiently to make him her Extraordinary Counsel. In this capacity he had no option but to play a major part in the prosecution of the Earl of Essex, a former favorite of the Queen, whose long-drawn-out fall from grace ended in execution after a botched coup attempt. The episode raised quite a lot of eyebrows since Bacon had entered the service of Essex only a few years previously, hoping, it has been said, thereby to regain some of the political momentum that he had lost over the tax levy incident.

Bacon's prospects improved considerably when James I succeeded Elizabeth in 1603. A knighthood and a sequence of increasingly important political appointments eventually led to his being made Lord Chancellor in 1618. In 1621, however, at the time of his greatest success and influence, he was arrested and charged with accepting bribes. After pleading guilty he was fined heavily and sent to prison in the Tower of London. The fine was later waived, and he spent only four days in the Tower, but he was never again allowed to hold any political office. In mitigation it must be said that in accepting gifts from two petitioners, Bacon was merely following the common practice of the day and that, in any case, he had found against the suppliants. Yet he accepted the blame and disgrace without making any excuse, and admitted that he ought to have known and done better.

In spite of the burdens of his political and legal work, Bacon had always been a prolific writer on matters of state, law, history, religion, philosophy, science and the general conduct of life. In his letter of 1592 to Lord Burghley, which is well-known among the few people who take an active interest in Bacon, after admitting to feeling old at the age of thirty-one, he wrote:

"I confess that I have taken all knowledge to be my province, and if I could purge it of two sorts of rovers, whereof the one, with frivolous disputations, confutations and verbosities, the other with blind experiments and auricular traditions and impostures, hath committed so many spoils, I hope I should bring in industrious observations, grounded conclusions and profitable inventions and discoveries... This, whether it be curiosity, or vain glory, or nature, or (if one take it favourably) *philanthropia*, is so fixed in my mind as it cannot be removed."

These remarks foreshadow Bacon's long struggle to rescue philosophy and science[13] from the decadence into which they had fallen since the heyday of scholasticism in the thirteenth and fourteenth centuries, and acknowledge that his motivations for such an effort will be open to differing interpretations. One of the fruits of his labors was *The Advancement of Learning*, published 1605, in which he powerfully defended the importance of learning in all aspects of life, pointed out deficiencies in the current state of knowledge and made suggestions for its improvement. This treatise stands out among his philosophical works as the only one to be published in English. The use of Latin in all other such works ensured that they could be read all over Europe. From 1621 onwards his enforced retirement meant that he was able to devote all his time to working on the project that had occupied him for many years—the renewal of learning and the design of a community whose object would be the discovery and use of scientific knowledge to improve the human condition.

Bacon's scientific curiosity led to his death in 1626. Being interested in the preservative properties of ice he stopped his carriage on a snowy day in order to buy a chicken from an old woman, thereby catching a cold from which pneumonia developed.

The financial mess which the ex-chancellor bequeathed to his heirs was a sign of one of his personal weaknesses, a taste for magnificence which he could not afford. This, again, might be seen as a manifestation of his powerful ambition to hold high office and to enjoy the same kind of establishment as his wealthy contemporaries. He seems to have been so out of touch with his actual financial condition that although his will specified all kinds of lavish bequests, he died in debt to the tune of £22,000, an enormous sum in those days.

Bacon's was, in fact, an unfinished life. At King James's court and in his home there were unresolved conflicts; Alice, his young wife, whom he had married when he was forty-five and she fourteen[14], seems to have been having an affair with a member of Bacon's household. In a codicil to his will Bacon wrote, "Whatsoever I have given, granted, confirmed or appointed to my wife... I do now, for just and great causes, utterly revoke and make void, and leave to her her right only." Alice could not wait even one little month and married Sir John Underhill within three weeks of her husband's death. Meanwhile, in spite of his immense struggles and his great capacity for hard work, his scientific project remained unfinished. That he regretted having devoted so much time and energy to political and legal causes, when he might have been giving himself to contemplation and philosophy, is implicit in an unpublished prayer written for his own private use near the end of his life.

"And now, when I thought most of peace and honour, Thine hand is heavy upon me, and hath humbled me according to Thy former loving kindness; keeping me still in Thy school, not as an alien, but as a child. Just are Thy judgments upon me for my sins, which are more in number than the sands of the sea, but have no proportion to Thy mercies; or what are the sands of the sea? Earth, heavens, and all these, are nothing to Thy mercies! I confess before Thee, that I am debtor to Thee, for the precious talent of Thy gifts and graces, which I have neither put into a napkin, not put out as I ought, to exchangers, where it might have made best profit; but misspent it in things for which I was least fit; so I may truly say, my soul hath been a stranger in the house of her pilgrimage. Be merciful unto me, O Lord, for my Saviour's sake; and receive me into Thy bosom, or guide me in Thy way."

(iii)

Intentions

The most profoundly religious among us are apt to try to make bargains with the Almighty; we want to take Jesus Christ into our lives, but at the same time we want a nice house, two cars, a swimming pool, a home theater system, a high-speed internet connection, a corner office, plenty of sex and the very latest in smart-phones. "Give me chastity and continence, but not just now", as St. Augustine reported himself to have said as a teenager.[15] Bacon enjoyed political power and gracious living, and may not always have been scrupulous in his efforts to attain them, but any serious reading of his essays and, in particular, his *Confession of Faith*, leaves no doubt about the depth and sincerity of his Christian beliefs. Even his flaming enthusiasm for scientific reform was held in check by his conviction that science comes second to religion in the whole scheme of things. Whatever the delights and material rewards of scientific work might be, his reforms were to be made in charity to his fellow human beings and in the hope of gaining some insight into God's intentions for mankind.

Bacon believed that the grievous conditions under which most human beings lived, labored, suffered and died were the result of the Fall. Among the items in his *Confession of Faith*[16], written about 1603, we find:

"That God created Man in his own image, in a reasonable soul, in innocency, in free will, and in sovereignty: That he gave him a law and commandment, which was in his power to keep, but he kept it not: That man made a total defection from God, presuming to imagine that the commandments and prohibitions of God were not the rules of Good and Evil, but that Good and Evil had their own principles and beginnings: and lusted after the knowledge of those imagined beginnings, to the end to depend no more upon God's will revealed, but upon himself and his own light as a God: than which there could not be a sin more opposite to the whole law of God…"

"That upon the fall of Man, death and vanity entered by the justice of God, and the image of God in man was defaced, and heaven and earth which were made for man's use were subdued to corruption by his fall; but that instantly and without intermission of time, after the word of God's law became through the fall of man frustrate as to obedience, there succeeded the greater word of the promise, that the righteousness of God might be wrought [achieved] by faith…"

"That Jesus the Lord became in the flesh a sacrificer and sacrifice for sin… A pattern of all righteousness; a preacher of the Word which himself was… A cornerstone to remove the separation between Jew and Gentile[17]… A Lord of Nature in his miracles; a conqueror of death and the power of darkness in his resurrection…"

Bacon thought that it might be possible for true religion and scientific advancement to mitigate the effects of the Fall, but, as the following passage from *The Great Instauration* shows, he was mindful of the tendency for science to be at odds with religion.

"At the outset of my work I most humbly and fervently pray to God the Father, God the Son and God the Holy Ghost, that, remembering the sorrows of mankind and the pilgrimage of this our life, in which we toil through few and evil days, they will vouchsafe through my hands to endow the human family with new mercies. And this I also humbly ask, that things human may not run counter to things divine, and that from the opening of the paths of the sense-world and the increase of natural light there will arise no unbelief or darkness in our minds towards the divine mysteries, but rather that the understanding thereby being purified and purged of fancies and vanity, yet nonetheless obedient and wholly submissive to the divine oracles, we may give to faith that which is faith's. Lastly that with knowledge rid of the poison instilled by the serpent, whereby the human mind becomes swollen and puffed up, we may not be wise above measure and sobriety, but may seek the truth in Christian love."

Let me emphasize a crucial principle: "From the opening of the paths of the sense-world and the increase of natural light there will arise no unbelief or darkness in our minds towards the divine mysteries."

In case this is not clear enough, Bacon adds the admonition:

"That men confine the sense within the limits of duty in respect of things divine: for the sense is like the sun, which reveals the face of the earth, but conceals the face of heaven... And that in flying from this evil they fall not into the opposite error, which they will surely do if they think that the investigation of nature is in any way forbidden. For it was not that pure and uncorrupted natural knowledge whereby Adam gave names to the creatures according to their kind, which brought about the fall. It was the ambitious and proud desire of moral knowledge to judge of good and evil, to the end that man might revolt from God and give laws to himself..."

It will be helpful for the reader to bear this distinction in mind, since it states Bacon's view of the proper limits of human knowledge very clearly.

At the end of the *Novum Organum* he makes a plain statement of what he hopes his work will achieve for humanity.

"For man by the Fall fell at the same time from his state of innocency and from his dominion over creation. Both of these losses, however, can even in this life be to some degree repaired; the former by religion and faith, the latter by arts and sciences. For the curse did not make creation entirely and for ever rebellious; but in virtue of that ordinance, 'in the sweat of thy face shalt thou eat thy bread', by every kind of effort (certainly not by disputations and idle magical ceremonies), [rebellious creation] will at length in some measure be subdued to providing man with his bread, that is, to the uses of human life."

(*Novum Organum*, Book 2, Aphorism 52)

Since references to Bacon's work often ignore his Christian writings while concentrating heavily on his scientific program, it cannot be emphasized too strongly that Christian faith was the senior member in the partnership between spiritual striving and research in the physical world.

"Although scientific discourse and revealed theology were apparently different in kind, Bacon seems to have believed that the latter placed limits in choice on the former. Natural philosophy was not to be invaded by revealed theology, but was nevertheless an activity bounded by it; any theory which seemed to violate the boundaries was *ipso facto* suspect.

"Theological respectability was never enough to persuade [Bacon] to adopt a theory. Lack of such respectability was always sufficient cause for him to reject one."[18]

Unlike Paracelsus and other sixteenth and seventeenth century thinkers, including Newton, Bacon seems to have been preoccupied with the Bible more as an instrument for human salvation than as a predictive tool for earthly events.

(iv)

The Scientific Context

Bacon, who was a profoundly learned man, was deeply dissatisfied with the state of science as he found it. The natural histories recorded and taken seriously by his predecessors and contemporaries and the manner of reaching supposedly scientific conclusions caused him deep distress. In Aphorism 17 of Book I of the *Novum Organum* he complains of "willfulness and wandering in the construction of axioms" and "in the formation of notions; not excepting even those very principles that depend on ordinary induction."

Later (Aphorism 25) he remarks, "The axioms[19] now in use have been derived from a meagre and narrow experience and from a few particulars of most common occurrence; and these axioms, having been framed, for the most part, so as just to fit them, it is no wonder they do not lead to fresh particulars; and if they chance to come up against an instance not previously known or noticed, the axiom is rescued by some frivolous distinction, whereas the more correct course would be for the axiom itself to be corrected."

A brief look at the kind of thing that Bacon actually encountered may be helpful. Two samples will have to suffice, one of method and one of anecdote, but the reader should be in no doubt that whole books could be filled with such instances.[20]

In their excellent translation of the *Novum Organum*[21], Peter Urbach and John Gibson note that "generalization from particular instances… was a standard part of the logic of [Bacon's] day. Thomas Wilson, in his influential textbook of logic, *The Rule of Reason, conteining the art of logique, set forth in Englishe* (1551) provides a typical example: 'Rhenyshe wine heateth, Malmesey heateth, Frenchewine heateth, neither is there any wyne that doth the contrary: Ergo all wine heateth.'" This is an example of what Bacon means by "ordinary induction"; first you bring a few specific examples to support your thesis, and then you anticipate your conclusion by asserting that no contrary examples exist; finally you state your conclusion as if you had proved it. It certainly explains the almost monastic severity with which Bacon prescribed the processes of valid induction. But specious logic wasn't the Chancellor's only bugbear, as the following remarks show:

"So in natural history, we see there hath not been that choice and judgement used as ought to have been; as may appear in the writings of Plinius, Cardanus, Albertus, and divers of the Arabians; being fraught with much fabulous matter, a great part not only untried but notoriously untrue, to the great derogation of the credit of natural philosophy… Wherein the great wisdom and integrity of Aristotle is worthy to be observed; that he made so diligent and exquisite a history of living creatures…"[22]

One of my favorite pieces of "fabulous matter", passed from author to author, is mentioned by C. S. Lewis in *The Discarded Image*[23]; "Sailors, says Theobald[24], mistake [the whale] for a promontory, land on him and light a fire. Excusably, he dives and they are drowned. In the Anglo-Saxon[25] they mistake him, more plausibly, for an island, and he dives not because he can feel the fire, but out of sheer malice. 'When the brute, skilled in ruses, perceives that the voyagers are fully settled and have pitched their tent, glad of fair weather, then of a sudden at all adventure, down he goes into the salt flood.'" Such excursions of natural history persisted into Bacon's time and beyond. He comments on the excessive credulity with which all kinds of fabulous tales are received; reports "which, though they had passage for a time, by the ignorance of the people, the superstitious simplicity of some, and the politic toleration of others, holding them but as divine poesies; yet after a period of time, when the mist began to clear up, they grew to be esteemed but as old wives fables, impostures of the clergy, illusions of spirits, and badges of the antichrist, to the great scandal and detriment of religion."[26] The uncritical acceptance of unattested anecdotes, if not of "old wives' fables", is a phenomenon still to be noted, especially among those who have what might be termed a spiritual agenda.

To find the deepest roots of Bacon's dissatisfaction a little more history is necessary. Like all good students we must go back to the ancient Greeks.[27] This will have the advantage of providing a context for a discussion of a great change in human consciousness which, according to Rudolf Steiner, began just before the dawn of Greek philosophy and eventually brought the Renaissance and Francis Bacon to European civilization.

(v)

The Pre-Socratic Philosophers

The earliest Greek philosophers appeared in the sixth century B.C., which was roughly six hundred years after the siege of Troy, between two and three hundred years after the composition of the Iliad, and about 100 years after the lifetime of a grumpy Boeotian farmer called Hesiod. Hesiod's father left him and his brother a small plot of land in a hamlet called Ascra, at the foot of Mount Helicon, which is the traditional home of the Muses. Hesiod, who appears to have been an introverted misogynist, referred to Ascra as a cursed place, cruel in winter, hard in summer, and never pleasant, and spent his long winter evenings writing the poetry from which later Greek writers derived a great deal of their mythology. His *Theogony* concerns the origins of the world and of the gods, and shows a special interest in their family relations. According to the fifth century historian Herodotus, Hesiod's retelling of the old stories became the generally accepted version.

Against the mythological background provided by Homer and Hesiod we can place a little political history. Around 1000 B.C., Greek colonists, driven from the mainland by the Dorians, established colonies in Ionia, on the west coast of what is now Turkey. In spite of several invasions, which culminated in occupation by the Persians in 546 BC, their twelve cities remained prosperous. These included Miletus, Samos, Ephesus and Colophon, places that some rather well known people came from or went to, including St. Paul. The Ionian revolt against King Darius I in 500 B.C. precipitated the Persian Wars. While all this was going on, Greek philosophy is traditionally supposed to have begun in 585 B.C., when Thales of Miletus correctly forecast an eclipse of the sun. What makes the Greek philosophy of this period so striking, however, is not that people were suddenly able to perform such mathematical feats as predicting eclipses. The Babylonian astronomers had been doing that for centuries. Later on, when Aristotle referred to the new philosophers as physicists, he meant that they had studied everything that happens in the natural world. The Babylonians had worked for the most part with purely mathematical relations, like the rhythms of the solar system, but the Greeks got into the deepest philosophical questions. How and why did the universe begin? What is it made of and how does it work?

Old farmer Hesiod had answered some of these questions before, and had done so in terms of the creative deeds of gods. Many of the stories appear to have reached us in corrupt forms, so it is not surprising that some of the activities of the Olympian Pantheon do not seem particularly godlike. When Xenophanes of Colophon (c.570—c.475 BC) complained that Homer and Hesiod attributed to the gods all the things that among men are regarded as shameful and blameworthy, including theft, adultery and deception, he did so on the ground of impiety. But he might himself have been charged with impiety, for he actually rejected the whole pantheon of anthropomorphic gods in favor of a single great god who perceives and works through the sheer power of thought.

Xenophanes was not alone in dismissing the Olympian deities in favor of something less personal, more reliable and more intellectual. Although they differed radically with one another in their interpretations of the structure of the world, the pre-Socratics generally agreed that *it is lawful and that its processes can be understood.* History is not a one-damn-thing-after-another sequence of unrelated events, and nature is not just a playground for a troupe of whimsical gods. The very word, *Kosmos,* used by Heraclitus where we would say *Universe,* means an arrangement that is not only orderly, but beautiful too[28]. This does not mean that the pre-Socratics were atheists—only that they wanted nature to be self-explanatory and God, or the gods, to be rational and not to interfere too much.

The word *self-explanatory* is important in this context. Science, we like to say, is based on observation, but the modern idea of scientific observation is very different from the ancient one. Unlike Francis Bacon, who declared that his natural philosophy should be "not only of Nature free and untrammelled... but much more of nature constrained and vexed"[29], the Greek philosophers took the world very much as they found it and let it speak to them as it would. Some of them, furthermore, had great difficulty in believing what it said. For Parmenides of Elea (born c. 519 BC), the brave new world of thinking superseded all other experience. I'm not sure that he ever stated the so-called Principle of Intelligibility explicitly—*Nothing can be which cannot be thought*—but it is so clearly evident in his philosophy that it has become associated with his name[30]. His view that the only dependable reality lay in the world of thought, and that the world of sense perception was one of illusion, seems extreme to us; according to him, creation and dissolution are impossible and the world must be regarded as a single, eternal, unchangeable object. This makes any recognizable form of science impossible.

Melissus of Samos and Zeno of Elea, the two philosophers usually grouped with Parmenides as members of the Eleatic School, adopted this view of the cosmos. Whereas Parmenides had expressed his philosophy in obscure poetry, Melissus put its essence into plain prose and added some thoughts of his own. The following brief sample, from a discussion of the apparent and deceptive multiplicity of objects in the world, includes two striking comments:

"…Things look different to us every time we see them. So clearly we do not see them correctly, and the apparent existence of all these different things is an illusion. For if they were true reality, they would not change, but each would be as it had always seemed to be: for nothing is stronger than what is true…"

We do not see correctly and *nothing is stronger than what is true.* The latter principle could be taken as a motto for the whole Greek philosophical endeavor. The belief that soundly argued philosophical conclusions are compulsory, whatever the appearances, continued for many centuries, in spite of the contradictions which frequently arose between different schools and individuals. Truth, it seems, wears many faces.

* * *

Parmenides and his followers didn't have it all their own way. Heraclitus (fl. 500 BC), the 'obscure' and the 'riddler', who came from Ephesus and regarded fire as the fundamental process of the universe, thought that change was the world's only constant characteristic. That, at least, is what is often said but, as usual with Greek philosophy, things are not quite so straightforward. Diogenes Laertius, writing about 200 AD, reports that Euripides gave Socrates a copy of Heraclitus' book and asked him what he thought of it. He replied: "What I understand is splendid; and I think that what I don't understand is too—but it would take a Delian diver to get to the bottom of it."

Hippolytus, a much later historian, gives a sample: "Heraclitus says that the universe is divisible and indivisible, generated and ungenerated, mortal and immortal, Word and Eternity, Father and Son, God and Justice. He praises and admires the unseen part of his [God's] power above the known part. That he is visible to men and not undiscoverable he says in the following words: 'I honor more those things which are learned by sight and hearing…' " No wonder that Socrates was baffled and Parmenides, like Averroes[31] and Aquinas more than a millennium and a half later, felt it necessary to state quite forcefully that contraries cannot be simultaneously true. Modern readers may well feel that they have even more reason for bafflement than Socrates. It is generally agreed, however, that Heraclitus believed that the world is in a state of continuous change and that it is possible to use one's senses and intelligence to understand the way things work, although most people do not do so. The world views of Parmenides and of Heraclitus could hardly have been in more extreme contradiction.

Democritus, who was born in Abdera in the north of Greece, probably around 460 BC, was a hugely prolific author on atomism[32], science, literature, the nature of knowledge, and ethics. All his writings are lost, but his philosophy of atomism, which has been represented as an attempt to reconcile the philosophy of permanence with the perception of change[33], was preserved by the Epicureans and became influential in Western European thought. Aristotle's book on Democritus has not survived, but Simplicius[34] quotes an enlightening fragment from it. After bringing out the idea of an infinite number of permanent particles situated in an infinite void, Aristotle continues:

"Democritus thinks that the particles are too small to be individually visible, and that they have many different shapes and sizes… The atoms mingle together in the void, and as they move about they collide and stick together in a cluster. This does not, however, truly produce a new, single substance, for two or more things can never become one…"

This gives some justification for placing Democritus in the camp of Parmenides, rather than that of Heraclitus. The appearance of change is genuine, but it *is* only an appearance. The great drawback of the theory, in the eyes of Parmenides and Melissus, was that void, or non-being, was an essential part of it. Obviously the atoms had to have something to move about in, but to the Eleatics this necessitated the unacceptable tactic of treating *non-being* as a form of *being*, or in other words, nothing as something. Perhaps the most distressing difficulty, however, concerns the question of whether it is really possible to know anything at all. The problem is stated briefly by Galen, the physician, who lived in the second century AD and was deeply interested in the philosophy of science:

"The greatest charge against any argument is that it conflicts with what is evident. For arguments cannot even start without evidence: how then can they be credible if they attack that from which they took their beginnings? Democritus too was aware of this; for when he had brought charges against the senses, saying, 'By convention color, by convention sweet, by convention bitter; in reality atoms and void', he had the senses reply to the intellect as follows: 'Poor mind, do you take your evidence from us and then try to overthrow us? Our overthrow is your fall.'

"So one should condemn the unreliability of an argument which is so bad that its most persuasive part conflicts with the evident propositions from which it took its start."

Sextus Empiricus, who flourished in the third century AD and seems to have been the greatest living authority on Scepticism, echoed Galen's critique:

"Democritus sometimes does away with what appears to be the senses and says that nothing of this sort appears in truth, but only in opinion; truth among the things that exist lying in the fact that there are atoms and void. For he says, 'By convention sweet and by convention bitter, by convention hot and by convention cold, by convention colour: in reality atoms and void.' That is to say, sense perceptions are thought and believed to exist but they do not exist in truth—only atoms and void do... We really know nothing about anything...' He does away in effect with all knowledge, even if it is only the senses which he explicitly attacks. But in the *Rules* he says that there are two forms of knowledge, one by way of the senses and the other by way of the understanding. The one by way of the understanding he calls genuine, considering it to be a reliable guide in the search for truth; the one by way of the senses he names dark, denying that it is unerring with regard to the discernment of what is true."

So, by way of an atomic theory which seems to have been designed to overcome a philosophical *impasse*, Democritus leads us back more or less to square one and places us firmly in the arms of Parmenides and Melissus. We arrive at what is true by means of reason, ignoring the deceptive claims of our senses.

Galen's cyclical argument has often been repeated; it is stated most persuasively in J. B. S. Haldane's *Possible Worlds*[35].

"If my mental processes are determined wholly by the motions of atoms in my brain, I have no reason to suppose that my beliefs are true... and hence I have no reason for supposing my brain to be composed of atoms."

This problem, fundamental to physical science, provides a link with Rudolf Steiner and the nineteenth century. The effort to explain and connect all phenomena, including physiological sensations, by means of what Steiner characterized as an abstract substratum of auxiliary concepts, like atoms, light waves and energy, resulted in a tendency to dismiss those sensations as purely subjective. Steiner, like Galen, found this tendency very objectionable.

"It is these reflections that compelled me to reject as impossible every theory of nature which, in principle, extends beyond the domain of the perceived world, and to seek in the sense-world the sole object of consideration for natural science."[36] "The theory must be limited to the perceptible and must seek connections within this."[37]

* * *

Why have I spent so much time on the pre-Socratics and their problems? One reason is that the significance of the emergence of philosophy in the ancient world, as understood in terms of Steiner's view of evolution, will become clear in Section (viii). Others are that Bacon thought far more highly of the pre-Socratics than he did of Aristotle, that his relationship to the atom is of great interest and that in his *Novum Organum* he refers specifically to the problem of knowledge as understood by the Greek philosophers; and yet another is that Steiner's insight into the ancient problem of knowledge became one of the starting points for his development of Goethean science.

(vi)

Aristotle to Bacon to Steiner[38]

According to Bacon, Aristotle was "far more anxious about how anyone delivering an opinion should explain himself" than about the "inner truth of things." (*Novum Organum*, Aphorism 63)

"For the Homoiomera of Anaxagoras, the atoms of Leucippus and Democritus, the heaven and earth of Parmenides, the strife and friendship of Empedocles, the resolution of bodies into the undifferentiated nature of fire and their refashioning into solids, as held by Heraclitus, all have something in them of the natural philosopher and a taste for the things of nature and experience... Whereas in Aristotle's Physics you hear little but the words of dialectic; and in his Metaphysics too, under a more imposing name and more evidently as a realist than as a nominalist[39], he has gone over the same ground again.

"Nor should it count for much that in his essays On Animals and in his Problems and other treatises he often cites experiments. For he had come to his conclusions beforehand, without taking proper account of experience in setting up his decisions and axioms; but after laying down the law according to his own judgement, he then brings in experience, twisted to fit in with his own ideas, and leads it about like a captive."

One thing that Bacon seems not to have considered is that he and Aristotle faced somewhat similar situations. Each found the science of his time in a state of confusion, although for entirely different reasons. Early Greek philosophy was bursting with energy in the exercise of newly emerging patterns of thinking, whereas late mediaeval and Renaissance science seemed to Bacon to be exhausted and decadent. Steiner's view of the situation is presented in the Hodder and Stoughton edition of Steiner's *The Redemption of Thinking*[40]. According to Canon A. P. Shepherd and Mildred Robertson Nicoll, who edited and annotated this volume,

Aristotle "knew that for him and for mankind in general the source of human ideas must be in the human mind itself, arising out of man's own physical experience and his contemplation of sense phenomena. He therefore devised for this purpose a system of logic..." In other words, "Away with all that stuff about the falsity of the sense world and the impossibility of really knowing anything! The worlds of thinking and sense perception must work together. The book of nature is open to you; you just have to learn to read it correctly."

For almost two millennia many philosophers did their best to follow Aristotle, but by the fifteenth century the impulse had entered a period of stagnation—hence the mess that Bacon encountered. In *The Redemption of Thinking*, Steiner sums up Bacon's position in a way that invites comparison with Canon Shepherd's assessment of Aristotle's intentions:

"With [Bacon], Nominalism has become such a thoroughgoing and avowed philosophy that he says: 'We must sweep away man's false belief in a reality which is, in point of fact, nothing but a *name*. Reality presents itself to us only when we look out on the world of the senses. The senses alone provide us with realities, the realities of empirical knowledge.'"

A further comparison, this time with Steiner's words from the Goethe prefaces, shows that there is great potential for confusion[41] in his views of Aristotelian, Baconian and Goethean science:

"The theory must be limited to the perceptible and must seek connections within this."

To make this clear, and to give a taste of what is to come in later stages of this study, I isolate the key phrases.

Aristotle, according to Steiner, *via* Shepherd and Nicoll: *the source of human ideas must be in the human mind itself, arising out of man's own physical experience and his contemplation of sense phenomena.*

Bacon, according to Steiner: *The senses alone provide us with realities, the realities of empirical knowledge.*

Steiner, on Goethean science: *...to seek in the sense-world the sole object of consideration for natural science. The theory must be limited to the perceptible and must seek connections within this.*

How odd that what sounds like the same fundamental idea should give rise to three such different views of the world! Well, perhaps not; it will be seen later that things look rather different when Bacon is allowed to speak for himself.

* * *

According to Steiner, Bacon did not realize that different soul energies are predominantly active in different ages—a dark saying, the meaning of which may become clearer with further examination of Steiner's view of human evolution—but that Bacon did feel, correctly, that the methods of Aristotle could no longer be used.[42] Aristotle's scientific work appeared to Bacon as a conglomeration of specious proofs and conveniently chosen supporting observations. It was Aristotle, moreover, who provided the major philosophical impulse for the scholastics of the late Middle Ages, for whom Bacon had so little respect.

In Bacon's time the mediaeval ethos still clung to science, as it did to the arts—why write a new story, or a new song, when there were so many oldies but goodies waiting to be brushed up for current consumption? Furthermore, as C. S. Lewis (in *The Discarded Image*) points out, beyond a liking for rhetoric, parables and proverbs, there was another reason for the acceptance of all kinds of tales of strange creatures in remote regions and of ordinary beasts behaving with oddly human motivations—in other words, tales of the kind that met with Bacon's strong disapproval.

"If, as Platonism taught—nor would Browne[43] have dissented—the visible world is made after an invisible pattern, if things below the Moon are all derived from things above her, the expectation that an analogical or moral sense will have been built into the nature and behaviour of creatures will not be *a priori* unreasonable. To us an account of animal behaviour would seem improbable if it suggested too obvious a moral. Not so to them. Their premises were different."

* * *

So far, I have provided a backdrop for the entrance of Bacon's plan for the reorientation and reorganization of philosophy in general and science in particular—the *Novum Organum*. Rudolf Steiner provided another, quite different background, which I now outline before coming to the *Novum Organum* itself.

Part II

Steiner: Karma, Consciousness and Bacon

"The study of problems connected with karma is by no means easy and discussion of anything that has to do with this subject entails — or ought at any rate to entail — a sense of deep responsibility. Such study is in truth a matter of penetrating into the most profound relationships of existence, for within the sphere of karma and the course it takes lie those processes which are the basis of the other phenomena of world-existence, even of the phenomena of nature. Without insight into the course taken by karma in the world and in the evolution of humanity it is quite impossible to understand why external nature is displayed before us in the form in which we behold it."

(Rudolf Steiner, Dornach, 1924)

(vii)

The Karmic Connection

Steiner gives a strongly negative critique of the *Novum Organum* in *The Riddles of Philosophy* (1914). He repeats this assessment and takes his objections considerably further in the lecture cycle *The Riddles of Humanity* (1916). The most radical treatment is to be found in the lecture cycles that are published under the title *Karmic Relations*, where Steiner speaks at length of Bacon's connection with the Arabian culture of the ninth century. According to Steiner, reincarnation and karma are basic facts without which no understanding of the human race and its history is possible. For those who take Steiner seriously, his words about the karma of the individual who became Francis Bacon provide an entry point to the understanding of post-Renaissance European history.

First, however, a word of caution: there are two (at least) important points to be considered before embarking on a study of *Karmic Relationships*. One, which was plainly stated by Steiner, is that we should not dip into the lectures simply in order to find some intriguing information about a particular individuality, but that individual destiny is to be understood in accordance with the laws and operation of Karma as a whole.

"What has been said in the lectures here since the Christmas Foundation Meeting should not really be passed on to any audience otherwise than by reading an exact transcript of what has been said here.

"A free exposition of this particular subject-matter is not possible at the present stage. If such a course were proposed I should have to take exception to it. These difficult and weighty matters entail grave consideration of every word and every sentence spoken here, in order that the *limits within which the statements are made shall be absolutely clear....*

"It is difficult to speak about these things because such lectures ought really to be given only to listeners who attend the series from beginning to end. Understanding will be difficult for anyone who comes in later." (Introductory note to *Karmic Relationships*, from a lecture of June 22, 1924.)

Fifteen years ago, I wrote the following about the second of the two important points mentioned above:

"The other, which is, I believe, implicit in the work, is that Steiner did not expect to be dropping his insights into a cultural vacuum. Steiner's audience may not have been familiar with every historical figure mentioned in the lectures, but I strongly suspect that the probability of some prior knowledge was much greater then and there than it is here and now. The kinds of things that people are interested in have changed very much in the past ninety years."

Now I see the situation in a different light. It is true that things have changed radically over the past ninety years, and even in the seventy years or so since the time when I was a boy. At that time, the state of popular culture in England was such that stand-up comedians could make references to Shakespeare and the Bible with some confidence that the audience would get the point. A musical skit could be based on tunes from Rossini, Bizet and Verdi, and a popular song could include the words, "There was a guy called Omar, and he wore a ruby 'at." I am pretty sure that something similar could be said about the situation in the German-speaking nations. I do not think, however, that people would have responded so knowingly to allusions to Parmenides, Averroes, Alanus ab Insulis, Dionysius the Areopagite or Hermes Trismegistos. Steiner was always ready to challenge popular ideas, but his statements about the more obscure figures of recorded and unrecorded history were, and are, usually accepted simply at face value by his followers. Furthermore, it is my experience that anthroposophists tend to be resistant to incursions from non-anthroposophical sources. The Karma Lectures are full of references to people who are either totally unknown to most readers or known just as names. The burden of my song is that in such cases, if all you know about these personages is what Steiner said about them, your knowledge is extremely limited. If, as Steiner insists, you study the whole Karma series you will see that the point is in the whole historical panorama of relationships, not in this or that fascinating detail about X or Y. If you really want to know about X or Y you need to do some digging on your own, and to obtain a wider context for your studies, including the diverse views of other witnesses. Students of Rudolf Steiner would do well to emulate the discriminating eclecticism of Justin Martyr; "Whatever things have been well said by all men belong to us Christians too."[44]

What I have said in the preceding paragraph applies in full measure to Francis Bacon; people who are familiar with the name are generally aware only of an unrepresentative symbol rather than a complex personality. It must be added that Steiner did not expect the full implications of his perceptions to be understood at once; understanding may grow with time, thought and contemplation—or it may not. If I simply set out to find confirmation of what I think Steiner meant, or what I should like him to have meant, I shall surely find it. That, as Bacon observed, is the way such pre-programmed researches tend to go. If my grasp of Steiner's intentions is less than perfect, I may well end up with a specious confirmation of something that he didn't actually say or mean. And I must acknowledge the possibility that my earnest efforts may lead to a big, fat question mark.

This explanation or apology was necessary, as in the following sketch of some aspects of Steiner's view of the esoteric history of consciousness from the time of the pre-Socratics to the Renaissance, I shall refer extensively to the karma of Francis Bacon as described by Steiner. The cat is already out of the bag, however[45]; any inhibitions that people may have felt about quoting snippets from the Karma Lectures disappeared some time ago.

(viii)

Steiner on the Evolution of Consciousness

Rudolf Steiner saw the work of the pre-Socratic philosophers as the first flowering of what he called the Age of the Intellectual Soul—the Age in which the capacity for independent thinking was to be developed: if Steiner is correct, dilemmas of the sort that the pre-Socratics encountered were direct consequences of changes in human consciousness which we shall shortly be considering and which will take us from ancient Greece to Renaissance England and Francis Bacon by way of mediaeval Arabia.

Steiner's picture of human evolution is in many ways the opposite of Darwin's. In Darwin's theory and all its progeny there is nothing purposive; the apparently miraculous organization of even the simplest organisms is the result of statistical inevitability and the self-replicative properties of certain molecular structures. The stages of development reached by present generations of people, animals and plants have been deeply affected by conditions of earth and sky, but any appearance of purpose can be traced back to the effects of natural selection and the properties of particles produced by the Big Bang.

According to Steiner, however, human beings were present in a remote age of the world at the very beginning of evolution, long before our present states of matter appeared. The whole process has been one of physical densification and increasing self-awareness, and has proceeded under the guidance of successive levels of spiritual beings, who have gone through their own parallel stages of evolution and have appeared to humanity as gods and angels.[46]

Encounters with angelic beings have been part of the recorded religious experience of the human race all over the world; but as consciousness in and of the physical world increased, contact with the spiritual world became more and more tenuous. Early Christians, encouraged by tradition and the words of St. Paul, pictured nine orders grouped in three choirs: Seraphim, Cherubim and Thrones; Dominations, Virtues and Powers; and Principalities, Archangels and Angels.[47] By the time of the Renaissance, the angelic hierarchies had gone some way towards acquiring their general modern status as poetic images or decorative figures for Christmas cards. Steiner, however, speaks of these divine powers as having been a constant, active and perceived presence in the creation and evolution of the world and of humanity. Under their guidance human beings were to achieve a level of independence that would eventually allow interaction with the spiritual world to take place in freedom. Therefore a separation had to begin, and its early manifestations include the complementary needs to take hold of life on earth in a new, practical and thoughtful way and to keep some vision and understanding of the spiritual nature of man. One of the manifestations of these processes was the arrival of the pre-Socratic philosophers, who took on the task of replacing divine intimations with independent thought. The situation became so fluid that for many years it would not have been clear what such a seemingly transparent phrase as "independent thought" actually meant.

We are so used to experiencing our thinking as a process that we control, and our thoughts as our own, even when acquired from someone else, that it is hard not to assume that this has always been so. Business records preserved from ancient Egypt seem to have been compiled out of a mercantile disposition not so very different from that of nineteenth century England. From the Babylonian astronomers to the Greek mathematicians the practical handling of number and geometrical form was conducted in ways that appeal very much to the modern consciousness, and it is easy to overlook the metaphysical excursions and spiritual intimations of those whose perceptions took them beyond the transactional world. And yet the flavor of the ancient civilizations is in some ways quite removed from anything that we experience today. The objects of everyday experience were physical, certainly, but not *merely* physical. According to Steiner, thoughts were not merely *about* the objects of perception but were perceived as *belonging* to and inherent in those objects. Ancient Greeks who had followed the appropriate path of knowledge were conscious of the spiritual beings who had stewardship of the workings of nature:

"If an ancient Greek had wanted to account for the origin of his thoughts through knowledge of the Mysteries, he would have had to say the following: I turn my spiritual sight up toward those beings who, through the science of the mysteries, have been revealed to me as the beings of form [Exousiai]. They are the bearers of cosmic intelligence; they are the bearers of cosmic thoughts. They let thoughts stream through all the world events, and they bestow these human thoughts upon the soul so that it can experience them consciously."[48]

Exousiai is another name for the *Powers*, the fourth hierarchy above the human being.

Steiner describes how, in a process centered in the fourth century AD and reaching completion in the fourteenth, the Exousiai gave up their rulership of the cosmic intelligence to the Archai—the Principalities—one step closer to the human being. At the same time the Exusiai maintained their stewardship of the whole world of sense impressions—colors, forms and sounds. The ancient Greek had perceived the angelic thought-forms streaming from natural objects. During the time of which we are speaking this capacity gradually disappeared. In earlier times people had experienced the thoughts and the actions of the hierarchies as part of their perception of the natural world. Now thinking would come to be an inner experience, while sense perceptions would still be felt as something external. This, however, is to put a complex matter very simply. In the third and fourth lectures of *Driving Forces of the Spiritual Powers in World History*, Steiner explains the web of relationships between the members of the Exousiai and Archai, in which these spiritual powers were not always at one in their vision of the destiny of the human race. Some wished to hold back the development of individual thinking, while others wished to hasten it. An adequate description of all the ramifications of this situation would take us far beyond the scope of this book, but one significant point must be mentioned, to understand which we must bear in mind that according to Steiner's world-view, spiritual beings, as well as human beings, are in a constant process of evolution. As Steiner puts it:

"Certain Spirits of Form [Exousiai] could not bring themselves to surrender the world of thoughts to the Archai... And so, among the spiritual Beings who hold sway over human happenings, there are the normally evolved Archai in possession of the world of thoughts, as well as backward Exousiai who still retain some sway over the world of thoughts... The position is therefore as follows: a man who through his karma is rightly qualified, receives the impulses at work in his thinking through the Archai. Thinking, although it remains objective, becomes his personal asset. He elaborates the thoughts more and more as his own personal possession. Other individuals do not reach this point; they take over the thoughts either as received from their parents or ancestors or as conventional thoughts prevailing in their national or racial community."

The interplay between the more fully evolved human beings and those whose thinking is still under the influence of the backward Spirits of Form is seen in the many migrations, invasions and intellectual currents of the Dark and Middle Ages. The following is of particular interest:

"In that era of vanishing antiquity and the dawning Middle Ages… certain spiritually minded personalities in the Near East, belonging to Arabian culture, were the first to be influenced by the Archai. The gist of these thought impulses spread especially across Africa, over to Spain, to the whole of Western Europe. It is a highly stimulating current of thought…"

It was, Steiner says, a persistent current that influenced, among others, Spinoza, Galileo and Copernicus. Meanwhile, impulses from the backward Exousiai were spreading from Asia into Eastern Europe. The current from Arabian culture, strongly influenced by its debt to classical Greek philosophy and moving though Africa and Spain into Western Europe, is the one that chiefly concerns us here, and, in spite of Steiner's words, it appears not to have been entirely free from some form of regressive influence.

* * *

A different account of the changing relationships of thoughts and sense perceptions to the human being is given in the *Letters to Members* of 1924, now published as *The Michael Mystery*, where Steiner speaks about the awakening in human souls of the light of personal, individual intelligence, the feeling, "I construct my thoughts". Hitherto people had experienced their thoughts as belonging to supersensible spirit-beings. "To that power, from whom proceed the Thoughts of things, they gave the name of *Michael*… Michael was the regent of the cosmic intelligence. From the ninth century on, people ceased to have the impression that their thoughts were inspired by Michael. Thoughts had fallen from Michael's dominion, and sunk from the spiritual world into the individual souls of men." "Since this transference of thoughts, man feels a freer association with the world of thoughts. This also gives the illusion that man himself produces his own thoughts." We do not *create* thoughts, but we have the ability, potentially at least, to control our thinking and give it whatever structure we desire. We may design and build the house that we live in, but we do not suppose that we have created the substance of which it is built.

The friendly reader will note that we have two accounts of the descent of the cosmic intelligence, given within a year or so of each other, that appear to be quite separate and radically different. I am sorry to say that I cannot be of much help. As far as I know, no one in the anthroposophical community has ever had anything to say about what seems to me to be a major problem. Here, however, is some background that may be useful to people who are not familiar with Steiner's many descriptions of the work of the Archangel Michael. Bear in mind that the most of what follows was given in the final year of Steiner's life, not long after the lectures in which he ascribed the descent of the divine intelligence to the work of the Exousiai and the Archai.

Michael is one of seven Archangels who guide and direct the fundamental tendencies of successive ages in relation to man, each one occupying the leading position for a period of between three and four hundred years. Michael had been involved in – in fact, we might say "had supervised" – the changing relationship of the divine intelligence to the human being from the very beginning, and at the crucial time when the earliest stirrings of Greek philosophy took place he became the leading Archangel. His reign began in the pre-Socratic period, lasted through the age of Socrates, Plato, Aristotle and Alexander the Great and ended soon after the death of Alexander in 323 B.C. Steiner describes Aristotle and Alexander as Michaelic figures who continued to work from the spiritual world for the healthy evolution of humanity. Michael's influence did not end at that point, but he had to work from a more remote region, and his relationship to the administration of the cosmic intelligence changed.

In his lectures on the Karma of the Anthroposophical Society, Steiner spoke of a great battle between the powers under the leadership of the Archangel Michael, who wish for the free and healthy evolution of the human race, and those led by Ahriman[49], who wish to bind human beings in the material world and prevent their free communion with the world of spirit.

While Michael was preparing for his next period of rulership, the Ahrimanic spirits of materialism from the lower regions of the earth were doing their utmost "to prevent Michael's dominion from prevailing on Earth. And at that time the Ahrimanic spirits whispered to those who would lend their ear: The Cosmic Intelligence has fallen away from Michael and is here, on the Earth: we will not allow Michael to resume his rulership over the Intelligence…

"Towards the end of the 19th century Michael himself would once again assume dominion upon the earth, but this new Michael Age must be different from the others. For what Michael had administered through many aeons had now fallen away from him. But he was to find it again when at the end of the seventies of the 19th century he would begin his new earthly rule. He would find it again at a time when an Intelligence intensely exposed to the Ahrimanic forces and bereft of spirituality had taken root among men...

"Such was the crisis from the beginning of the 15th century until our day, which expresses itself as the battle of Ahriman and Michael. For Ahriman is using all his power to challenge Michael's dominion over the Intelligence that has now become earthly. And Michael, with all the impulses that are his, though his dominion over the Intelligence has fallen from him, is striving to take hold of it again on earth at the beginning of his new earthly rule.... So Michael finds himself obliged to defend against Ahriman what he had ruled through the aeons of time for the benefit of humankind. Mankind stands in the midst of this battle; and among other things, to be an anthroposophist is to understand this battle to a certain extent at least."

The relationship of the Archangel Michael to the Archai and Exousiai is deeply mysterious. According to Steiner, Michael is alone among the Archangels in maintaining what, in earthly terms, we would call a total commitment to the continued healthy evolution of the human race. We can think of him, Steiner says, as the countenance of Christ, as the being who helps us to take Christ into our thinking if we so will, providing the upward path that leads the human being back to the spirit.

In view of Michael's essential role in the descent of the intelligence as described in the *Letters to Members* and the karma lectures, I find it incomprehensible that he is not mentioned at all in the report given in *The Driving Forces* a year and a half earlier.

* * *

Steiner tells us in the *Driving Forces* that the descent of the divine intelligence was centered on the fourth century A. D. and completed by about fourteenth, from which it follows that the change began in the seventh century B. C. and encompassed the Age of the Intellectual Soul. Its inception accounts for the first stirrings of the impulse to develop objective and logical explanations for the phenomena of the natural world, which appeared two centuries before the Golden Age of Greek philosophy. Its completion is reflected in the growing feelings of independence and self-confidence with which Renaissance people tackled the problems of the world around them.

We don't need Steiner's help to see that our knowledge of the pre-Socratic philosophers of the fifth and sixth centuries B.C., the spiritual perceptions still evident in their work, and the difficulties they got into, clearly indicates that it would be a mistake to assume that they were just like present day scientists, only less well equipped and informed. Historians and aestheticians give us the impression that every historical event, artistic movement and individual achievement is motivated and influenced by preceding events and personalities and is really, in that sense, a continuation of something that has been going on already. Yet it is clear from exoteric history that something extraordinary happened; apparently an army of natural philosophers sprang deeply motivated, if not fully armed, out of the grass. There is an enormous contrast between the poetic and mythic explanations of previous generations and the efforts of the pre-Socratics to understand the world and its inhabitants. As Jonathan Barnes expresses the matter:

"There are similarities between certain aspects of these early tales and certain parts of the early philosophers' writings. But Aristotle made a sharp distinction between what he called the 'mythologists' and the philosophers; and it is true that the differences are far more marked and far more significant than the similarities… It would be silly to claim that the pre-Socratics began something totally novel and entirely unprecedented in the history of human intellectual endeavor. But it remains true that the best researches of scholarship have produced remarkably little by way of true antecedents. It is reasonable to conclude that Miletus in the early sixth century BC saw the birth of science and philosophy."[50]

Barnes ascribes this efflorescence of rational enquiry to "genius" rather than "supernatural talent." Steiner would say that in the process of evolution, as guided by the spiritual powers who carry the responsibility for human destiny, such an outbreak was inevitable at this particular time.

To the student of Rudolf Steiner it would seem quite natural that such a change in the character of human participation in the thought processes of the world, accompanied by a loss of perception of the divine world, and later by the spread of Christianity and the fading of classical civilization, would produce confusion and anxiety in the shape of conflicting desires to hang on to the old, to look for some transformation that would embrace both the old and the new, or to abandon the old altogether. Concerning the evolution of Greek thought, Steiner says, in *The Riddles of Philosophy*:

"One can observe... in the pre-Socratic thinkers the prelude; in Socrates, Plato and Aristotle the culmination; after them a decline and a kind of dissolution of thought life.... Greek thought life has an element that makes it appear "perfect" in the best sense of the word. It is as if the energy of thought in the Greek thinkers had worked out everything that it contains within itself.... *What* can be thought and how one can doubt about thinking and knowledge, all enters the field of consciousness in Greek civilization, and in the manifestation of thought the soul takes possession of its own being. Has Greek thought, however, shown the soul that it has the power to fulfill everything that it has stimulated in it?"

Perhaps this train of thought is easier to follow in the original German. There is plenty of room for debate about the perfection of Greek thought, but the real point seems to be that thinking potentially enabled the human being to become the master of his own consciousness. When we have sorted out the three "its" in the last sentence, the question becomes, "Thinking has generated new potentialities in the human soul; can these new potentialities be fulfilled through the power of thought?"

This question was answered in the negative by the neoplatonists of the early Christian era. Plotinus, the best known of the neoplatonists, was born in Egypt, probably of Greek lineage, in 204 A.D., and taught in Rome from 244 until his death in 270. In traditional Platonism, the life of thought was dependent on a supreme, autonomous intellect. Plotinus taught that beyond this principle, and thus above the life of thought, there is a greater being, unitary and simple—the One. Reality consists of a series of levels—the One, the Intelligence, the Soul. Each higher one radiates into the next lower, while remaining unchanged in itself. The physical world is generated by the soul projecting on matter, which, according to Plotinus, has no concrete existence, but merely acts as a vessel for the lowest activity of the soul, creating forms in ordinary space. Although matter often gives the appearance of evil, the whole cosmic process stems from the overflowing activity of the One, and is therefore the best of all possible worlds.

As Steiner describes the neoplatonic vision, beyond the life of thought is the striving for illumination, for the ascent into a world-being that transcends thought, for a mystical experience, independent of thinking, which will unite the soul with the world foundation. For Christian and Pagan alike there was a turning away from earthly preoccupations, towards spiritual ideals and perceptions. "The world conceptions arise out of the background of the religious life. What is alive in them is not self-unfolding thought, but the religious impulses that are striving to manifest themselves in the previously conquered thought forms."[51]

There, in a rather convoluted nutshell, is what became one of the thorniest problems of the thinkers of the Middle Ages. Can religious perceptions and ideals be expressed in a philosophically sound manner? Or, more bluntly, are religion and philosophy compatible? Is an Aristotelian Islam or an Aristotelian Christianity possible? The neoplatonist ideal faded but never disappeared, while the works of Aristotle, accompanied by a significant tincture of Neoplatonism, found their way into the Arabian world by a strange path, involving the Nestorian Church and the conflicting ideals of the early Christian, pre-Islamic period.

(ix)

Aristotle and Arabian Philosophy

Rudolf Steiner attached great importance to the connection that he perceived between Francis Bacon and the Arabian court of the Middle Ages—the court of the Abbasid Caliphate in Baghdad, where Harun al-Rashid reigned from 786 until 809 A.D. The greatest of the Abbasids, Harun al-Rashid was a patron of the arts and learning, and was, according to Steiner, the bearer of the individuality later to incarnate as Francis Bacon, thereby making Western Europe accessible to a renewed stream of Arabian thought. To understand the implications of this karmic connection, some knowledge of Arabian thinking will be required.[52] The Arabian philosophers in the period from Harun until the late Middle Ages thought and wrote about every conceivable aspect of experience, knowledge and existence; here I attempt to follow only the particular threads that appear to tie in with Steiner's observations on the origins of Bacon's world-view. The frequency and variety of Steiner's comments about Islam, Arabian philosophers and Francis Bacon, together with the perception that his statements are not demonstrably free from internal contradictions and differences with ascertainable fact, have made this a rather difficult process.

The first line of enquiry is a brief survey of some of the Arabian philosophers' attempts to deal with the problems of individual thinking and personal immortality, and Steiner's commentaries thereon. The second concerns Steiner's description of a darker and more deep-seated effort by spiritual powers to use what he refers to as "Arabism" as an instrument for the subversion of human evolution. After that, we shall see what emerges.

* * *

One constant characteristic of mediaeval Arabian philosophy is devotion to Aristotle, whose principal works were first translated into

Arabic in the reign of al-Ma'mun (813-833), the son of Harun al-Rashid. The dualities of faith and reason, religion and philosophy, and realism and nominalism, with their bitter conflicts and uneasy truces, pervaded Arabian and European thinking alike. A Steinerian view suggests that these struggles were deeply connected with the radical, although long drawn out, transformation of the human relationship to the world of thought, described in the preceding section. As far as this study is concerned, the most awkward questions, those with the most far-reaching consequences and the deepest connection with spiritual history, can be put in a deceptively simple way: do we form our own thoughts or are they the operations of an impersonal (or super-personal) cosmic intelligence? Does the imprint of our thoughts and experiences on our soul life become a permanent, individual possession, passing with our individuality into the afterlife?

Arabian philosophers tried to solve these problems in their own fashion, and appearances suggest, perhaps unexpectedly, that Aristotle caused a great deal of the trouble. Here is a brief explanation of how the Stagyrite got in on the act in the first place, and what it was in his philosophy that caused such alarm and despondency.

In the early centuries of the Christian era the city of Edessa, situated a few miles north of the present-day border between Turkey and Syria, and sometimes referred to as the "Athens of Syria", was a great centre of religious and philosophical activity. Conquered by the Romans in 49 A.D. and declared a Roman colony in 214 A.D., its culture remained basically Greek, but it harbored a strong community of Jews who lived side by side with the pagan community and even shared a burial ground with them. Although a Christian church was established early in the third century and the city adopted Christianity as its official religion, Greek and Jewish thought continued to flourish. What eventually got the Christian citizens of Edessa into trouble was a controversy over the combination of divine and human natures in Jesus. The dyophysite[53] tradition—the belief that in Jesus two distinct persons were present, one human and one divine—was very strong, but it came under increasing attack in the fifth century. To the monophysites the most outrageous consequence of dyophysitism, drawn by Nestorius, the dyophysite leader, was that the Virgin Mary was not the Mother of God, but the mother of Jesus' human nature only. In 489 A.D., after the unity of Christ's person had been established as the orthodox view, Zeno, the Emperor of the East, drove the Nestorian scholars out of Edessa into Persia, where they were welcomed and encouraged to continue their work. They took with them not only their dyophysite theology but also their enthusiasm for Greek philosophy, particularly that of Aristotle. Their departure led to the establishment of a school of logic and theology at Nisibis, not far from Edessa, and a medical school at Gandisapora[54] (Gundishapur), in the east of Persia, whence knowledge of Greek medicine, science and philosophy spread throughout the land. The Monophysites followed the same path as the Nestorians (dyophysites), and Athenian philosophers banished by Justinian in 529 AD were also welcomed at Gandisapora.

Arabian students quickly outstripped their Nestorian mentors, and in the eighth and ninth centuries Aristotle's principal works were translated, first into Syriac and later into Arabic. Students flocked to the centers of learning at Baghdad and Gandisapora from far and wide, laying Islam open to foreign ideas and culture. Orthodox Moslems viewed these developments with grave suspicion, disapproved of al-Ma'mun's predilection for philosophy and considered that the Caliph was not a sound candidate for eventual salvation.

One of Aristotle's gifts to posterity was the set of writings known as the Organon, a set of instructions on how to think, the title of which Bacon borrowed for his *Novum Organum*. Aristotle wrote about every topic that a philosopher might reasonably be interested in, including the nature of perception and thinking, but I do not have the impression that he was heavily preoccupied with the problem of human individuality, which was to become such a bugbear for later workers. From Steiner's point of view, it is important to remember that during the eleven centuries that elapsed between the death of Aristotle and the heyday of Arabian philosophy, the gulf between the human being and the world of the hierarchies grew immeasurably wider and deeper. Individual consciousness and immortality became big topics for mediaeval philosophers and theologians, and a lot of the discussion centered on a few passages in the Aristotle's *De Anima* (*Concerning the Soul*) of which I quote one.

"But since, in the whole of nature, to something which serves as matter for each kind of thing, there is also something else which is the cause and that which produces because it makes them all, the two being related as art to its material, of necessity these differences must be found also in the soul. And to the one intellect, which answers to this description because it *becomes* all things, corresponds the other intellect because it *makes* all things, as a sort of disposition such as light does. For in a manner light, too, makes colours which are potential into actual colours. And it is this intellect [later known as the active intellect] *which is separate and unaffected and unmixed*, being in substance activity... It is not the case that this intellect sometimes thinks and sometimes does not. When separated it is just that which it is *and it is this alone which is immortal and eternal. But we are not mindful because [the active intellect] is not capable of being affected, whilst [the passive intellect] is perishable; and without this there is no thinking.*"[55] [My italics]

To the best of my knowledge, Rudolf Steiner never made any reference to the *De Anima*. It may seem clear enough to a student of anthroposophy that Aristotle's *active intellect* is an aspect of the cosmic intelligence described by Steiner, but the philosophers who acknowledged the pre-eminence of Aristotle and wished to reconcile his work with their religion were not anthroposophists, and the interpretation of this and related passages became a matter of great difficulty and supreme importance to Moslem and Christian thinkers. To some it was clear that the active intellect is a cosmic principle that penetrates the human soul from above but does not become the individual property of the human being. That which is imprinted on the passive intellect may be individual, although this is a controversial point, but the passive intellect is perishable, making the immortality of the individual a very dubious proposition. Individuation, as Aristotle had said, depends on matter[56], so how can our individuality survive in a spiritual region devoid of matter? As one who thinks, feels and acts, am I an individual or do my thoughts, feelings and impulses come from an exterior source and belong to the whole group of which I am a member? If I am an individual on earth, is my individuality established strongly enough that it will survive death? As might be expected, Moslem and Christian theologians came down firmly on the side of individuality and individual survival; but after a promising start things became very difficult for the philosophers.

It is, perhaps, advisable to note that some modern philosophers regard Aristotle's active intellect as "an incurably dualist intrusion" or an "irrelevant intrusion", involving the "notorious distinction between the active and the passive intellects" and the very odd "suggestion that the former is separate from the body." To these philosophers it is inconceivable that Aristotle introduced this idea because it was something that he experienced as reality, so they conclude that he must have invented it for use as a convenient mechanism.[57] As far as subsequent philosophy was concerned, it was very *in*convenient.

To anyone who accepts Steiner's view of history, it will be evident that Aristotle was speaking of the situation as it was soon after the beginning of the descent of the divine intelligence. When the great Arabian philosophers appeared on the scene, this process was still a long way from completion so, on this view, the relations between perception, thinking, intuition and revelation must have been in a state of flux. In any case it is clear that such a state existed, whether or not it came about through the activities of the hierarchies as described by Steiner.

Acknowledging that religion and philosophy were fundamentally different ways of understanding the universe and the human being, and believing that they could not be contradictory, several generations of Arabian philosophers did their best to reconcile the two approaches. These philosophers generally had two things in common; they were devoted to Aristotle, and they were sincere Moslems. The problem of being a true philosopher and a true Moslem at the same time involved many different aspects of existence, including God's relationship to the world as creator and maintainer, but the most excruciating difficulties—at least, as far as this study is concerned—are connected with Aristotle's words about the active and passive intellects. In later centuries Christian philosophers faced analogous problems, and in due course we shall see how Thomas Aquinas provided some answers.

* * *

Al-Kindi (d. 870 A. D.), known as "the philosopher of the Arabs", was a man of noble birth who held an important position in the Caliphate at a time when many translations of the Greek philosophers were being made. Unlike some of the later Arabian thinkers he believed that there was no problem in reconciling reason and revelation, that human reason can arrive at theological truth and that the knowledge expressed by sacred writings and inspired prophecy takes precedence over the results of philosophy. He was therefore able to establish philosophy as a respectable pursuit among Moslems who were wary of its non-Islamic sources. It seems that Aristotle's words didn't land him in the kind of philosophical quagmire that later philosophers had to plough through. The real trouble began with serious efforts to understand the interaction between a universal, active intellect and an individual human soul. How can our passive intellect become the vehicle of our individuality and transport us into the afterlife? The simplest way of describing the history of this question is to say that no matter what the philosophers did with it they could rarely satisfy themselves and never satisfy the theologians. Here are a few examples.

In the 10th century the Brothers of Purity, a group working in Basra, al-Kindi's home town, attempted to produce a survey of all knowledge and, in the process, to reconcile theology and philosophy, or as we might now say, faith and reason. Their work, Aristotelian in substance but touched by neoplatonic thought, was acceptable to neither side.

At the same time al-Farabi (c. 875-950), who had been taught by a Christian Aristotelian and had greater access to reliable texts and commentaries, was laying a foundation for Avicenna's philosophy. Al-Farabi incurred the wrath of the orthodox Moslem theologians by insisting that philosophy was the highest activity of the human mind. Echoing Melissus, he maintained that philosophical truth is logically necessary ("Nothing is stronger than what is true.") and the same for all who possess it, whereas there is no definitive expression of symbolic (pictorial) truth. Those who are incapable of philosophizing must receive symbolic truth in the form best suited to their training, their nationality and their position in society.

According to Al-Farabi, the active intellect is the tenth in a hierarchy of pure intelligences, at the top of which is the neoplatonic One. He considered that the active intellect, which provides the connection between the realm of pure intelligence and the individual human mind, was universal rather than personal, and the passive intellect, which is to say the human mind as modified by perception and experience, was mortal. It was therefore extremely difficult to make belief in personal immortality philosophically acceptable. The difficulty of resolving such problems without inconsistency led eventually to the charge that some of the Arabian philosophers held the "double-truth" theory, according to which it is possible to accept philosophical and theological truths that contradict each other.

In spite of all his efforts, al-Farabi failed to establish that the acquisition of philosophical truth by way of the active intellect, or a good approximation to it by means of symbols, might make personal immortality possible. Having spent most of his life in a great struggle to understand the nature of mind and being, in the bitter end he was unable to see the independent existence of intellect in the human individual as anything but a delusion.

Avicenna, who was born near Bukhara in 980, was the son of a provincial Governor, and grew up amid violent political upheavals that caused him to flee from court to court to avoid capture by the victorious Mamhmad of Ghazna. In his autobiography he tells us that he was largely self-taught, even in medicine, the field in which he became most famous. He reports that he had read Aristotle's *Metaphysics* forty times without understanding it, before finding a commentary by al-Farabi, from which he learned what it means to search for the nature of being—in other words, to be a metaphysician. Steiner saw Avicenna and his great successor, Averroes, as epitomizing Arabian attitudes to the human condition.

"Through Avicenna and Averroes, something was introduced that was to enter human civilization with the beginning of the fifteenth century, namely, the struggle for the consciousness soul.[58] What Avicenna and Averroes brought across, what Aristotelianism had turned into in Asia, so to speak, struggles with the comprehension of the human I, which was received like a revelation from above as a mystery wisdom. This gave rise to the view that for so long provoked such weighty disputes in Europe, namely, that man's ego is not actually an independent entity but is basically one with the divine universal being...

"This is the reason for Avicenna's conception that what constitutes the individual soul originates with birth and ends with death... The I, on the other hand, could not be transitory in this manner. Therefore, Avicenna said: Actually, the ego is the same in all human beings. It is basically a ray from the Godhead which returns again into the Godhead when the human being dies. It is real, but not individually real."[59]

Clearly, the struggle for the divine intelligence, as described in the *Letters to Members* and the Karma Lectures, and the struggle for the consciousness soul, as described in the above quotation, are aspects of the same evolutionary process. It must be noted that the view of the soul's passage through life and death that Steiner ascribes to Avicenna is contrary to the theology of Islam, which insists on personal immortality.

It is instructive to compare Steiner's characterization of Avicenna's position with the account provided by Frederick C. Copleston in his *History of Mediaeval Philosophy*.[60]

(Since I place considerable reliance on Copleston's report, which differs from Steiner's over certain key issues, I add the following excerpt from an obituary in the Guardian, 1994.

"Frederick Copleston's life is largely the record of his publications and of the many academic honours which his prolific publications deserved and received as a result. His nine-volume History of Philosophy (1946-75), together with his single-volume writings on Nietzsche and Schopenhauer, his Darcy lectures, Philosophies and Cultures (1980), and his Gifford Lectures, Religion and the One (1982), are an impressive, still much-used and highly regarded account of the history of philosophy and philosophers from the pre-Socratics to the present day. The esteem in which the learned world held Copleston was marked by his election as a Fellow of the British Academy in 1970, by his being made an Honorary Fellow of St John's College, Oxford (his old Alma Mater), in 1975, by a much-prized Honorary D. Litt. from St Andrews University and finally in 1993 by his appointment as CBE. *His mammoth History is marked by an enviable objectivity, and by his willingness to be fair and to let the facts speak for themselves.*")

References to God and the theology of creation provide further insight into the schism between the philosophers and the Moslem theologians. Copleston explains Avicenna's reasoning from the existence of possible beings to that of an absolutely necessary being, God, and continues:

"The absolutely necessary being is for Avicenna not only the ultimate cause for all other beings, but also a personal being who knows all that proceeds from him. To this extent, therefore, Avicenna effects a harmonization between philosophy and the religious beliefs of Islam."

The difficulties soon begin to pile up, however. As Copleston notes, "According to Avicenna, God knows all things by knowing his own essence. Indeed it is the divine self-knowledge which generates the world." This is what makes it impossible for Avicenna to accept the traditional Moslem concept of creation.[61]

"God is unchangeable and transcends time. The philosopher cannot conceive of him as becoming one day a creator, after a period in which he created nothing. If God is the absolutely necessary being and also, as Avicenna believes, absolute goodness, this goodness must communicate itself eternally."

In other words, creation could not have been a process that took place in a finite period of time; contrary to Moslem orthodoxy, it must have been from eternity. It follows from this that the whole hierarchy of intelligences, intermediary beings between God and the material world, proceeds from God eternally.

"These intelligences differ from one another in virtue of their different degrees of proximity to God. The tenth intelligence is the giver of forms. That is to say, it is through its activity that forms are received in matter as pure potentiality."

(The reader will recall that al-Farabi had equated the tenth intelligence with Aristotle's active intellect.)

In Avicenna's world, as Copleston reports, the relationships between God and his creatures are *necessary*, in the philosophical sense of the word, and the result is a completely deterministic universe, leaving no room for human freedom.[62]

Avicenna's views about God and creation were incompatible with the Moslem (and, of course, Christian) picture of God's activities, and his thoughts on personal identity and immortality were theologically equally dubious.

"The tenth intelligence, the giver of forms, also has the function of illuminating the human mind. That is to say, it exercises the function of Aristotle's active intellect [and Steiner's 'ray from the Godhead.'] In his account of the way in which we achieve knowledge, Avicenna follows Aristotle; but whereas the Greek philosopher's remarks on the ontological status of the active intellect are notoriously obscure and open to various interpretations, Avicenna makes it perfectly clear that in his opinion the active intellect is not simply a function or a power of the human mind, but a separate intelligence. In particular, its activity is required for the apprehension of the universal concept or essence."

That is to say that without the aid of the active intellect we should be unable to distinguish categories or forms. If this were not so, the passive intellect would be able to exist in its own right and by its own power, a possibility that Avicenna could not entertain.

"This doctrine does not, however, entail the denial of personal immortality. *For Avicenna the pronoun 'I' refers to the soul rather than the physical body. Personal identity can thus be preserved without the body. And the rational soul is immortal...* It is true that Avicenna regards the pictures found in the Koran as mythical... but though he demythologizes popular conceptions of the next life, he accepts the Moslem doctrine of personal immortality, as far as the soul is concerned." (My italics)

In spite of all the possible confusions over the meanings of "I", "ego" and "soul", it is clear that Avicenna's view of immortality, as stated in his own words, is not consistent with Steiner's reporting of it.

These issues were integral to the philosophy of Avicenna, who was a deeply religious man. In tackling them he was attempting to fashion a true and consistent view of the universe and not merely trying to keep his philosophy respectable. History suggests that such efforts are necessary and that they usually end up pleasing no one. The Moslem theologians, as represented by al-Ghazali (1058-1111), reacted strongly against al-Farabi and Avicenna, demolishing their systems point by point and making it very difficult for the active pursuit of philosophy to continue in Baghdad. Al-Ghazali himself, not satisfied with Islamic orthodoxy, turned to Sufism and became the great philosopher of that movement. Like the works of most of the prominent Arabian philosophers, his *Intentions of the Philosophers* and *Incoherence of the Philosophers*, first expounding and then criticizing the work of al-Farabi and Avicenna, soon appeared in Western Europe in Latin translation, providing fuel for the subsequent European fire.

(x)

Averroes

A dramatic outward sign of the westward migration of people, ideas and impulses came at the beginning of the eighth century with the Moorish invasion of Spain. In 711 AD, the Moors, a nomadic people of North Africa who had become fanatical Moslems, swept into the Iberian Peninsula, routing the Visigoths. The latter were the descendants of Goths who had defeated the Roman Emperors of the East and the West in the fourth century and, having gone 2 and 0 against Roman Emperors, went on to occupy most of Spain and part of southern France. After losing their lands north of the Pyrenees, the Visigoths had become Christians and merged with the Spanish population. The incursive Moors established an Emirate, and later a Caliphate, in the Andalusian city of Cordoba, which rivaled Baghdad in wealth and splendor and became a center of both Moslem and Jewish culture. Averroes was born in this city in 1126 and, being a member of a wealthy family descended from a long line of religious judges, he grew up in one of the best homes in Cordoba.

Not much is known about Averroes' early life, but a short biography written not long after his death tells us that he was well educated in theology and Islamic law, and had a wide knowledge of Arabic literature. His greatest enthusiasm was for Greek philosophy and medicine, and he was thoroughly familiar with the works of Aristotle.

When Averroes was still a young man, the Moorish rulers were displaced by a Berber group of a more puritanical nature. Under the new regime, schools and libraries established by the Moors in Andalusia were abolished, books were ritually cursed and burned, and great crowds in mosques, listening to lectures on science, literature, law and religion, were dispersed. Surprisingly enough, however, the new ruler and his successor, Abu Ya'qub Yusuf, were deeply interested in all kinds of learning, including the study of philosophy. Abu Ya'qub surrounded himself with scholars, among whom was his chief physician, Ibn Tufayl, who introduced Averroes to the Prince in about 1168.

On meeting the leader of a dynasty so feared for its puritanical orthodoxy, the middle-aged Averroes feigned ignorance of philosophy. He soon discovered, however, that the Prince was thoroughly at home with philosophical issues. Here is part of the account of this incident, given by Averroes to one of his pupils, quoted in the introduction to G. F. Hourani's translation of Averroes' *On the Harmony of Religion and Philosophy*.[63]

"When I entered into the presence of the Prince of the Believers, I found him with Abu Bakr Ibn Tufayl alone. Abu Bakr began praising me, mentioning my family and ancestors and generously including in the recital things beyond my real merits. The first thing that the Prince said to me... was "What is the opinion of the philosophers about the heavens? Are they eternal or created?" Confusion and fear took hold of me and I began making excuses and denying that I had ever concerned myself with philosophic learning... but the Prince of the Believers understood my fear and confusion. Turning to Ibn Tufayl, he talked about the question of which he had asked me, mentioning what Aristotle, Plato and all the philosophers had said, and also bringing in the objections that the Moslem thinkers had against them... Thus he continued to set me at ease until I spoke and he learned what was my competence in the subject. When I withdrew he ordered for me a donation in money, a magnificent robe of honor and a steed."

The story continues with the commission to write the commentaries on Aristotle's works that would become so well known, highly regarded and influential that in Christian circles he would be referred to as the Commentator.[64]

"Ibn Tufayl summoned me one day and told me, 'Today I heard the Prince of the Believers complain of the difficulty of expression in Aristotle and his translators, saying that if someone would tackle these books, thoroughly understand them, summarize them and expound their aims, it would be easier for people to grasp them.'"

As Hourani notes, "Until the interview with the Prince, Averroes was unaware of his favorable interest in philosophy, and feared some harsh penalty for himself if he were known to be occupied in such a study. Nothing could more plainly illuminate the public unpopularity of philosophy than the Prince's extreme discretion and the philosopher's apprehensions."[65]

Eventually Averroes became the Sultan's royal physician and chief judge of Cordoba. I have given this brief excerpt from the story of his dealings with the Prince because it provides an inkling of his character as a real human being rather than the lop-sided image prevalent since the thirteenth century.

Averroes aimed at an accurate exposition of Aristotle's philosophy, which he regarded as the culmination of human intellectual activity, a position in harmony with that of Rudolf Steiner.[66] Averroes thought that this would help to free philosophy from the bad reputation it had acquired among conservative theologians, publishing, among other works, *The Incoherence of the Incoherence*, in response to al-Ghazali. Like Plato, al-Kindi, Dewey and the British government of the 1940's, he thought that the style and content of education should be adjusted in accordance with the capacities of those receiving it. Most people can cope only with knowledge in the imaginative, pictorial form given in the Koran. Those who are able to follow a train of thought and to reach probable conclusions can receive instruction based on the Koran and theology, while those who seek truth in its rational essence, through strict logical demonstration, can use the material of the Koran for logical penetration. As the embodiment of revelation, the Koran can be understood at different levels. Philosophy is not dangerous to belief as long as it is kept from those who do not understand. These ideas were condemned by the Moslem theologians and later contributed to the mistaken belief that Averroes adhered to the "double truth" theory. Averroes, however, was simply following a principle which runs through teaching of almost every kind, whether esoteric or exoteric, namely that it is unwise to give people knowledge which they are not equipped to handle.

Averroes takes up the idea that God creates all things by knowing them, since by knowing himself he knows all that is possible. By taking God's thought to be creative rather than representational Averroes goes further than both Aristotle and Avicenna, giving a picture somewhat more in accordance with Moslem belief. However, since God and his thought are eternal and unchanging, the world must be eternally created. Like Avicenna, Averroes insists that it is nonsense to speak of a time before creation. The depiction of creation as an event in time is simply the best that popular theology can do for people whose thinking is pictorial rather than philosophical.[67] As far as the European theologians were concerned, the most controversial feature of the philosophy of Averroes—the one which raised most virulently the spectre of double truth—was his treatment of the problems of individuality and personal immortality. What, precisely, is it that survives?

Averroes finds that Aristotle uses the word *intellect* in a number of different ways. The passive intellect—the seat of pictorial imagination—Aristotle considers mortal. The active intellect is a universal, eternal intelligence existing independently of individual human minds. The active intellect impresses forms or concepts on the *potential* intellect. The potential intellect, which contains only forms imprinted by the active intellect, cannot be personal. Like the active intellect, the potential intellect must be one and eternal. We can therefore ask, as Thomas Aquinas did, how it comes about that different people think different thoughts and have different ideas and opinions. Averroes, however, in his Great[68] Commentary on the *De Anima*, has already made this objection himself.

"If what was understood by me and by you were one in every way, it would be the case that when I understood something, you too would understand the same thing; and there would be many other impossible consequences."

He tries to solve the problem by introducing the concept of *acquired intellect*, the intellect created by the interaction of the active intellect and the individual's life of sense-experience and imaginative pictures. This interaction individualizes the potential intellect of the human being; each of us has a mind stocked with personal ideas, memories and imaginative pictures. Does this acquired intellect survive death? It seems that Averroes must answer this question in the negative, since he agrees with Aristotle that the process of generation implies the inevitability of corruption and that, since it is only through matter that individuals can arise within a species, there can be no such thing as an individual disembodied soul. But Averroes clearly embraces the Moslem belief in human individuality and immortality.

Somehow, in the midst of all these difficulties, Averroes managed to keep his head above water and to devote a whole treatise to the harmony of philosophy and religion, in which he states explicitly that truth cannot contradict truth and that philosophy and revelation must be in accord. There are a couple of historical ironies connected with this work. One is that it may have contributed to his persecution and banishment, since one of his offences was that he "sought to reconcile religion and philosophy." Another is that although it was translated into Hebrew around 1300 it never made it into Latin or any other language until late in the nineteenth century, and even then it seems to have been generally ignored. So a great deal has been said and written about Averroes without the knowledge of some of his most mature thinking, and there is no indication that either Thomas Aquinas or Rudolf Steiner was aware of the treatise. However, Hourani's English translation of it has been available since 1961, so anyone interested in this key historical figure has access to it. Evidence of the influence of this translation can be seen in the differences between Copleston's treatments of Averroes in his 1952 *Mediaeval Philosophy* and 1955 *Aquinas*, on the one hand, and his 1972 *A History of Mediaeval Philosophy*, on the other.

It is doubtful whether Averroes' explanations satisfied their author, and they seem never to have satisfied anyone else. In later years his name became firmly, although with very dubious justification, attached to the unicity theory—that each person's apparently individual thinking is really an expression of the great impersonal active intellect.

* * *

Rudolf Steiner does not mention Averroes' attempts to satisfy his Islamic beliefs by making personal intelligence and immortality plausible, but he treats the Cordoban with respect and gives an insight into his difficulties.

"In Spain it was taught by the Moorish scholars, and above all by such an individuality as Averroes, that the [Cosmic] Intelligence holds sway everywhere. The whole world, the whole cosmos is filled with the all-pervading Intelligence. Human beings down here on earth have many different properties, but they do not possess a personal intelligence of their own... So that the human being as he walks about on earth, shares in the universal Cosmic Intelligence which is common to all. And when he dies, the Intelligence that was his returns to the universal Intelligence. Thus all the thoughts, conceptions and ideas which man possesses in the life between birth and death flow back into the common reservoir of the universal Intelligence. One cannot therefore say that the thing of outstanding value in man's soul, namely his Intelligence, is subject to personal immortality. Indeed it was actually taught by the Spanish, Moorish scholars that man does not possess personal immortality. True, he lives on, but, said these scholars, the most important thing about him during his life is the fact that he can unfold intelligent knowledge, and this does *not* remain with his own being. We cannot therefore say that the intelligent being possesses personal immortality. You see, this was the very point in the fury of the battle which was waged by the Schoolmen of the Dominican Order. It was to maintain and uphold the personal immortality of man. And in that time, such a striving could appear in no other way than it did when the Dominicans declared: Man is personally immortal, and the teaching of Averroes on this subject is *heresy*, absolute heresy."

It is worth interrupting Steiner to remind the reader that the teaching of Averroes appeared just as heretical to the Islamic theologians of his time as it did to the Christian scholars of the following century. Steiner continues:

"Today we have to put it differently, but for that time one can understand that a man like Averroes in Spain, who did not assume the personal immortality of man, was declared a heretic. Today we have to study the matter in its reality. We have to say: In the sense in which man has become immortal, as to his Spiritual[69] Soul, he has indeed attained immortality — the continued consciousness of personality after passing through the gate of death — but he has attained this only since the time when a Spiritual Soul took up its abode in earthly man... The evolution of mankind brought with it the individual and personal immortality of man. And it was by the Dominican Schoolmen that this personal immortality was first emphasised, while on the other hand an ancient truth — one that was no longer true for that age in the evolution of the human race — was put forward in the Academies conducted by the Moors in Spain. For we today must not only be tolerant of our contemporaries. We must be tolerant of those who went on propagating ancient teachings. Such tolerance was not possible in that time. Hence it is important for us to repeat this to ourselves again and again: The personal immortality maintained by Dominican Schoolmen has only been true since the time when the Consciousness Soul slowly and gradually entered into mankind."[70]

Here is a possible explanation for the bugbear of double-truth as it appeared in the Middle Ages—something that was true in a previous age of the world is not true now, and something that is true now was not true then. Averroes was doing his best, but, according to Steiner, he lacked a correct historical perspective.

Steiner's comments are specifically about the problem of personal, individual immortality, to which the question of unicity is antecedent. The Consciousness Soul Age began "officially", so to speak, in 1413, but Steiner makes it clear that its influence might well have been felt two centuries earlier, so that he can refer to the teaching of Aquinas, who died in 1274, as belonging to the new age of the world. Averroes had died in 1198, at the very end of the time when the ancient wisdom to which Steiner refers, was still in its final stage, but his attempts to justify his belief in personal immortality might be said to show that he had intimations of the changing relationship between man and cosmos. This is, perhaps, the best that can be done to express the situation in anthroposophical terms.

* * *

Aristotle's description of the intellects and their relation to the individual was, to say the least, open to interpretation. By the time of Averroes, it had been interpreted and applied in a number of different ways, and the same could be said about almost any topic treated by the philosophers. Al-Farabi, following Aristotle, had said that philosophy was the highest activity of the human mind, yielding truth through strict demonstration and insight. If this is the case, how is it that four centuries of Arabian philosophers, all taking Aristotle as their starting point, produced so many different varieties of truth? This is not to be taken as an indictment of the Arabians; the same kind of thing can easily be said about European and American philosophers. When St. Thomas Aquinas attacks Averroes, the immediate object of the attack seems to be inconsistency rather than untruth. False conclusions may be contested simply because in the light of an over-riding principle their falsity is apparent, but the disputation is still likely to proceed by way of charges of incorrect reasoning or misquotation of authorities. The geography of the wire-drawn reasoning upon which so much of the philosophy of the Middle Ages is built is more like that of an old eastern city, with its nests of little streets, lanes and alleys, some of them blind, than that of a wide plain crossed by a great highway leading from a pleasant suburbia of observation and insight to the austere uplands of truth. In the old town it is easy to get lost, to arrive at one's destination without knowing exactly how one got there, or to arrive at some unexpected but even more desirable location. It usually helps if one knows where one is trying to go. The philosophical process is always subject to the necessity of choice, the possibility of error and the influence of a desired or anticipated conclusion.

My point is not only that this is so but also that any philosopher who was not carried away by the perception of his own perspicacity must have been aware of it. Revelation is in no better case; that which is revealed may be partial, imperfectly seen or subject to interpretation. It may also proceed from powers inimical to the health and welfare of the human race. Perhaps the only way forward is to examine how we reach our own convictions. When I say that I believe in the Father, the Son and the Holy Spirit I am not reporting the result of ratiocination or privileged revelation; I am speaking of an inner conviction which may have been sparked by a moment of illumination and strengthened by contemplation, but which gradually attains a mysterious level of sureness beyond the reach of philosophy. If the belief of Averroes in personal immortality was of this kind it would not be constrained by philosophical objections. In the words of Wallace and Thatcher[71], "*The real grandeur of Averroes is seen in his resolute prosecution of the standpoint of science in matters of this world, and in his recognition that religion is not a branch of knowledge to be reduced to propositions and systems of dogma, but a personal and inward power, an individual truth which stands distinct from, but not contradictory to, the universalities of scientific law.*"

(xi)

The Academy of Gandisapora

When I reached this point in my odyssey, I had a deceptively clear image of the situation of the Arabian philosophers as explained by Steiner; their perception of the human condition looked back to the period before the descent of the cosmic intelligence and the development of individuality, placing them in the service of spiritual powers, the backward Spirits of Form, who opposed the Michaelic impulse in human evolution. Whatever the influences to which the Arabian philosophers were subject, their efforts seemed to me to have been genuine and deeply felt. They tried to deal with these problems in a way that made individuality and immortality part of the solution, but they were unable to do so in a philosophically convincing way. The apparently paradoxical aspect of the situation is that those who were most deeply convinced of the power and validity of thinking were the ones who had the greatest difficulty in understanding the autonomy of the individual human being. It would be natural, though fruitless, to try to imagine how the philosophers would have fared if they had been freed from the attentions of the orthodox Moslem theologians.

According to Steiner's view of evolution, this blossoming of Arabian philosophy took place at a time when the cosmic intelligence was descending into the minds of human beings and when the divine thoughts which had had their place in the objects of sense perception had moved a step closer. The theologians and philosophers, who tried to make some sense of the relations of mind, soul, intellect, form and the physical world, were like marksmen shooting at a moving target, while under the impression that it was standing still.

Although this picture seems to be based on Steiner's esoteric findings, it is, in more than one way, excessively comfortable. It bypasses the fact that Steiner talks as though Moslem theology and the various world views of Moslem philosophers were all of a piece, which is the exact opposite of the truth; and it makes no attempt to deal with the discrepancies between the stated views of Avicenna and Averroes and Steiner's reporting of them. An equally serious deficiency is the lack of any reference to another branch of the story that is not to be found in any exoteric sources, and has to do with the dark side of the Academy of Gandisapora.

The quotations given in Sections (ix) and (x) might lead one to suppose that Steiner regarded Avicenna and Averroes as well-meaning but mistaken, and saw their efforts, and the general thrust of Arabian philosophy as tending to resist the onset of the consciousness soul age. At other times, however, he made it clear that he saw the Arabians as participating in a deliberate effort to subvert the proper course of human evolution and send it in a very different direction. In a lecture entitled *How do I find the Christ?*, given in October 1918, he described how the Academy of Jundi-Shapur (Gandisapora) became involved in such a scheme:

"The year A.D. 333 marked the zenith of the epoch of the Intellectual or Mind Soul; thereafter the descending path of that epoch could have been used for the purpose of guiding the human race into a course altogether different from the one intended by those Divine Beings who have been connected with man from the beginning. This deviation was to be brought about through the endowment of man with something that ought properly to come to mankind only at a later epoch, namely, the Consciousness Soul and its functions. Through a kind of premature revelation these faculties were to be bestowed upon humanity in the year A. D. 666.

"This is in line with the invariable practice of the Beings who are the enemies of the Gods[72] who love mankind. What the good spiritual Beings desire to bring about at a later time, these other Beings want to bring forward to an earlier period, before mankind is ready to receive it...

"What was it that these Beings desired to achieve by these means? They wanted to give to man too soon the Consciousness Soul, whereby they would have cut man off from the path to his future destiny and would have claimed him for a quite different kind of evolution.

"This project was not fulfilled in this particular form, phenomenal, majestic, but diabolical, as had been the intention of these evil spiritual Beings; but the traces of it have nevertheless taken effect in history. This came about because of human deeds, of which one can only say that while men on Earth perform these deeds, they are acting always as the agents of certain spiritual beings… When the year 666 was approaching, there had gathered in the Persian Academy of Jundi-Shapur a matchless scholarship that had come over from ancient Greek culture and had taken no account of the Mystery of Golgotha…

"If this aim of the Academy of Jundi-Shapur had fully succeeded, numbers of men of supreme learning, and endowed with extraordinary genius, would have travelled through North Africa, Western Asia, and Southern Europe, and then through all Europe, spreading the Jundi-Shapur culture of A.D. 666. The primary purpose of this culture was that at that premature time man should be made to rely entirely upon his own personality, because the Consciousness Soul had been brought into full operation within him.

"This attempt failed. Because of Christ's incarnation, death and resurrection the world had already assumed a configuration different from that which alone would have enabled such a thing to come to pass. Therefore the whole thrust which it was the intention of the Academy of Jundi-Shapur to give to Western culture was blunted. Only a little survived in what Arabian scholars brought over to Spain, and even that did not penetrate in the form or in the way that had been intended. In its place there arose Mohammedanism — Mohammed and his teaching. Islam came in the place of what had been intended to go forth from the Academy of Jundi-Shapur."

I note, for what it's worth, that in 666 A.D. Islam was already in full swing throughout Arabia.

To quote from the synopsis attached, presumably editorially, to the beginning of this lecture, "The effort of Jundi-Shapur, however, had some effect. It left a poison in the physical organism of Western humanity in scientific materialism, resulting in a widespread tendency to deny the Divine."

The significance of Gandisapora is brought out in slightly different terms in No. 27 of the *Letters to Members*[73]:

Ancient learning, in the form given by Aristotle, "was caught in the tide of that eastern stream which one may name Arabism. Arabism is, in one aspect of its character, a premature development of the Consciousness

Soul. Through a soul-life working prematurely in the direction of the Consciousness Soul, Arabism afforded the opportunity for a spiritual wave to pour itself from Asia through this channel over Africa, Southern Europe, Western Europe, and so to fill certain members of European humanity with an intellectualism which ought only to have come later. Southern and Western Europe received, in the seventh and eighth centuries, spiritual impulses which should really not have come until the age of the Spiritual [Consciousness] Soul...

"The Arabism by which European spiritual life was invaded kept human souls in their life of Knowledge back from the spiritual world. Prematurely, it brought into action that intellect which can only take hold of external Nature.

"And this Arabism proved very powerful. Upon whomsoever it laid its grasp, an inward and for the most part all-unconscious arrogance began to take hold of this person's soul. He felt the power of intellectualism, but did not realize that the mere intellect was unable to penetrate into reality. So he abandoned himself to that external reality which comes of its own accord to men and works upon their senses. He never thought of taking any step towards the spiritual reality.

"This was the situation with which the spiritual life of the Middle Ages was faced. It had inherited the mighty traditions of the spirit-world; but all its soul-life was so steeped in intellectualism through — one might say — the covert influence of Arabism, that knowledge found no access to the sources whence the inherited traditions, after all, drew their substance.

"Thenceforth, from the early Middle Ages on, there was a constant struggle between what was instinctively felt in men's minds as a link with the Spirit, and the form which Thought had assumed under Arabism."

It is to be noted that Steiner describes two apparently discrepant tendencies in the work of the Arabian thinkers: in his remarks about Avicenna and Averroes he indicates a tendency to retard the evolution of humanity towards the state of individual consciousness and autonomy appropriate to the Consciousness Soul Age, whereas the effect of Gandisapora was to begin the development of an intellectuality appropriate only to a much later stage of the development of the consciousness soul. The former was the result of a relatively benign ignorance or misunderstanding of the evolution of consciousness, whereas the latter was a deliberate attempt at subversion. It would have been very helpful if he had shown us how, or whether, these two tendencies interacted, but as far as I know, no such explanation is to be found.

Exoteric history tells the story of the march of Arabian culture across North Africa to Spain and Southern France, but Steiner provides something more, in the shape of an explanation of the esoteric means by which "Arabism" penetrated Western European culture. In the ninth century, the individualities previously incarnated as Aristotle, Alexander the Great, Harun al-Rashid and his counsellor came together in what is often referred to as a spiritual conference. The amalgam of Christianity and Aristotelianism, which was to incarnate in Western Europe largely through the work of Aquinas, was under the care of Aristotle and Alexander, but Harun al-Rashid and his counsellor could not embrace it.

"All that Alexander and Aristotle had experienced formed itself into the impulse which remained alive in them — the impulse to ensure that the new Michael Rulership, to which with every fibre of their souls Alexander and Aristotle had pledged their troth, would bring a Christianity not only firmly established but more inward, more profound…"

"Neither Harun al-Rashid nor his Counsellor was willing to accept this — the Counsellor with less emphasis, but fundamentally it was so in his case too. They desired, first and foremost, that the world should be dominated by the impulse that had taken such firm root in Mohammedanism. The participants in this spiritual struggle in the 9th century A.D. confronted each other in resolute, intense opposition — Harun al-Rashid and his Counsellor on the one side and, on the other, the individualities who had lived as Aristotle and Alexander.

"The aftermaths of this spiritual struggle worked on in the civilisation of Europe, are indeed working to this day. For what happens in the spiritual world above works down upon and into the affairs of the earth. And the very opposition with which Harun al-Rashid and his wise Counsellor confronted Aristotle and Alexander at that time added strength to the impulse, so that from this meeting two streams went forth — one taking its course in Arabism and one whereby, through the impulses of the Michael Rulership, Aristotelianism was to be led over into Christianity.

"Harun al-Rashid was born again as Bacon of Verulam. His wise Counsellor too was born again, almost at the same time, as Amos Comenius[74], the educational reformer. It is a trend that has no direct connection with Christianity."[75]

It seemed to me at first, especially in the light of Steiner's benevolent attitude towards Avicenna and Averroes, that this "spiritual conference" was an expression of the tendency to retard the progress of humanity into the consciousness soul age, and that Bacon's scientific method might be regarded, as I shall show later, as a new manifestation of the old unicity theory. However, Steiner's references to "Arabism" and his assessments of Bacon's work and intentions, indicate more of a relation to the impulse of Gundishapur—a brilliant and soulless acceleration into the new era. What we have here appears to be an extension of the bifurcated vision already mentioned.

In any case, "brilliant" is a word that can hardly be applied to the scientific method described in Bacon's *Novum Organum*; "dogged" and "plodding" spring more readily to mind.

* * *

In Volume I, Lecture 10 of *Karmic Relationships*, Steiner refers to the great age of Arabian philosophy beginning in the ninth century during the reign of Harun al-Rashid, and explains Arabism as follows:

"When we consider the form in which Mohammedanism made its appearance, we find, first and foremost, the uncompromising monotheism, the one, all-powerful Godhead — a conception of Divinity that is allied with fatalism. The destiny of man is predetermined; he must submit to this destiny, or at least recognise his subjection to it. This attitude is an integral part of the religious life. But this Arabism — for let us call it so — also brought in its train something entirely different. The strange thing is that while, on the one hand, the warlike methods adopted by Arabism created disturbance and alarm among the peoples, on the other hand it is also remarkable that for well-nigh a thousand years after the founding of Mohammedanism, Arabism did very much to promote and further civilisation."

This is, indeed, remarkable, since the civilizing influences of art, music and science often had to proceed against the determined opposition of the Moslem authorities, a matter of fact which, as far as I am aware, Steiner never mentions.

Steiner continues:

"We see Harun al-Rashid, whose praises have so often been sung by poets, at the centre of a wide circle of activity in the sciences and the arts. Himself a highly cultured man, he gathered around him men of real brilliance in the field of science and art. We see him in Asia — not exactly ruling over culture, but certainly giving the impulse to it at a very high level.

"And we see how there emerges within this spiritual culture, of which Harun al-Rashid was the soul, something that had been spreading in Asia in a continuous stream since the time of Aristotle. Aristotelian philosophy and natural science had spread across into Asia and had there been elaborated by oriental insight, oriental imagination, oriental vision. Its influence can be traced over the whole of Asia Minor, almost to the frontier of India, and its effectiveness may be judged from the fact that a widespread and highly developed system of medicine, for example, was cultivated at this Court of Harun al-Rashid.

"Profound philosophic thought is applied to what had been founded by Mohammed with a kind of religious furor; we see this becoming the object of intense study and being put to splendid application by the scholars, poets, scientists and physicians living at this Court in Baghdad."

This would not lead one to imagine that the philosophical and cultural aspirations of all these brilliant people were in any way problematical for the orthodox theologians, or that a Caliph with a leaning towards the arts and philosophy might be regarded as "not being a sound candidate for eventual salvation." Steiner's abstention from any comment on the divergences between the views of the Moslem philosophers and those of their theological contemporaries is hard to understand—he could hardly have been unaware of the situation.

* * *

Leaving aside problems for which I can conceive of no solution, it is time for a proper introduction to the scholastic philosophers, a brief visit with St. Thomas Aquinas, and an attempt to throw some light on the conflict between Aquinas and the Averroists. As with the discussions of Arabian philosophy, what follows is not intended as a rounded picture; my object now is only find what kind of trail—if any—leads from the multifarious thought processes of the Arabian philosophers to the philosophico-religious aspirations of Francis Bacon.[76]

(xii)

Scholasticism; Aquinas and Averroes

In the thirteenth century, the appearance of Latin translations of Aristotle and the commentaries of Avicenna and Averroes, and the growth of universities, particularly in Paris and Oxford, provided impulses for what has been called the Golden Age of Mediaeval Philosophy. The philosopher-theologians of the time became known as scholastics or schoolmen, and one of the hottest issues among the scholastics was one that had already exercised the minds of the Arabian philosophers: is it possible and legitimate to use the powers of reason to deepen the understanding of what is believed through faith?[77]

Perhaps the most striking symptom of humanity's need to supplement revelation with reason was the ongoing effort to provide proofs of the existence of God. In the eleventh century, St. Anselm, one of the forerunners of scholasticism, had based his proof on the human idea of a perfect being from whom nothing is lacking. From Aquinas in the thirteenth century to C. S. Lewis[78] in the twentieth and Timothy Keller[79] in the twenty-first, such attempts have continued.

Half a century after Anselm, Peter Abelard, who is unfortunately known mainly for his disastrous love affair with Héloïse, applied Aristotelian logic to questions of faith, and anticipated Aquinas in his discussions of *universals*, which we shall come to very shortly. Like their Arabian predecessors and contemporaries, Anselm and Abelard were in continual trouble with both church and political authorities. This is particularly remarkable in Anselm's case since he became a church authority himself—no less than Archbishop of Canterbury—but we must remember that issues that seem remote, abstract or irrelevant to us in the twenty-first century were matters of great moment during the period when the transitional state of consciousness—the long-drawn-out transition from the mediaeval outlook to that of the Renaissance—made it extraordinarily important to establish an orthodoxy and keep the mass of untutored believers safe from philosophical subtleties and scientific heresies. Present-day controversies about evolution and intelligent design are pale descendants of the bitter doctrinal antagonisms that sent heretics to the stake only a few centuries ago.

Like some of his Arabian forbears, Thomas Aquinas (1224-1274) aimed at a synthesis of reason and faith. A philosophy of earthly things is possible and desirable, but accounts for only a part of human experience. The line between philosophy, which proceeds through the working of natural reason, and theology, which takes divine revelation as its starting point, is permeable—dotted, perhaps. *Since both faith and reason come from God it is not possible that they should in any way contradict each other.* It is therefore legitimate to use the methods of philosophy in the development of a theological system, as Aquinas did in producing the *Summa Theologica*, his powerful and influential synthesis of Christianity and Aristotelian philosophy. Theology depends on divine revelation for much of its substance, but the existence of God can be proved through natural reason. St. Thomas deploys the living power of human thought to penetrate the realities of nature and God. Our thoughts are individual and we owe them to God; their origin is heavenly and they still trail clouds of glory. It is thinking that makes us human and links us with both God and nature. This is why we call ourselves *homo sapiens* or, in earlier times, *animal rationalis*—an animal with a rational soul. Followers of St. Thomas believe that thinking is where the divine spark enters us, and that denial of the validity of thinking is incompatible with Christianity.[80] What brings him to the fore in this study is his conflict with Averroes.

Averroes, believing that neither the active nor the potential intellect was specific to the individual human being, had tried to reach an understanding of human individuality in terms of an *acquired* intellect. Aquinas used Averroes' commentary on the *De Anima* as a source of corroboration, but was evidently unaware of the Commentator's rejection of the unicity theory, which appeared only in Great Commentary.[81] St. Thomas was also unaware of Averroes' rejection of the double truth theory in the *Harmony*, but even if he had known these things, he would still have found fault with Averroes' interpretation of the ambiguous passages in the *De Anima*.

The human mind, according to Aquinas's Aristotelian approach, depends on sense experience for all its natural knowledge; the individual intellect functions actively to gather elements of universality from sense perceptions and to impress the *idea* on the intellect in its passive mode. If Averroes had interpreted Aristotle correctly he would not have required such an elaborate and philosophically dubious analysis to save the clear perception that understanding is a function of the individual human being.

It is hard for us now to see how embracing the correct solution of such a seemingly abstract philosophical problem might be essential for salvation. It was not, however, abstract at the time, and the anxieties of the Christian Fathers about doctrinal rectitude were of a magnitude comparable with those of the Moslem theologians. Suspicions of adherence to the unicity theory, or worse, to the double-truth theory, were apt to result in penances, heresy trials and excommunications. It is unfortunate that those suspected of such departures from orthodoxy were lumped together as "Averroists", since their views—as perceived, at any rate, by the establishment[82]—were not altogether in line with those of Averroes. Many of them lived and worked at the University of Paris and, at the behest of Pope John XXI, the Bishop of Paris instituted an inquiry, leading to the condemnation of 219 propositions. This mixed bag of malefical[83] statements was drawn not only from an august company of philosophers, including Aristotle, Avicenna and Averroes, but also from the theologians, including Aquinas himself. Orthodoxy, as embodied by conservative religious government, was unable to tolerate the free operation of human intelligence and insight. That this intolerance was partly in the interest of preserving the concept of human individuality adds a nice touch of irony to an act of repression.

The philosophies of Averroes and Aquinas were not completely antithetical. St. Thomas struggled with the problems of creation and causality in a way very reminiscent of Averroes. For Averroes the relationship between philosophical truth and theological or revealed truth was more complex than is often realized. Obviously he considered that the *symbolic* representation of theological truth was on a lower level, but that is a different matter.

So, as we used to say in the twentieth century, the beat goes on. From above we have revelation and faith; from below, observation and reasoning. The neoplatonists and the Moslem theologians had gravitated more to the former, the Arabian Aristotelian philosophers more to the latter, and neither a true marriage nor even a smooth transition had ever been achieved. Averroes did his best to establish the harmony of religion and philosophy, but it is doubtful whether he found his solution completely satisfactory and it is probable that no one else did, not even those who were considered to be his followers.

(xiii)

Realists and Nominalists

Among the many related questions faced by the scholastics was the problem of *universals*. As I remarked a moment ago, "The human mind, according to Aquinas's Aristotelian approach, depends on sense experience for all its natural knowledge; the individual intellect functions actively to gather elements of universality from sense perceptions and to impress the *idea* on the intellect in its passive mode."

This naturally leads to the question, "Do these elements of universality arise from something akin to thought or intention that is immanent in the objects of perception, or are they superimposed by the observer's intellectual processes?" This is a way of characterizing the schism between realists and nominalists which Steiner considered so important, and which caused just as much trouble as the problems of individuality and immortality.

The popular explanation of the realist position in mediaeval philosophy is that the idea, universal, or general concept of a class of objects, such as oak trees, lions or triangles, is believed to exist independently both of our thought processes and of the individual objects. The universal is, in other words, a real, actual entity outside our minds. There were, however, various stages in the perception of universals. At the extreme realist end of the spectrum is Plato's teaching, in which the universal is a *form* (also referred to as an *idea* or *archetype*) existing in a spiritual dimension, independent of our thinking and functioning to generate individual manifestations on earth. At the opposite end of the spectrum is the *nominalist* view; outside the human mind, universals have no existence whatsoever, and only individual objects have actual existence. Faced with a multitude of miscellaneous objects we find that some resemble one another sufficiently to be placed in a separate bundle. Carnivores with golden manes and tufted tails can be placed in the category of lions. If we are *nominalists* we believe that this category is something that we have invented and *named*. Individual lions exist, but the category has no existence outside the mind.[84] If we are realists in the Platonic sense, however, we believe that these creatures resemble one another because they are all generated from an idea or form in the spiritual world. Mediaeval thinking was strongly influenced by Aristotle's modified form of realism, in which, rather than existing as a separate, generative archetype, the universal form or idea is immanent in each individual.

Steiner relates all this confusion to the action of the Exousiai in giving up their rulership of the cosmic intelligence to the Archai, one step closer to the human being, while maintaining their stewardship of the whole world of sense impressions—colors, forms and sounds. How do we understand the objects of perception, now that the thoughts that were once as intimately wedded to them as their colors and shapes seem to have passed into a philosophical limbo? In Steiner's words:

"This uncertainty runs through the teachings of the Scholastics... The Realists, with Thomas Aquinas and his circle at their head, still felt the old connection between Thought and Thing... they looked on Thoughts as actual realities, existing in the Things. The Thoughts of a man they viewed as something real, flowing from the Things into his soul. The Nominalists felt strongly that the soul makes her own thoughts… [that] thoughts were only the names men made for things….

"Even though thoughts had fallen from his domain and into that of men, [the Realists] yet wanted as thinkers to go on serving Michael as Prince of Intelligence in the cosmos. The Nominalists, in the unconscious parts of their souls, completed the falling away from Michael. They regarded not Michael, but man as the owner of the thoughts."[85]

Whatever one's opinion of Steiner and the operations of the hierarchies, it is clear that the problem of realism and nominalism is not merely an abstract question of the status of universals, but a vital issue of the reality and validity of thinking in relation to sense perception, faith and revelation. If we ask which of the scholastics believed in Platonic archetypes the answer is almost certainly none of them. Probably the closest is the view of St. Anselm, who regarded the purpose of any created being as whatever God made it for; before the creation, the idea or form of the being existed as a universal in the mind of God, giving creatures the obligation to praise God by fulfilling His purpose as well as they possibly can.

Aquinas and his followers were realists in the sense that they experienced the formative principles as having their own independent existence, so that our thinking draws something *real* from the perceived world.

(xiv)

Thomism in Decline

I mentioned that one of the foundations of Aquinas's synthesis is the principle that although philosophy falls short of the highest regions of faith and revelation, natural reason can still be applied to theological matters. This is the point at which the earliest attacks on his system began. The

Scottish philosopher John Duns Scotus (c.1265-c.1308), known also as the "Subtle Doctor", emphasized the gap between theology and philosophy, placing more emphasis on faith and will and less on reason. He was, however, a realist in the same sense as Aquinas, and relied extensively on Aristotle. His name, Duns, was transformed into the word "dunce", originally meaning "a maker of excessively subtle distinctions."

A greater challenge to Thomist philosophy and theology took place in the early fourteenth century with an increasing tendency for philosophy to become analytical rather than synthetic—in other words to take apart rather than to build up—and to work against the realism of Aquinas. The key figure here is William of Ockham (1285-1347), known as the "more than subtle Doctor" and most famous for his "razor", which he used not to trim beards but to excise unnecessary concepts. As far as we are concerned, the most important victim of this process was the realist concept of the Universal as something outside the human mind and inherent in the objects of nature. Like many philosophers before him, Ockham considered himself the true interpreter of Aristotle. He accepted Aristotle's theory of form, but he thought that it had been misused or misrepresented by some of his fellow scholastics, including Aquinas. Like Francis Bacon, three centuries later, he maintained that we can extract all the juice we need from our sense impressions by using our powers of observation and organization. In supposing the independent existence of universals we are needlessly multiplying entities, a practice already frowned upon by Aristotle, and, as William put it, committing "the worst error in philosophy."

This is a reasonable position to take if it seems to us that people arrive at the Universals inductively and then take the extra step of *supposing* that they exist independently; "It is vain to do with more what can be done with less." It would be a very different matter for those who were able actually to *experience* the formative operation of thought within the phenomena of nature. Steiner considered that true Aristotelian realists were able to do this and that five hundred years after Aquinas, Goethe made this kind of experience the basis for a new form of science. The reality of the fourteenth century, however, was that philosophers were less inclined to pursue the idea of locating thought or spirit in natural being. Their essentially nominalistic approach resulted in what was regarded as the "new philosophy", in contrast to the old realist philosophy of the thirteenth century, which had included the work of both Thomas Aquinas and Duns Scotus. Aquinas was still a respected figure but he was not given the prominence accorded to him in modern times by the Roman Church, which, in the person of Pope Leo XIII, adopted Thomism as its official philosophy in 1879, the same year as the beginning of Michael's current stint as ruling Archangel.

By the late fifteenth century the Scholastics' efforts to bring Aristotelianism and Christianity, reason and faith, into a single, consistent world experience had fallen into decadence and gradually petered out. The transition into nominalism had deprived their thinking of substance and, with nothing real to think about, their thought processes turned in upon themselves and produced the "cobwebs of learning, admirable for the fineness of thread and work, but of no substance or profit" that Francis Bacon saw as characteristic of the scholastic movement as a whole.

* * *

The tendency among anthroposophists automatically to regard the realists as the good guys and the nominalists as the bad is not helpful to the understanding. In Steiner's terms, there was a very good reason for the latter point of view to emerge—the ancient unity of object and thought had been dissolved in an earlier age when the Exousiai released the cosmic intelligence while keeping responsibility for sense impressions. Furthermore, being a realist was no guarantee of supporting the great synthesis of Aquinas. As we have seen, Duns Scotus, who was a moderate (i.e. Aristotelian) realist, was one of the first to undermine the harmony of faith and reason, a central point in the doctrine of St. Thomas. It is necessary to recognize that the philosophical and theological traumas that human beings had to deal with in the Middle Ages were not merely the results of people being good or bad, perceptive or opaque to the needs of truly human evolution. No doubt some were good and sensitive, some were bad and dense, and many were simply confused; but, whether or not we accept Steiner's picture of evolution, the underlying truth is that the problems that they had to deal with were cosmic in scale and none of the proposed solutions really worked.

However vital the question of Realism versus Nominalism may be to those who wish to understand the spiritual realities of the world, it seems to be of very little importance to modern historians of philosophy, possibly because among professional philosophers very few, if any, realists of any kind remain.[86] I have gone into the matter in some detail because Steiner regards Francis Bacon's philosophy as the epitome of Nominalism; this is something that requires careful examination.

*　*　*

One characteristic that Bacon did not share with the Arabians and the scholastics was reverence for Aristotle. His contempt for the thought processes of the scholastics was exacerbated by their absorption of Aristotle's philosophy into the body of religious orthodoxy, which put a considerable damper on subsequent experimentation and discovery. He thought that the pursuit of true science had lapsed into a system of exercises in dialectic, and likened the decay of knowledge to the putrefaction of natural substances, since it brought forth "subtile, idle, unwholesome, and (as I may term them) vermiculate questions.... This type of degenerate learning did chiefly reign among the schoolmen [scholastics]; who having sharp and strong wits and an abundance of leisure, and small variety of reading; but their wits being shut up in the cells of a few authors (chiefly Aristotle, their dictator) as their persons were shut up in the cells of monasteries and colleges; and knowing little history, either of nature or time; did out of no great quantity of matter, and infinite agitation of wit, spin out unto us those laborious webs of learning which are extant in their books. For the wit and mind of man, if it work upon matter, which is the contemplation of the creatures of God, worketh according to the stuff, and is limited thereby; but if it worketh upon itself, as the spider worketh his web, then it is endless, and brings forth indeed cobwebs of learning, admirable for the fineness of thread and work, but of no substance or profit."[87]

As far as his status with regard to Nominalism is concerned, I must remind the reader of Steiner's comments:

"With [Bacon], Nominalism has become such a thoroughgoing and avowed philosophy that he says: 'We must sweep away man's false belief in a reality which is, in point of fact, nothing but a *name*. Reality presents itself to us only when we look out on the world of the senses. The senses alone provide us with realities, the realities of empirical knowledge.' ...For him the spiritual world has evaporated into something which can never well up from the inner life of man with any scientific certainty or security."

Realism and nominalism are mentioned not at all in *The Advancement of Learning* and only once in the *Novum Organum*. Bacon remarks that the notions of the pre-Socratic philosophers "have all of them some taste of the natural philosopher — some savor of the nature of things, and experience, and bodies; whereas in the physics of Aristotle you hear hardly anything but the words of logic, which in his metaphysics also, under a more imposing name, and evidently more as a realist than a nominalist, he has handled over again."

Realism *versus* nominalism was no longer an issue—the debate had been settled in favor of the latter. Bacon's target was not realism, but the whole scholastic movement and its decadent aftermath, the manifestations of which deeply offended his sense of rightness. The problem of living amid the literary detritus of spent world-views is that what is real, valid and still fruitful becomes extremely elusive. The whole tangled mass of sixteenth century learning, if I may change the metaphor, had become a jungle too thick either to be penetrated or to be cultivated, and this is what Bacon wanted to cut away. The remarks attributed by Rudolf Steiner to Francis Bacon in the foregoing quotation are not Bacon's own words, but represent Steiner's perception of his frame of mind and intentions. Bacon's scientific method flowed vigorously into the nominalist stream, but I have found no evidence that he was particularly concerned with the old nominalist-realist debate. His view of the world recalls that of Anselm and, with its clear implication that categories are created by God and not by man, has something in common with that of the traditional realists: "The ideas of the divine mind… are the creator's true stamp on created things, printed and defined on matter by true and precise lines." He hoped that his elaborate system of scientific research would actually draw these ideas from nature into the human mind, thereby revealing to some extent God's purposes, and he thought that by these means he might establish "forever a true and lawful marriage between the empirical and the rational faculty [i.e. between the sense world and the thought world], the unkind and ill-starred divorce of which has thrown into confusion all the affairs of the human family."[88]

It must be remembered that Bacon was under the impression that what he was trying to reverse was the result of human frailty whereas, according to Steiner, the situation had developed from the decision of divine powers to allow the separation of thought from thing, and from disagreements in the spiritual world about how the process should continue, all of which would certainly have been sufficient to throw "into confusion all the affairs of the human family". Believing that God's designs were present in the objects of perception, Bacon was under no illusion about the quantity, quality and intensity of the work needed to enable us to catch a glimpse of them.

Part III

Bacon's Scientific Method

"Boethius[89]... distinguishes intelligentia from ratio; the former being enjoyed in its perfection by angels. Intellectus is that in man which approximates most nearly to angelic intelligentia; it is in fact obumbrata intelligentia, clouded intelligence, or a shadow of intelligence. Its relation to reason is thus described by Aquinas: 'Intellect is the simple (i.e., indivisible, uncompounded) grasp of an intelligible truth, whereas reasoning is the progression towards an intelligible truth by going from one understood point to another....' We are enjoying intellectus when we 'just see' a self-evident truth; we are exercising ratio when we proceed step by step to prove a truth which is not self-evident. A cognitive life in which all truth can be simply 'seen' would be the life of an angel. A life of unmitigated ratio where nothing was simply 'seen' and all had to be proved would presumably be impossible." (C. S. Lewis, The Discarded Image, C.U.P., 1964.)[90]

"To God, truly, the Giver and Architect of Forms, and it may be to the angels and higher intelligences, it belongs to have an affirmative knowledge of forms immediately, and from the first contemplation. But this assuredly is more than man can do, to whom it is granted at first to proceed only by negatives, and to end at last in affirmatives after exclusion has been exhausted." (Francis Bacon, Novum Organum, Aphorism 15.)

"How often have I said to you that when you have eliminated the impossible, whatever remains, *however improbable*, must be the truth?"

(Sherlock Holmes, *per* Sir Arthur Conan Doyle)

(xv)

The Great Instauration

In 1620, Bacon published most of what we know about his method in his *Instauratio Magna* (The Great Instauration). *Instauratio* may be interpreted as *restoration* or *institution*, and Bacon may have had both senses in mind, since he aimed at restoring man's lordship over nature, while specifically proposing to create new forms of philosophy and logic for scientific purposes. The work was intended to consist of six sections, but the 1620 publication included only a dedication to King James, an outline of the projected contents of the whole work, the *Novum Organum*, or *New Organon*, which consists of a preface and two books of aphorisms, and an introduction to the *Natural and Experimental History*.

According to the original plan, the six parts were to be:

Part I: The Division of Knowledge.
Part II: The New Organon (Novum Organum) or Direction concerning the Interpretation of Nature.[91]
Part III: The Phenomena of the Universe: or a Natural and Experimental History for the Foundation of Philosophy.
Part IV: The Ladder of the Intellect.
Part V: The Forerunners: or Anticipations of the New Philosophy.
Part VI: The New Philosophy: or Active Science

Part I recalls Bacon's remark to Lord Burghley: "I confess that I have taken all knowledge to be my province..." His division corresponded to what he understood to be the principle activities of the human mind: memory, imagination and reason.

Part II, the *Novum Organum*, although unfinished, gives a concrete idea of the strictly inductive science that Bacon contemplated. Part III appeared posthumously in the form of the *Sylva Sylvarum*, also unfinished. Bacon referred to the *Novum Organum* as "the chiefest of his works" and explained its premature publication as a precaution against his advancing years—"I number my days and would have it saved." There is, however, reason to believe that he was anxious to get on with the natural and experimental histories, which he valued at least as highly, and which he regarded as complementary to the inductive system and potentially more influential.

In Part IV, Bacon intended to give examples of the use of his method, and Part V was to give some "Anticipations of the New Philosophy." Earlier writings suggest that this would have included a speculative account of a geocentric universe in which the material, inner earth was divided from the aerie, active heavens by a region of mixed substance in which the phenomena of nature were to be observed. Bacon admitted, or rather, asserted, that to complete the final section of the Great Instauration, to which the first five sections were supposed to be "subservient and ministrant", was a task "both above my strength and beyond my hopes." As the earlier parts of the work show, he believed that the task of bringing the New Philosophy to full fruition was beyond the powers of a single individual. It could come about only when those aspects of life connected with the three human capacities that he recognized—memory (past and present), imagination (philosophy and the arts) and reason (the community of scientists)—worked together. The whole work was one part of a twofold effort in some degree to restore human beings to the status that they had enjoyed before the Fall, the other part being a life of Christian faith and piety through which we might become once more the children of God.

(xvi)

The *Novum Organum*

At last we come to a description of Bacon's proposed system for the advancement of science, and I have to warn the reader that while I shall do my best to keep these explanations brief, it must be admitted that Bacon's style and method do not encourage brevity. Anyone who ploughs through all 182 aphorisms may well feel that Bacon's idea of an aphorism was very elastic—some of them go on for several pages—and that Bacon could have conveyed the essence of his message much more briefly.

The opening paragraph of the *Novum Organum* tells the reader exactly where Bacon is coming from:

"Those who have taken upon them to lay down the law of nature as a thing already searched out and understood… have therein done philosophy and the sciences great injury. For as they have been successful in inducing belief, so they have been effective in quenching and stopping inquiry… Those on the other hand who have taken a contrary course, and asserted that absolutely nothing can be known… have certainly advanced reasons for it that are not to be despised; but yet they have neither started from true principles nor rested in the just conclusion; zeal and affectation having carried them much too far. The more ancient of the Greeks… took up with better judgment a position between these two extremes — between the presumption of pronouncing on everything, and the despair of comprehending anything; and though frequently and bitterly complaining of the difficulty of inquiry and the obscurity of things, and like impatient horses champing at the bit, they did not the less follow up their object and engage with nature, thinking (it seems) that this very question — viz., whether or not anything can be known — was to be settled not by arguing, but by trying. And yet they too, trusting entirely to the force of their understanding, applied no rule, but made everything turn upon hard thinking and perpetual working and exercise of the mind."

Despairing of the state of scientific method and knowledge, Bacon goes on to emphasize the carefully regulated practice of observation and to propose a clean sweep of the traditional habits of mind.

"Now my method, though hard to practice, is easy to explain... I propose to establish progressive stages of certainty. The evidence of the sense, helped and guarded by a certain process of correction, I retain. But the mental operation which follows the act of sense I for the most part reject; and instead of it I open and lay out a new and certain path for the mind to proceed in, starting directly from the simple sensuous perception."

He asserts that by attaching so much importance to logic, people had already conceded that the mind was in need of help, but that the "remedy had come too late to do any good when the mind is already occupied with unsound doctrines and beset by vain imaginings."

"And therefore that art of logic...has had the effect of making the errors permanent rather than disclosing truth. There remains but one course for the recovery of a sound and healthy condition — namely, that the entire work of the understanding be commenced afresh, and the mind itself be from the very outset not left to take its own course, but guided at every step; and the business be done as if by machinery."

Bacon presses the mechanical analogy; to try to erect a great edifice of science using only the unaided powers of individual minds is as mad as to try to erect a huge obelisk with the power of the human body when mechanical assistance is available. Readers who recoil from this dismissal of the mind as an organism capable of grasping the nature of things, and its replacement by a mechanically applied method, will not be appeased by the grudging, if not openly insulting, manner with which he allows for the continuation of traditional methods.

"Be it remembered then that I am far from wishing to interfere with the philosophy which now flourishes... For I do not object to the use of this received philosophy, or others like it, for supplying matter for disputations or ornaments for discourse — for the professor's lecture and for the business of life. Nay, more, I declare openly that for these uses the philosophy which I bring forward will not be much available… It cannot be caught up in passage. It does not flatter the understanding by conformity with preconceived notions. Nor will it come down to popular acceptance except by its utility and effects.

"Let there be therefore two streams of knowledge, and in like manner two kindreds of students in philosophy — not hostile or alien to each other, but bound together by mutual services; let there in short be one method for the cultivation, another for the discovery, of knowledge. And for those who prefer the former, either from hurry or from considerations of business or for want of mental power to take in and embrace the other (which must needs be most men's case), I wish that they may succeed to their desire in what they are about… But if there be any man who… aspires to penetrate further; to overcome, not an adversary in argument, but nature in action; to seek, not pretty and probable conjectures, but certain and demonstrable knowledge — I invite all such to join themselves with me, that… we may find a way at length into her inner chambers. And to make my meaning clearer and to familiarize the thing by giving it a name, I have chosen to call one of these methods or ways Anticipation of the Mind, the other Interpretation of Nature."

"To overcome nature in action" and "to seek certain and demonstrable knowledge" are Bacon's immediate goals, and they are inextricably intertwined.

(xvii)

Novum Organum, Book I: A Brief Look

The source of the one thing that everyone "knows" about Francis Bacon is the third aphorism of Book I.

Human knowledge and human power meet in one; for where the cause is not known the effect cannot be produced. We can only command nature by obeying her, and that which in contemplation is as the cause is in operation as the rule.

(Book I, Aphorism 3)

This is how the aphorism appears in the complete edition of Bacon's works, translated by James Spedding, Robert Ellis and Douglas Heath, and published between 1857 and 1874. The usual thoughtless quotation, "Knowledge is power", is generally given in complete ignorance of the kind of power that Bacon was talking about, as if it implied power of a political, economic or social nature. I shall have more to say about this when we come to *The New Atlantis,* so at this point I merely emphasize that Bacon is referring to the ability to understand natural processes and use them to produce desired results: *We can only command nature by obeying her.*

In the early stages of the book most of the "aphorisms" are actually aphoristic—it is only later that they become really lengthy—and it is worthwhile to quote some of those in which he reminds the reader of his view of the obstacles to scientific progress.

9. *The cause and root of nearly all the evils in the sciences is this—that while we mistakenly admire and extol the powers of the human mind, we neglect to look for true ways of helping it.*

10. *The subtlety of nature is greater many times over than that of the senses and the understanding, so that all the specious meditations, speculations and glosses in which men indulge are to no purpose, only there is no one at hand to observe it.*

11. *Just as the sciences we now have are of no use in discovering works, so neither does the logic we now have help us in discovering new sciences.*

Here, stated in its most concentrated form, is Bacon's opinion of the human mind, an opinion that, to some people, might justify a decision not to bother to read any further. Can it possibly be true that our God-given intelligence is such a feeble thing that it cannot be trusted to understand the workings of a natural world that has the same origin? This is a question that may well be asked by anyone who believes that in the beginning God created the heavens and the earth, and that He went on to create man and woman to dwell on the earth and wonder at the heavens. Intelligence has one foot in the heavens and the other on the earth. Intelligence and nature are the gifts of God, so why should not the one understand the other?

Bacon's opinion, however, was not generated from principles but from observation. It seemed to him that the problems that he saw in the science of his time were due partly to limited intellectual capacity and partly to having gone the wrong way about the job in the first place. If one person's mind is too weak, why not look for a way of combining the efforts of a large number of minds? Just as twenty people, properly equipped with ropes and pulleys can raise huge objects that would seem immovable to the individual weight-lifter, twenty people, if properly organized, might be able to generate a kind of science beyond the capabilities of the individual.

The catch here lies in the phrase, "if properly organized." Even if it were possible to turn geese into swans by multiplication, someone would still have to give the geese their assignments and collect their results. Evidently, in giving his assessment of the powers of the individual goose, Bacon has made a tacit exception of himself; he would not be a goose but a goose driver. This structural quirk is almost laughably obvious in Aphorism 10, where he complains about the ways in which scientific work is done, and adds, "Only there is no one at hand to observe it."

It may be noted that the same quirk is sometimes evident in Rudolf Steiner's lectures and writings.

* * *

Aphorism 19 hints at a way of proceeding that might replace the "fashionable" method.

There are and can be only two ways of searching into and discovering truth. The one rushes from the senses and particulars to axioms[92] of the most general kind, and from these principles, the truth of which is taken for granted, proceeds to judgement and to the discovery of intermediate axioms. And this is the method that is now fashionable. The other derives axioms from the senses and particulars by a gradual and continuous ascent, to arrive at the most general axioms last of all. This is the true way, but as yet untried.

A classic case of the "fashionable" method mentioned in Aphorism 19 is the emergence of the Democritan atomic theory in the fifth century BC, in which far-reaching conclusions about the constitution and operation of matter are drawn from a combination of metaphysical questions and anecdotal data. The theory appears as speculation rather than knowledge, and was, as Bacon would have said, barren of works—2,300 years elapsed before it was put to any practical use. It is hard to find a handy, self-contained example of the method proposed by Bacon, since it has never been tried by anyone except its author, and the example which he gives, and which we shall examine, is longwinded and not very convincing.

The principles of Bacon's method are only partly accounted for in Aphorism 19, quoted above. We learn more from the following aphorisms:

... At the beginning and for some time, I look only for light-bearing experiments, not fruit-bearing ones, following, as I have often said, the example of the divine creation, when on the first day, God made the light only, and devoted a whole day to that alone, without introducing any material work in that time. If, therefore, anyone should think that such things are of no use, he should consider whether he also thinks light to be of no use... (Aphorism 121)

.... The ideas of the divine mind... are the creator's true stamp upon created things, printed and defined on matter by true and precise lines. In this respect, therefore, truth and utility are the very things themselves;[93] *so works themselves are of greater value as pledges of truth than as comforts in life.* (Aphorism 124)

Bacon has been accused of placing utility ahead of understanding, but plainly he was not after an easy conquest and a quick profit. It takes time to develop an understanding of the natural world, and once it is obtained, this understanding, validated by operation, brings us into contact with the working of the divine mind. The relationship between truth and works is cyclical, and truth, he emphasizes, is more important than comfort. This gives another bearing on the meaning of "power", as shown in the following summary:

Contemplation of systematically obtained observations leads to understanding; understanding leads to operation; successful operation certifies the validity of the understanding. The poverty of the human mind in comparison with the richness of nature is to be balanced by the systematic examination of a wealth of observations. *Power over nature, in this context, means the ability to produce desired effects in physical objects.*[94]

(xviii)

Novum Organum, Book II: A Taste

Bacon gives the most succinct and colorful description of his method in Aphorism 123 of Book I of the *Novum Organum*:

I may say of myself that which someone said in jest: "It cannot be that we should think alike, when one drinks water and the other wine." Now other men, in both ancient and modern times, have in scientific matters drunk a crude liquor which, like water, wells up spontaneously from their understanding or is drawn up by logic, as if by wheels from a well. Whereas I toast mankind in a liquor strained from countless grapes, from grapes ripe and fully seasoned, collected in clusters, gathered and then squeezed in the press, and finally purified and clarified in the vat. And therefore it is no wonder that they and I do not think alike.

The picture of one his tables of instances as a bunch of grapes is much more appetizing than the reality. "First", he says (Book II, Aphorism 10), "we must prepare a natural and experimental history, sufficient and good; and this is the foundation of all, for we are not to imagine or suppose, but to *discover*, what nature does or may be made to do." Secondly, since "this history is so various and diffuse that it confuses and distracts the understanding... we must form tables and arrangements of instances, in such a method and order that the understanding may be able to deal with them." However "The understanding, if left to itself... is incompetent to form axioms[95] unless it be directed and guarded. Thirdly, therefore, we must use true and legitimate induction, which is the very key of interpretation."

Starting in Aphorism 11, he uses "the investigation of the form of heat" as his example. The first step is to create a list of *Instances Agreeing in the Nature of Heat*, a muster, as he says, "of all known instances that agree in the same nature, though in substances the most unlike." He produces a list of 27 instances, which he calls the *Table of Essence and Presence*, in which warmth is produced, ranging from the effects of sunrays and burning objects to the spontaneous combustion of damp vegetation and horse dung. Opposed to this (Aphorism XII) is the *Table of Deviation, or of Absence in Proximity*, in which Bacon gives examples of circumstances apparently similar to those in his first list but in which warmth is not produced. The rays of the moon, the stars and comets have no warming power and rotting wood does not produce heat. At this point, the modern reader may well be wondering what possible process of induction can draw anything useful from these tables of somewhat miscellaneous and contradictory data. Bacon hasn't finished yet, however. He now presents a *Table of Degrees or Comparison in Heat*, containing "instances in which the nature under inquiry exists to a greater or lesser degree." "No nature", he says, "can be taken to be the true form, unless it always decreases when the nature decreases and always increases when the nature increases."

Among the forty-one instances he gives are the observations that animals are always cold on the outside in winter or cold weather but are thought to be warmer inside, and that the heat from the heavenly bodies depends on their perpendicularity, their proximity and their conjunction with stars. Before going on to show us how to use the tables he admits to a considerable degree of dissatisfaction with them (Aphorism 14):

How poor we are in [natural] history anyone may see from the foregoing tables, where I not only insert sometimes mere traditions and reports (though never without a note of doubtful credit and authority) in place of history proved and instances certain, but am also frequently forced to use the words "Let trial be made" or "Let it be further inquired."

He also gives a stern warning about the word *form*, specifically excluding the Platonic archetype. In Aphorism 1 of Book II he says that our object is to "discover the form of a given nature, or its true specific difference, or nature-engendering nature or source of emanation (for these are the terms that come nearest to the description of the thing)." In Peter Urbach's words, Bacon is talking about the "internal state of a body that is responsible for a corresponding observable nature." Bacon emphasizes that he is not talking about the archetypes of such things as lions, eagles, roses or gold, but about the "laws and determinations of absolute actuality which govern and constitute any simple nature, as heat, light, weight… Thus the form of heat or the form of light is the same thing as the law of heat or the law of light." (Aphorism 17)

If, having absorbed (perhaps) three long tables of instances and received an explanation of the nature of form, we feel ready to learn exactly what the form of heat is, we are in for a disappointment, a little like the disappointment we have felt on those occasions when we thought that Rudolf Steiner was finally going to tell us what spirit "really" is. The process of induction is only just beginning. As Bacon has remarked in Aphorism 15, *"To God, truly, the Giver and Architect of Forms, and it may be to the angels and higher intelligences, it belongs to have an affirmative knowledge of forms immediately, and from the first contemplation. But this assuredly is more than man can do, to whom it is granted at first to proceed only by negatives, and to end at last in affirmatives after exclusion has been exhausted."*

The nature of form, he insists, is such that it is always fully present in every aspect: any manifestation of a supposed form which is sometimes present and sometimes absent must therefore be excluded. "Any contradictory instance overthrows a conjecture as to the form." We may for instance have been inclined to accept light and brightness as manifestations of the form of heat, but we must reject them since heat often occurs without brightness, as in the case of boiling water, and brightness without heat, as in the case of moonbeams. Bacon is not satisfied that these exclusions are sufficient to lead to a definitive statement of the form of heat, but he feels that the questing intelligence needs a little encouragement, so he produces what he calls the *Indulgence of the Understanding* or the *Commencement of Interpretation* or, returning to grapes, the *First Vintage*. This goes on for several pages before arriving at a statement of "the form or true definition of heat."[96]

Heat is a motion, expansive, restrained and acting in its strife upon the smaller particles of bodies. But concerning the expansion we make this qualification: while it expands in all directions, it has at the same time an inclination upward. And the struggle of the particles is qualified also: it is not sluggish, but hurried and violent.

Remembering that "that which in contemplation is as the cause is in operation as the rule", we can expect this statement of understanding to be followed by a statement of operation:

Viewed with reference to operation it is the same thing: If in any natural body you can excite a dilating or expanding motion, and can so repress this motion and turn it back upon itself that the dilation shall not proceed equably, but have its way in one part and be counteracted in another, you will undoubtedly generate heat.

Having tasted this sample of Bacon's grape juice, you may be inclined to wonder what all the fuss is about or to question whether His Lordship has discovered something in keeping with his grandiose plans for the betterment of mankind and insight into God's purposes. For one thing, it sounds a little reminiscent of Democritus and his struggling and colliding atoms; and for another, the statement of operation doesn't conjure up any pictures of useful practical activity. I am not saying that Bacon was wrong. The activity of pumping up a bicycle tire fits Bacon's description quite well and certainly generates heat in the barrel of the pump. But when the thermal effects of expansion and contraction became important matters for practical physicists and refrigerator designers it was not because of anything that Bacon had said or done. Like Bacon, however, we must avoid jumping to hasty conclusions—someone with a more positive outlook might easily describe his conclusions about heat as a remarkable anticipation of nineteenth century kinetic theory. But then, of course, the same could be—and has been—said about Democritus.

One problem is that we have no clear idea what Bacon meant by "particles" in this context, and it is highly probable that he hadn't either. Earlier references seem to indicate that his particles were larger than atoms but too small to be individually visible. That he rejects the Democritan idea of immutable atoms moving in the void is clear from Book II, Aphorism 8, where, speaking of the results of his system of investigation, he says:

Nor shall we thus be led to the doctrine of atoms, which implies the hypothesis of a vacuum and that of the unchangeableness of matter (both false assumptions); we shall be led only to real particles, such as really exist.

There are, moreover, difficulties connected with the motions and interactions of particles that other people from Democritus to Descartes had worried about and Bacon never touches. He seems to have introduced the notion of sub-sensible particles without citing any experimental evidence on their behalf, and the validity of the statement of operation does not depend on their existence.

Bacon's scientific books are full of insights and encompass a whole natural history—albeit one that often has a distinct mediaeval flavor—but they were "barren of works"—at least, the kind of works that he envisaged for them.

*   *   *

If we stop for a moment to ask what would have been required to make these ideas of heat fruitful, two things immediately come to mind, the first being that Bacon's work is devoid of mathematics. I have never come upon any indication that he ever took a measurement of anything in his life.

There is an element of historical irony here. At exactly the same time as Bacon was making such a long-drawn-out fuss about the ancient methods of inquiry, the Dutchman Willabrod Snell (1591-1626) was in the process of discovering the laws of refraction. This he did, not with recourse to lengthy tables of instances, exclusions and so on, but by working with rays of light and using his geometrical insight. A few years later Descartes stated the laws in their modern trigonometrical form. Meanwhile, Kepler had given exact mathematical expression to the laws of planetary motion and would have had them much more easily—and the laws of refraction too—if he had been proficient in trigonometry; and Galileo had laid the foundations for Newtonian dynamics. Within half a century of Bacon's death a whole generation of physicists appeared, including Huygens, Hooke, Boyle and Newton, who discovered mathematically expressed laws of optics, heat, mechanics and gravitation by methods that had nothing to do with anything in the *Novum Organum*. As far as "works" are concerned, there is no doubting the fruitfulness of these discoveries, but they might not have satisfied Bacon. In his view mathematically stated laws were merely descriptive. He was almost certainly unaware of Kepler's Laws of Planetary Motion, at least in the complete form that every student learns today, but even if he had known them his response might well have been, "Yes, but *why* do the orbits have this form? What is the physical reason?"[97] And he would have wanted to know *why* rays of light bend according to Snell's Law.

The second observation is that although he admired Democritus and sometimes spoke about particles, he seems to have had no conception of them as explanatory or predictive tools. In Bacon's view philosophy concerned itself far too much with the very big and the very little—"the first principles of things and the highest generalities of nature; whereas utility and the means of working result entirely from things intermediate. Hence it is that men cease not from abstracting nature until they come to potential and unformed matter, nor, on the other hand, from dissecting nature till they reach the atom; things which, even if true, can do little for the welfare of mankind."[98]

It is not without interest and relevance to note that Bacon's strictures apply to the two components of physical science that are least comprehensible to most people today—the theory of relativity (big) and the quantum theory (little). The "things intermediate", which we find in our living rooms and garages, obey ordinary, old-fashioned physical laws. It is only when we get involved with things far beyond the range of normal perception that the rot sets in.

If you take these two characteristics together—Bacon's lack of interest in both mathematics and atoms—and imagine them applied to the theoretical physics and chemistry of the past three centuries, you will find that there is very little left. Bacon wanted to know what was going on inside the objects he studied that made them behave the way they did. Science has tried to do this by applying Newtonian mechanics, electrical principles, quantum theory and relativistic principles to the motions and transitions of atoms, bits of atoms and waves, and if Bacon had lived another few hundred years, he might have realized that atoms and great generalizations were far more useful than he had expected. Or he might have said, "That's all very well, but why are atoms the way they are?" And later on, "Why are electrons, quarks and photons the way they are?" He would have agreed with Newton's answer—"Because that's the way God made them"—and he might still have felt dissatisfied. A lot of energy and time has been expended in the effort to find the answers to questions of that kind, without having much effect on the general course of scientific and technological development. Bacon would undoubtedly have been pleased with the kinetic theory of matter and its application to refrigeration[99], but he would have been disappointed to find that most of the technology of refrigeration and the whole of classical thermodynamics are completely independent of any particular notions about what he called "the form of heat", in other words, what's going on inside the materials. Something similar applies to the development of electrical circuits and vacuum tubes—our ideas of what goes on inside them have changed radically over the past hundred-and-fifty years, but the circuits still work just as well. It wasn't until we got into the technology arising from solid state physics that what Bacon would have called the "form of electricity" came into its own.

Underlying all such observations is the question of whether the method described in the *Novum Organum* is likely under any circumstances to generate a true and useful science. The answer, a resounding "No", seems to me to be at once obvious and hard to explain. The fact that in spite of all the talk of Baconian institutions the method was never put into operation is a strong indication of its futility. We can compare its diffuseness—like the absent-minded shopper in the supermarket, we don't know what we're looking for until we see it—with the concentration required of a quantum physicist or a Goethean scientist. One way of stating the problem is to point out that if you want a view of the world you have to have a place to stand, something that Bacon was at pains not to provide. Another way was provided by William Whewell[100] in his *Philosophy of the Inductive Sciences* (John W. Parker, London, 1840).

"For an Art[101] of Discovery is not possible. At each step of the progress of science, are needed invention, sagacity, genius; elements which no Art can give. We may hope in vain, as Bacon hoped, for an organ which shall enable all men to construct scientific truths, as a pair of compasses enables all men to construct exact circles. However large were his anticipations, the actual progress of science since his time may aid in giving comprehensiveness to our views. And with respect to the methods by which science is to be promoted, the structure and operation of the Organ by which truth is to be collected from nature, we know that, though Bacon's general maxims still guide and animate philosophical enquirers yet that his views, in their detail, have all turned out inapplicable: the technical parts of his method failed in his hands and are forgotten among the cultivators of science."

Like Whewell, we can observe that Bacon's proposed system went nowhere, while we continue to admire the Chancellor for his pertinacity and probity in dealing with his data. It is this last aspect that has become so important in modern science. Every lead must be pursued and every contrary instance means the abandonment or modification of a theory. It is not clear, however, that Bacon was entirely responsible for these precepts. Kepler did not need Bacon to tell him that a discrepancy of a few minutes of arc meant the abandonment of a cherished system.[102]

This discussion raises several questions: "Why was Bacon so influential?" or "Why do so many people *think* that he was influential?" In Steiner's terms, "How does his work reflect its Arabian lineage?" "Is it possible that his influence had little or nothing to do with his scientific work or anything else that he actually thought or did, but that he was a mere stepping stone for spiritual powers—the daemons of materialism mentioned in the Karma lectures?" Did the daemons look at Bacon's work as a whole and say, "Aha! If we suppress all the soul elements and religious insights that come from the human and generous side of this man's character and keep only the elements from which human feeling has been rigorously excluded, we shall be able to promulgate a kind of science which will soon exclude perception not only of the spirit (which we have already abolished[103]) but also of the soul, and which may eventually cast doubt on the reality of consciousness." Or did these consequences arise through purely human agencies, without the aid of daemons?

I'll do my best to respond to these questions (eventually), but there are two other pressing matters to deal with first.

(xix)

Knowledge and Power—*The New Atlantis*

Carved into the stonework over the main entrance of a certain school on the Upper East Side of Manhattan are the words "Knowledge is Power—Bacon". It is easy to imagine what the students think—or, at least, what they are intended to think—when they see this inscription. "If I study hard and learn a lot, I shall become powerful—perhaps financially, perhaps politically, perhaps scientifically." Recently I have encountered the formula written with an equals sign, "Knowledge = Power", given with the sort of pseudo-scientific relish usually applied by popular quoters of $E = mc^2$, and with even less understanding of its meaning and origin. Misquotation does not stop at this point, however; it seems that the knowledge-power equation has penetrated the advertising world. "Information is power. (Now who couldn't use more of both?)"[104]

This triple degradation of Bacon's original message is typical of attitudes towards Bacon, at least until fairly recently. The first ingredient is ignorance; hardly anyone actually *reads* Bacon's works, so opinions are almost always second, third or fourth hand. Many people are under the impression that he wanted to use whatever knowledge he had to enable him or some trained band of nefarious scientists to exercise political, economic, military or technological control over their fellow human beings. It is therefore important to emphasize that on the only occasion when Bacon explicitly stated that knowledge is power (*Nam et ipsa scientia potestas est.*) he was talking about *God's* knowledge and power and providing an echo of philosophical and theological discussions that had taken place centuries earlier.[105]

The second ingredient is the tendency to turn the fruits of highly nuanced discussions into statements of arithmetical equivalency. Understanding is not really wanted—only the bottom line, as in "Time equals money." And the third is the degradation of knowledge, which implies some kind of soul-spiritual relationship to that which is known, into mere information. Information does not become knowledge until it has been transformed by inner experience.

According to John Channing Briggs, Bacon's linking of the two attributes became "the famous and problematic justification for human beings to equate knowledge and power"[106]. The connection is, however, as old as, or older than, history. Before the time of Bacon, power over one's fellow human beings was often sought through esoteric knowledge, if knowledge was involved at all, but there has always been a strong tendency for human capacities of any sort—occult, religious, scientific, political, economic, military—no matter with what idealism they have been attained, to be subverted and misused in the interest of personal power or advancement. Clearly this is not the kind of power that Bacon was talking about, but it is easy to see how our modern consciousness, unpenetrated by any actual knowledge of Bacon's work, has come to represent his studied exposition of scientific method by a single degenerate slogan.

Bacon, aware of the countless thousands who eked out a slender living by the sweat of their brows, believed that by his efforts people might to some extent be freed, both physically and spiritually, from the curse of Eden. In our world "power" almost always means either physical power—mechanical, electrical, muscular—or domination of a moral, intellectual, political or economic nature. We have, perhaps, forgotten another context in which the word appeared in Bacon's time: "But as many as received him, to them gave he power to become the sons of God, even to them that believe on his name." (John; i, 3; Authorized Version, 1611) In this context "power" means "ability" or "potentiality". Faith and knowledge give us the potential to re-enter the Kingdom of Heaven and to regain the rule over nature given by God to man, and lost through the sin of Adam and Eve. In Bacon's words:

"Lastly, I would like to address one general admonition to all—that they reflect on the true ends of knowledge, and that they seek it neither for intellectual satisfaction, nor for contention, nor for superiority to others, nor for profit, fame or power, or any of these baser things; but that they direct and bring it to perfection in charity, for the benefit and use of life. For the angels fell through desire for power; men through desire for knowledge. But of love and charity there can be no excess, neither did angel or man ever run into danger thereby."

(*The Great Instauration*, Preface)

* * *

A great deal of the "knowledge is power" discussion has centered on Bacon's unfinished tale of the *New Atlantis*. Bacon's *Sylva Sylvarum: or a Natural History* was published posthumously in 1627 by his chaplain and literary executor, William Rawley, and in the same volume, Rawley printed the *New Atlantis*, with a short introduction from which the following remarks are quoted.

"This fable my Lord devised, to the end that he might exhibit therein a model or description of a college instituted for the interpreting of nature and the producing of great and marvellous works for the benefit of men.... And even so far his Lordship hath proceeded, as to finish that part. Certainly the model is more vast and high than can possibly be imitated in all things; notwithstanding most things therein are within men's power to effect. His Lordship thought also in this fable to have composed a frame of Laws, or the best state or mould of a commonwealth; but foreseeing it would be a long work, his desire of collecting the Natural History diverted him, *which he preferred many degrees before it.*" [My italics]

In view of the amount of attention paid to *New Atlantis*, we should note that it was not planned as part of the Great Instauration, that Bacon considered its completion far less important than getting on with the *Natural History* and that there are other reasons for not completing a project besides dying. This should be borne in mind when weighing the somewhat uneven tenor of his comments on the democratic nature of the scientific endeavor and the free accessibility of its discoveries. The following remarks show the extent of disagreement on this topic among scholars.

"In his *Instauratio Magna* and elsewhere, Bacon had called for an open, democratic approach to the study of nature whereby the knowledge produced by all members of the society would be freely communicated for the benefit of all. *In contrast, secrecy is a pervasive theme of the New Atlantis.* Information is not only kept from the strangers to the island. The fellows of Salomon's house withhold information from the public at large and from the government itself." [My italics]

(Rose-Mary Sargent, in *The Cambridge Companion to Bacon*

"The transition between the voyage narrative and the description of Salomon's House, which constitutes the real substance of the *New Atlantis*, owes something to the form of the sacred dialogue, as found for instance in the second book of Esdras, ch. 3ff, in which the author describes how a divine spirit reveals to him some portion of hidden wisdom. So the Father of Salomon's House, left alone with the narrator, says, 'God bless thee, my son; I will give thee the greatest jewel I have. For I will impart unto thee, for the love of God and man, a relation of the true state of Salomon's House'. Such dialogues are also a form of apocalypse, an unveiling or disclosure of things ordinarily hidden from human eyes. *Once again, Bacon's emphasis is on the open communication of scientific knowledge, as against the secrecy practised by the occult tradition.*" [My italics]
(Brian Vickers, *Francis Bacon*, Oxford Authors, Ed. Vickers)

As Sargent points out, commenting on the dualities of openness and secrecy, democracy and meritocracy, "such tensions are an inherent part of cooperative research."

This is not one of those cases where it is easy to say, "Well, you must read the book yourself and decide." It is true that the *New Atlantis* is what is known as an easy read, although I have never met anyone else who has actually read it, but its importance in relation to the whole body of Bacon's philosophical and scientific writings is questionable. Quite apart from the matter of secrecy, it has been interpreted in so many different ways[107]—as a popular utopia, a religious allegory, a sociological critique, and an imperialist, capitalist, political manifesto, not to mention a concrete plan for a scientific society—that I am doubtful whether the possibility of a definitive interpretation exists, and fairly confident that the effort to find one would turn out to be a wild goose chase leading only to a mare's nest.[108]

Bacon's whole *oeuvre* has been subjected to widely differing interpretations, and we should briefly consider some of these.

In the seventeenth century there was a great deal of support for some of Bacon's ideas and a determined effort to put them into operation, notably in the formation of the Royal Society in London, which, however, bore only a passing resemblance to the "College of the Six Days Work" described in *New Atlantis*. By the middle of the nineteenth century the need for an experimentally based, gradualistic science was taken for granted, but the detailed approach described by Bacon was derided or ignored. As Paolo Rossi writes in the *Cambridge Companion*, "Two different, negative appraisals centered on Bacon's philosophy." According to one, Bacon was a champion of "what science has never been and will never be: a kind of knowledge obtained by observation, a process of accumulation of data, an illusory attempt to free the human mind from theories and presuppositions". According to the other, "Bacon was precisely the opposite—the symbol of what science has been up until now and should no longer be: the impious will to dominate nature and tyrannize mankind… it is the scientific and technological enthusiasm of the Lord Chancellor that leads to materialism, the mercantilization of culture, to modern industrial society, which is the realm of alienation and conformism, of the standardization and destruction of all human values."[109]

Both of these viewpoints appear in Steiner's assessment of Bacon; the former in his critique of Bacon's actual scientific method, and the latter in his assertions about Bacon's intentions for human society.

Rossi continues: "According to the [Anglo-American] philosophers of our century who extolled scientific knowledge against the nonsensical propositions of metaphysicians, Bacon has nothing to do with science. According to the continental philosophers… Bacon is the very essence of science…. Once again, Bacon was reduced to a *symbol*. The 'plumb and the weight' of the texts was avoided…. Bacon's precise distinction between 'experiments of light' and 'experiments of fruit' was disregarded. So, too, were ignored the many pages Bacon wrote against the utilitarian desire of immediate results and the foolish habit of abandoning the natural course of scientific enquiry and turning aside, like Atalanta, after profit and commodity."

After cataloguing some of the writers who have inveighed against the symbol rather than the reality, Rossi concludes; "Perhaps Francis Bacon was right; it is impossible to eradicate all the idols from men's minds. Among the idols we have so far been unable to eradicate are undoubtedly the following: *the propensity not to read the original texts; the tendency to reduce the philosophies of the past to some seemingly brilliant slogans; the construction on the basis of these of mythical philosophical portraits"* [My italics[110]]

* * *

In reading the *Novum Organum* we might almost get the idea of something rather like a beehive with no queen bee, a sausage machine with no one at the controls or a type of *Sorcerer's Apprentice* scene with the master-magician permanently absent. The scientist gives himself no airs and sits on a level with everyone else. The description that Bacon gives in *New Atlantis* is very different, insofar as there are evidently people of great importance in charge—"Fathers", who are richly dressed, lavishly attended and treated with enormous deference. The Father who explains the scientific establishment to the representative of the stranded mariners gives a list of assets—six-hundred-fathom caves, half-mile high towers, compost-makers, great lakes of both salt and fresh water, wells and fountains, spacious houses for climatic experimentation, chambers of health, experimental gardens, orchards, parks and whole zoos, brewhouses, bakeries, kitchens, dispensaries, optical-houses, sound-houses, perfume-houses, engine-houses and mathematical houses. It is depressing to find that the animals and plants to be found in these parks and gardens are there not so much for beauty as for experimental purposes. Operating this huge endeavor is a nine-fold hierarchy of workers, ranging from those who collect experimental results from all over the world, to those who draw up tables ("to give the better light for the drawing of observations and axioms"), those who design new experiments and finally to the "Interpreters of Nature", who raise the experimental discoveries to greater observations, axioms and aphorisms. Successful inventors are publicly honored and daily praise and thanks are given to God for his marvellous works.

At this point the story abruptly ends, with a note from Rawley: "The rest was not perfected." Was this because Bacon, having committed his wish-list or pipe-dream to paper, could not raise the enthusiasm to work out the legal system of Bensalem and describe the travelers' return? Could it be that he found this fragmentary description so discordant with his earlier picture of a scientific society that he abandoned it in distaste? After a bout of window-shopping or catalogue-browsing we usually realize that we can never afford all those things that we thought we wanted and that we probably don't really need them anyway. So we return to what seems practical and useful, often with a sigh that mingles unfulfilled longing with relief that we have escaped without doing anything stupid. So the ex-Chancellor returned to the study of natural history, "which he preferred many degrees before" the *New Atlantis*; and after, perhaps, wasting a little time on his aborted *Xanadu*, we come back to reality.

(xx)

Idols

The reality that Bacon experienced seemed to him to be loaded with unrealities that ignorant or ill-advised people had set up and worshipped as if they were gods. He refers to these entities as idols, first mentions them in an unpublished essay written around 1603, and gives them the full treatment in Book I of the Novum Organum, where he characterizes them as "certain empty dogmas" and contrasts them with "the Ideas of the divine… the true signatures and marks set upon the works of creation as they are found in nature." As Bacon's discourse on idols proceeds, taking up a large part of Book I, it embraces not only "empty dogmas", but also words, concepts and whole philosophies and histories. It will suffice for the moment to say that Rudolf Steiner viewed Bacon as the agent through whom renegade spiritual powers tried to destroy the human relationship to the divine origin and content of language, and the doctrine of idols as Bacon's main instrument in this process. A full discussion will be found in Part V of this volume.

Steiner's analyses of Bacon's proposals for a new system of science appeared at a time when he had already provided the foundations for a view of nature based on Goethe's scientific work. A brief study of Steiner's thoughts about the science of the early twentieth century and the scientific attitudes that he discovered and embraced in the work of Johann Wolfgang von Goethe, will provide some essential background for the understanding of his response to Bacon's life and work.

Part IV

Steiner, Goethe and Modern Science

"Nobody can attain a true knowledge of the spirit who has not acquired scientific discipline, who has not learned to investigate and think in the laboratories according to the modern scientific method. Those who pursue spiritual science have less cause to undervalue modern science than anyone."

(Rudolf Steiner, *The Boundaries of Natural Science*, Dornach, 1920)

(xxi)

Anthroposophy and Science

When I first encountered Rudolf Steiner more than fifty years ago I was given the impression that anthroposophists disapproved of almost everything that was modern. Twentieth century art and science were regarded as grossly and unrelentingly ugly and materialistic—the products of people entirely cut off from the spiritual world. It took some time for me to realize that these opinions were based largely on personal feelings and represented a very one-sided knowledge and interpretation of Steiner's view of the world. It is true that artists and scientists are infected with materialism, but so, of course, is everyone else, including anthroposophists.

People relying on English translations had some excuse for being ignorant of Steiner's scientific writings, but things began to change with the 1969 publication in English of Karl Stockmeyer's great work on the curriculum of the Waldorf Schools.[111] One very important feature is Steiner's insistence that an adequate preparation for life must include a knowledge of modern developments in physical science. At a meeting with the first Waldorf teachers in 1919 he specifically mentioned wireless telegraphy, X-rays and alpha, beta and gamma rays, and spoke eloquently about the need for people to understand the technological workings of modern life.

"We live in a world produced by human beings, moulded by human thought, of which we make use and which we do not understand in the least. This lack of comprehension for human creation, or for the results of human thought, is of great significance for the entire complexion of the human soul and spirit…"[112]

Wireless, X-rays and radioactivity were much newer to the scientists then than quarks and chaos theory are now.

Thirteen years later, the publication of *The Boundaries of Natural Science*, the translation of a series of lectures given in 1920, gave me more food for thought. In this cycle, Steiner links knowledge of modern scientific method with the development of spiritual science.

"...nobody can attain a true knowledge of the spirit who has not acquired scientific discipline, who has not learned to investigate and think in the laboratories according to the modern scientific method. Those who pursue spiritual science have less cause to undervalue modern science than anyone."[113]

Although this is not to be taken as an unqualified endorsement of modern science it is certainly a strong warning against ignorance and disdain. I had to wait another nine years for the publication of *Anthroposophy and Science*, a course given in 1921. Here Steiner deals with the mathematical treatment of the natural world, points to the feeling of certainty which arises from this, and remarks that the cause of this feeling is not immediately obvious. He continues:

"A clear knowledge of the feeling that accompanies the use of mathematics [in natural science] will lead us to acknowledge the necessity that a spiritual science must come about with an equal degree of certainty... This spiritual science will conform in every discipline to the scientific consciousness of the times; it will, in addition oppose all that is brought forward by modern science that is suspect, and it will answer questions that often go unanswered. Spiritual science will be on a very sure mathematical foundation."

"Especially in our age, in which there is real proficiency in the handling of facts in an outer experimental way... what is investigated experimentally *must be permeated with the results of spiritual research.*" Our experimental, mathematical way of dealing with our surroundings brings "order and harmony into the otherwise chaotic stream of everyday facts... [but] one has to admit that all the knowledge obtained in this way stands as a closed door to the outer world in that it does not allow the essence of this outer world to enter our cognition... As long as we remain in this field of knowledge, we cannot see through the outer appearances; we also, of course, do not claim to do so... Basically we need this kind of knowledge to maintain our normal human consciousness. How does one arrive at anthroposophical spiritual science when starting from the familiar science of the present day? I don't believe anyone will be able to answer this question in a truly scientific way who cannot first answer the question: How is our observational knowledge raised to the kind of knowledge that is permeated with mathematics?"[114]

The mathematical treatment of nature, he says, helps to give us a feeling of unity with an outer world that otherwise seems foreign. But the picture we have created no longer contains the reality which presented itself to us originally. The abundance of sense impressions—colors, sounds, smells, tastes, textures—is lost, and nothing in the world of mathematical representation can replace it. Mathematical knowledge takes us more deeply into our inner life, but when we impose our reassuring inner mathematics on the outside world we cut ourselves off from the world's essential being. The equations which enable us to design optical instruments and explain rainbows give no inkling that there is such a thing as the actual sensation of color.

Is it possible, however, "that what is first experienced mathematically as pale abstractions can be made stronger? In other words, could the force which we have to use to attain a mathematical knowledge of nature be used more effectively, with the result not just a mathematical abstraction, but something inwardly, spiritually concrete? ...This we can see as a third step in attaining knowledge. The first step would be the familiar grasping of the real outer world. The second would be the mathematical penetration of the outer world, after we have first learned inwardly to construct the purely mathematical aspect. The third would be the entirely inner experience, like the mathematical experience but with the character of spiritual reality."

I give these quotations because they indicate the direction in which Steiner thought a spiritually oriented science might go. This is emphasized in a remark made on Christmas Eve, 1922:

"...The scientific path taken by modern humanity [is] ... not erroneous but entirely proper. ...It bears within itself the seed of a new perception and a new spiritual activity of will."[115]

Caution is necessary, however. While it is true that scientific thinking cannot proceed at all unless it is propelled by will activity, the result of this propulsion is a momentum which carries the process beyond the phenomena and into a world of atomic constructs which Steiner considers, at best, to be of dubious value. *"I take my lesson from inert matter, which continues to roll on even when the propulsive force has ceased."*[116]

It will emerge later that Francis Bacon had made some very similar observations three centuries previously, but, for the moment we shall follow Steiner into his development of a form a science, inspired by Goethe's scientific work, in which the thinking does not "roll on" but dwells on the phenomena themselves and seeks necessary connections through contemplation.

(xxii)

A Goethean Alternative

Johann Wolfgang von Goethe was born in 1749, 22 years after the death of Newton and seven years before the birth of Mozart. He died in 1832, five years after Beethoven's death, a few years after John Dalton made the first atomic weight calculations, and one year after Charles Darwin boarded the Beagle. The dictionaries tell us that he was a "German poet, dramatist, novelist and scientist whose genius embraced most fields of human endeavor." Goethe considered that his scientific work was no less important than all his other endeavors, so he might not have been pleased to see it left until last on the list. It is generally agreed that he was a very skillful experimenter and an acute observer, but most of his contemporaries couldn't stand the way he thought and talked about science, which seemed to them to confuse the artistic and the metaphysical with the scientific. Apart from that pervasive objection, there were two big differences between Goethe's way of doing science and that of his contemporaries. One was that, like Bacon, they wanted to do things to nature in order to see what would happen, while he wanted to let nature speak for herself; the other is that while physical science was becoming increasingly mathematical, Goethe's work is devoid of mathematics. It may seem odd, therefore, to place a discussion of it immediately after quoting Steiner on the fundamental importance of the mathematical treatment of nature. It is generally thought that Newton's method is analytic and objective, while Goethe's world is poetic and subjective. Steiner believed that the meditative approach adopted by Goethe unites the objective and the subjective, enabling different phenomena to be linked together in the human consciousness with the kind of certainty and precision that we usually, although not always correctly, associate with mathematical methods. Goethe's approach is a step towards answering one of the questions asked by Rudolf Steiner in relation to the metamorphosis of scientific method into *spiritual* scientific method.

"… Could the force which we have to use to attain a mathematical knowledge of nature be used more effectively, with the result not just a mathematical abstraction, but something inwardly, spiritually concrete?"

Precision and certainty are not the only desirable qualities; nature will not speak to you unless you approach her with reverence and a pure heart, and Steiner found that Goethe's science is imbued with that kind of moral conscience. It is not only that the scientist must be moral; nature herself has moral qualities. Nature acts and suffers, and is to be loved and cared for, not exploited. Goethe's way of letting nature speak for herself is to study her forms and processes meditatively rather than trying to explain them with mechanical models; he wants to be at one with nature and experience what she does. This attitude can easily lead to a lazy, sub-mystical, feel-good wallowing in pleasant sensations, but in spite of Goethe's lack of mathematics, his ideal, at least as seen by Steiner, is to be disciplined, precise and rigorous.

In 1883, at the age of twenty-one, Steiner was invited to edit all Goethe's scientific writings as part of a collection of German masterpieces. While working on the first volume he realized that something lay behind Goethe's work that was never explicitly stated—not a system of science but a different way of looking at nature—different, that is from the kind of approach that had become the norm in the early nineteenth century. In ancient times, when people looked at nature they experienced the presence of God, or the gods, and of a varied collection of nature spirits, some mischievous and some benign.[117] Now the divine presence has become much harder to perceive, and the elemental beings have been repelled by concrete and exhaust fumes and by people who think of the land merely as a source of profit, amusement, relaxation and protection from the less affluent. Even in Newton's time nature seemed more alive than it does now and he could refer to mineral processes in organic terms as if a piece of metal had some life in it. We've all heard the story of the apple falling on Newton's head and giving him the idea of gravitation. Chaucer, in the fourteenth century, would have said that the apple fell because the tree had finished with it and because it was time for it to go back to the earth to continue the cycle of regeneration.

Every kindly thing that is
Hath a kindly stede ther he
May best in hit conserved be;
Unto which place everything
Through his kindly enclyning
Moveth for to come to.[118]

Goethe might well have said that the impact damaged Newton's brain and accounted for his subsequent wrong-headedness, although a more ancient commentator might have pointed out that the apple is a symbol of wisdom, and arrived at a different conclusion.

Now, most people believe that the motion of everything from an apple to a planet is determined by the inscrutable processes of gravity and inertia. People have given all kinds of answers to the question why there was so little progress in the physical sciences before 1600 and such a tremendous acceleration subsequently. Part of the answer is that instead of seeing natural processes as expressions of something akin to human sympathies and antipathies, the scientists began to treat both mineral and organic matter as if it were dead and subject only to impersonal forces. Gravity makes the apple fall; inertia keeps the planets in their orbits; the sap rises because of surface tension. If nature is inanimate we can do whatever we like to it (no need to say "her" any more) with no twinge of remorse or conscience. Francis Bacon was certainly not without a sense of wonder at the marvels of nature, and all his scientific work was done with the ideal of improving the lot of mankind, but he proposed a degree of ruthlessness in dealing with natural objects that a Goethean scientist would find unacceptable.

"Now as to how my Natural History should be composed, I mean it to be a history not only of Nature free and untrammeled (that is, when she is left to her own course and does her work in her own way)… but much more of nature constrained and vexed; that is to say when by art and the hand of man she is forced out of her natural state and squeezed and moulded."

It is only proper to note that long before Bacon proposed the "constraint and vexation" of nature as part of a scientific method, the land had been mined for gems and ores, and the ores had been smelted for useful metals. Wasteful agricultural methods were common and people who are now thought of as alchemists had tortured the substance of the earth with fire and water in order to extract its secrets. Still, it would be hard to think of a plan for the subjugation and exploitation of nature more directly opposed to the ideals of Goethean science than that of Francis Bacon. He speaks of contemplation, and, like him, we should very much like to "help the human mind"; but the mulling over of elaborate sets of data that he envisaged bears very little resemblance to the kind of contemplation through which Goethe came to his understanding of mineral, plant and animal morphology and the nature of light and color.

Having completed the first volume of the new edition, Steiner decided that before going on to the second volume he must make a further study and try to make explicit what Goethe had left implicit. His work bore fruit in 1886 in the form of *A Theory of Knowledge based on Goethe's World Conception*, a forbidding title for a book that does not make easy reading.

You may well feel that Goethe's approach to nature sounds as if it ought to be easier to understand than, say, a regular textbook of physics, but we are talking about two very different ways of thinking. My experience is that Goethean science is easier to *do* than it is to explain. In a well-written physics text—and I have to interrupt myself here to remark that as a very experienced physics teacher I am aware that that phrase is almost an oxymoron—but, as I was saying, in a well-written physics text, the argument goes from point to point in a logical manner and anyone of reasonable intelligence can follow it. Goethean science is not illogical or a-logical, but it does require a contemplative approach; you can't get the juice out of it just by reading about it.

The second volume of Goethe's scientific work did not appear until 1887 and another ten years elapsed before the project was completed. One of Steiner's duties as editor was to write an introduction for each section. These were published in English by the Anthroposophic Press in 1950, under the title *Goethe the Scientist*, and the degree of interest which the book stirred up can be gauged by the fact that it was remaindered and in 1964 and I was able to buy a copy for $1.[119] *Goethe the Scientist* provides an excellent introduction to Goethean science.

While working on the Goethe edition Steiner struggled with the nineteenth century version of the ancient problem of knowledge. In the early 1870's, when he began his scientific education, the atom was simply a more sophisticated version of Democritus' indestructible particle. Physicists had had some success with the kinetic theory of matter and the wave theory of light but there were still only the most rudimentary ideas of chemical combination, and there were distinguished scientists who were still very sceptical about atoms. Steiner, however, could see the way the wind was blowing and he was particularly distressed by efforts to explain all our perceptions and inner experiences in terms of atomic motion. So he found himself facing the roadblock that had first appeared in the ancient world—if our sense impressions are determined by atomic motions they must be valueless as a source of truth.

"It is these reflections that compelled me to reject as impossible every theory of nature which, in principle, extends beyond the domain of the perceived world, and to seek in the sense-world the sole object of consideration for natural science."[120]

Steiner refers to the battle that he has conducted against the basic conceptions of contemporary natural science, by which he means the view that "no understanding of the physical world can be gained otherwise than by tracing it back to 'mechanics of the atom'",[121] and states the first principle of Goethean science.

"The theory must be limited to the perceptible and must seek connections within this."[122] [Did I just hear someone say, "Wasn't that what Bacon was trying to do?"? Patience, Dear Reader!]

And as he put it in the *Philosophy of Freedom*, which he wrote while he was working on the Goethe Edition, and which describes his own approach to knowledge:

"Observation and thinking are the two points of departure for all the spiritual striving of man..."[123]

In order to make the correct reading of nature possible, Aristotle had created a system of logic; two thousand years later, Bacon designed a system that he thought would do the job better, and after another three centuries, Goethe, implicitly, and Steiner, explicitly, developed another new approach to science. We have the first principle, but what comes next? It's all very well to speak of seeking connections within the perceptible, but how do you actually do this? Bacon tried to get his connections by sorting through tables of instances, and modern scientists get theirs by means of atomic science, but how does a Goethean scientist do it? It is not to be expected that Steiner found, or would have wished to find, any sort of prescribed system of science in Goethe's writings, but he did find two ideas which act as signposts. One is the operation of metamorphosis and the other is the notion of the primal (or archetypal) phenomenon.

(xxiii)

Metamorphosis

Goethe frequently refers to a primordial creation and a continuing world in which a single being is enduringly manifest through a sea of continuous change. He is wrestling with problems that sound very similar to the ones that had preoccupied the pre-Socratic philosophers 2,300 years earlier, but he is doing it as a post-renaissance man with a highly developed impulse for independent thinking. As far as that goes it would be hard to say anything different about Dalton, Berzelius and other nineteenth century scientists, or indeed about all scientists who try to reveal the unity that lies behind nature's multiplicity. Goethe, however, came to his scientific work with a quite different frame of mind, not to be explained, as Steiner says, by simply presenting Goethe as a thinker. In Section VIII of *Goethe the Scientist* Steiner goes into the question of "how this genius came at all to be active in the scientific domain." "Goethe had to suffer much because of the false assumption of his contemporaries that poetic creation and scientific research could not be united in a single mind... What were the motives which drove the great poet to science?"

Goethe's artistic nature carried with it a strong inner impulse towards scientific thinking—scientific work was not merely a sideline but a necessary development. "There is an objective transition from art to science, a point where the two come together in such a way that perfection in one field requires perfection in the other."

Most nineteenth century scientists, believing that there was a great gulf fixed between science and art, found the conjunction of the two incomprehensible. This attitude shows up strongly in the course of a talk on Goethe's *Farbenlehre*, given by John Tyndall at the Royal Institution in 1880.[124] Tyndall, who was a distinguished physicist, a not inconsiderable poet and a great champion of Goethe the poet and dramatist, said the following. "The average reading of the late Mr. Buckle[125] is said to have amounted to three volumes a day. They could not have been volumes like those of the *Farbenlehre*. For the necessity of halting and pondering over its statements is so frequent, and the difficulty of coming to any undoubted conclusion regarding Goethe's real conceptions is often so great, as to invoke the expenditure of an inordinate amount of time. I cannot even now say with any confidence that I fully realize all the thoughts of Goethe. Many of them are strange to the scientific man. They demand for their interpretation a sympathy beyond that required, or even tolerated, in severe physical research."

These remarks help us to understand the indifference or hostility with which the *Farbenlehre* (loosely translated as *Theory of Color)* was received. Goethe's scientific works demand meditative reading, and it is clear that Steiner himself found that disentangling the essence of Goethe's message was no easy task. I am fairly sure that I am not alone in finding a similar difficulty with some of Steiner's works.

Goethe's manner of scientific research carried with it the ideal of uniting the objective and the subjective in the human soul. "For him, art and science sprang from a single source. Whereas the scientist immerses himself in the depths of reality in order to be able to express its impelling forces in the form of thoughts, the artist seeks by imagination to embody the same forces in his material."[126] Imagination is a power of perception and disciplined artistic creation, not a tendency to arbitrary fantasy. "'In the works of man, as in those of nature, what most deserves consideration is the intention', says Goethe. Everywhere he sought, not only what is given to the senses in the external world, but the tendency or intention through which it has come to exist… In nature's own formations she gets 'into specific forms as into a blind alley'; one must go back to what was to have come about if the tendency had been able to unfold without hindrance, just as the mathematician never has in mind this particular triangle, but the nexus of law which is fundamental to every triangle. Not what nature has created, but according to what principle it has created, is the important question. And then this principle is to be worked out as befits its own nature, not as this has occurred in the single form subject to a thousand natural contingencies. The artist has to 'evolve the noble out of the common, the beautiful out of the misshapen.'"[127]

No crystal, plant or animal grows freely out of its own inner necessity. Available space, weather, nutrition and the activities of competitors all mask the innate developmental principles. Studies of organic growth are hampered by the great difficulty of distinguishing between the essential and the accidental, but this is exactly what Steiner believed that Goethe had accomplished in his discovery of the archetypal plant, the plant, that is, that does not merely *represent* all actual plants but has the potential to *become* all plants; the plant which nature, so to speak, had in mind, unblemished by the vicissitudes of its environment.[128]

Goethe believed, and acted on his belief, that artistic vision could reveal those developmental principles. The process is contemplative, not analytical, and requires time and inner quiet. This is in tremendous contrast to both eighteenth century taxonomy and nineteenth century chemistry. The Linnaean system separates nature into compartments whereas Goethe experiences nature as a continuum. Nineteenth century chemistry is the story of people trying one conceptual model after another, in the hope of eventually finding something that will fit an increasingly complex set of experimental observations. In contemplating the forms of plants and animals Goethe perceived a formative principle of metamorphosis which enabled him to see each organism as a unity of interrelated parts and to perceive principles of growth and being that might apply to the whole process of nature rather than to the restricted fields of the botanist and the zoologist. In the formation of seed, leaves, calyx, corolla, stamens and pistil, fruit, and, again, seed, there is a series of alternating expansions and contractions. Mainstream scientists look for molecular processes to explain the expansions and contractions, but according to Steiner this stands the matter on its head.

"Nothing is to be presupposed which causes the expansion and contraction; on the contrary, everything else is the result of this expansion and contraction. It causes a progressive metamorphosis from stage to stage. People are simply unable to grasp the concept in its very own intuitive form, but demand that it shall be the result of a physical process. *They are able to conceive expansion and contraction only as caused, not as causing.* Goethe does not look upon expansion and contraction as if they were the results of inorganic processes taking place within the plant, but considers them as the manner in which the being of the plant is fully realized."[129]

(It is to be noted, for future reference, that this rejection of the idea of finding an explanation for a fundamental principle is also found in Bacon's *Novum Organum*.)

People who believe that nature consists of nothing but atoms and void, in the highly sophisticated forms which these concepts have acquired in the modern world, feel that they are getting closer and closer to a full explanation of the mechanisms of such processes. I speak with the voice of personal experience when I say that it is very hard, even for those who are intuitively drawn to Goethe's view of nature, to get out of the mechanistic habit. Goethe's way of expressing things has the cognate disadvantages of being easily ridiculed by the scientific *intelligentsia*, and being easily and uncritically accepted by half-baked *dilettanti*, so it is as well to remember that the test of a scientific principle is not how good or reasonable it sounds, but how well it fits the facts and, in particular, how fruitful it is in generating further penetration into the mysteries of nature.

Hard as all this may be to digest, it actually becomes harder. Steiner continues:

"Nature advances from seed to fruit in a succession of stages, so that the next following appears as a result of the next preceding. This is called by Goethe *an advancing on a spiritual ladder*." Speaking about the upwardly growing plant, Goethe says 'that a higher junction, as it arises out of the lower, and receives the sap mediated through this, must receive this still more finely filtered, must also enjoy the influence of the leaves which has been occurring in the interval, must develop itself more finely, and must bring fine sap to its leaves and buds.'"[130]

A nice analogy, one might say, between biological growth and spiritual development. But just as Goethe's view of natural processes was not *merely* scientific, this statement is not intended to be *merely* analogical. This is how nature works. Its forms result from organic growth *and* creative intention. This, perhaps, is the real meaning of intelligent design: not God creating an elaborate plan and bringing it into full being with a snap—or, perhaps, six snaps—of his fingers, but an ongoing process in which spirit is always working in the physical.

Since the seventeenth century most scientists, if they considered the spiritual at all—and a great many of them did—have been careful to keep it strictly separate from the scientific. For the increasingly atheistic society of the past couple of centuries the problem has largely vanished. But here is a man who speaks of the spiritual and the physical as all part of the same indivisible whole, who links the scientific with the artistic, and blurs the distinction between objective and subjective. He rejects the very bifurcation that made post-renaissance science possible. No wonder the general opinion was that Goethe ought to have stuck to his poetic last. Yet Goethe was not simply trying to put the clock back. He saw metamorphosis is a rule of nature, and if we can calm the inner mechanic long enough we may be able to see that there are rules or tendencies in nature that appear to operate independently of any detailed, microscopic or submicroscopic structure. This is, indeed, the case in certain branches of mainstream science, including classical thermodynamics.[131]

(xxiv)

The Primal Phenomenon

"Are not the Rays of Light very small bodies emitted from shining substances?" asks Newton, towards the end of his celebrated *Opticks*, published in 1704. "For such bodies will pass through uniform Mediums in right [straight] lines without bending into the shadow, which is the Nature of the Rays of Light." This was Newton's corpuscular theory of light, and it has certain corollaries, one of which concerns the relations of white and colored lights. It was natural for him to suppose that different colors are produced by the action of different particles and that sunlight is a mixture of these particles. He thought that by refracting the particles through different angles the prism separated colors that were already there. A century later, when Goethe was proposing a way of studying nature which rejected mechanistic explanations of any sort, Thomas Young and Augustin Fresnel were casting grave doubt on the validity of the corpuscular theory; but several more decades would elapse before the wave theory came into its own, so when Goethe vigorously attacked the view that white light is a mixture of the prismatic colors, it was against Newton that he vented his outrage. Goethe experienced sunlight as a glorious unity and found Newton's ideas very offensive. He believed that the prism produced colors by a process of metamorphosis and not by separating the components of a mixture.

Goethe's view was that colors are created through the interaction of light and darkness. Darkness seen through light generates cool colors as in the blue of the sky, in which we see the darkness of space through the sunlit atmosphere. Light seen through darkness brings warm colors, as when we see red of the setting sun through the intervening space. Goethe tries to show that these processes operate whether the colors we see are those of the prismatic spectrum, the rainbow or the daylight sky and the sunset, and his work embodies a principle that Steiner was later to make explicit; that the contemplation of such a set of phenomena can lead to the experience of connections that are necessary in just as strong a sense as the connections in a mathematical proof. Steiner calls such necessary relationships *primal phenomena* and considers that they are embodied in a new kind of clear and exact thinking that is to Goethean science as mathematical thinking is to orthodox science.

Newton believed that by using a very narrow beam of light he obtained the purest possible colors from his prism; Goethe considered that Newton's experiment, in which the sunlight passed through a narrow slit, was an act of "constraint and vexation", that the resulting spectrum was over-refined and that Newton's theory of color could only be the product of a sick mind. Using a wide beam of sunlight, he obtained from his prism two regions of color separated by a region of white. The region refracted through a smaller angle consisted of the warm colors, red, orange and yellow. The region refracted through a greater angle contained blue, indigo and violet. In thus identifying the colors it is necessary to observe that except at the outer limits of the spectrum their qualities are quite different from those of the colors produced from the narrow beam. Each spectrum has its own kind of beauty. Goethe's colors are full of life, energy and sparkle, and merge imperceptibly into the white central region. Newton's spectrum is remote and austere. Students seeing it for the first time are apt to gasp with wonder and astonishment.[132] Newton thought that his spectrum was pure, whereas Goethe considered it sterile, and we know that Goethe was not one to tolerate sterility. What you do depends on what you are trying to achieve.

Implicit in Newton's thinking are two assumptions that seem to have become part of the collective post-renaissance scientific unconscious. One is that nature is a complex of mechanical systems proceeding independently of human consciousness but, in principle, perfectly accessible to consciousness. The other is that a system can be analyzed into parts each of which functions in exactly the same way on its own as it does when it is part of the whole. Reason and experience gradually convinced the scientific community that these assumptions yield only first approximations to truth. Goethean scientists don't need to be persuaded of this since neither Goethe nor Steiner made these assumptions. Consciousness is the central element in science because it is where the phenomena meet and interact. As the relativists and quantum physicists of the early twentieth century realized, the observer is part of the process. This realization produced some pretty sensational new science but left the scientists' orientation towards the natural world very much where it had been before. The quality of *red* as a sensation in consciousness is not something that physicists spend any time on.

A significant part of the *Farbenlehre* is devoted to attacks not only on Newton's scientific work but also on his character, and the tendency towards an *ad hominem* approach did not die with Goethe. The obvious partisanship shown by Ernst Lehrs in his *Man or Matter*[133] frequently raises doubts about the cogency of his arguments. Goethe's confusion when he first looked through a prism, expecting a white wall to appear covered with colors, showed, among other things, that he had not read Newton's reports very carefully. Lehrs turns this misunderstanding into a sign of virtue. "[Goethe] did not, as Newton had, shut himself into a darkened room, so as to get hold of the color-phenomenon by means of an artificially set up apparatus." Fie on Newton! "Instead he turned first of all to nature..."[134]

As it happens, Lehrs has only just mentioned that the real reason why Goethe did not repeat Newton's experiment was that he lacked "the opportunity of arranging a dark chamber on Newton's lines, where the necessary ray of light from a tiny hole in the window covering was sent through a prism, [so] he postponed the whole thing, until in the midst of all his many other interests and duties it was forgotten." When, after frequent reminders from the unfortunate owner of the optical equipment that he had borrowed, Goethe finally picked up the prism, the "nature" that he surveyed through it was the interior of a white-walled room. What set him off on his new optical adventures was the observation, not unknown to previous investigators, that colors appear only at the boundaries between light and dark. None of this detracts from the value of Goethe's later work on optics. It only shows the tendency of the polemical approach to backfire.

*   *   *

To a physicist with an orthodox upbringing the creation of colors by the setting sun has nothing in common with the action of a prism in producing red at the less refracted end of the spectrum. The former is quantitatively understandable in terms of the mathematics of scattering; the latter, with much greater difficulty, in terms of electromagnetic conditions in the glass. The red arc of the rainbow is another kettle of fish with several new ingredients, but it is still susceptible to physical mathematics. To Goethe, Steiner and scientists inspired by their work, red is red whether we see it in a prismatic spectrum, in a rainbow or in a sunset, and the three phenomena are linked by the observation that, in each case, red appears when light is seen through intervening darkness. There is a deep division between the mind-sets of the orthodox and the Goethean scientist. The former wants to explain what happens in terms of events involving waves and particles or entities that have wave-like and particle-like properties; the latter does not wish to *explain* anything, but to understand his perceptions in terms of each other and what the circumstances of their production have in common.

The mention of sunsets is a reminder that it would be hard to think of a better example of the benefits and limitations of the mathematization of nature than the physics of scattering as it was developed in the late nineteenth century. We are used to the idea of a beam of light passing in a lawful way through a transparent medium, such as air or glass. If the medium were perfectly transparent the beam would be invisible from the side. A beam passing through a turbid medium, such as dusty or misty air, is visible from the side because some of the light is redirected by dust particles or droplets of water. *Scattering* is the term used when we have the impression that this redirection takes place more or less at random.

Lord Rayleigh[135] believed that sunlight, in its passage through the earth's atmosphere, is scattered by minute particles of dust, and he developed a theory according to which the degree of scattering varies inversely with the fourth power of the wavelength of the light. To put this in practical terms, we note that the wavelength of light at the red end of the spectrum is about 1.8 times the wavelength at the blue end. According to Rayleigh's mathematics this means that the blue will be scattered more than the red by a factor of 1.8^4, or about 10. There is a strong tendency, therefore, for the red light to pass on through the atmosphere into the beyond, and for the blue to be scattered in all directions, including earthwards, for the delectation of those who are lucky enough to be out and about on fine, sunny days. On their way home in the evening, those fortunate people may be able to see the sunset, at which time they will be looking directly at the sun and will receive light that has lost a great deal of the blue because of scattering, but retains a far greater proportion of the red. This is all worked out with mathematical precision on the basis of certain assumptions about the scattering process, and it fits the observations very well. For the Goethean scientist, the big problem about it is that it gives no inkling of the living, inner experience of color. "If one is honest one has to admit that all the knowledge obtained in this way stands as a closed door to the outer world in that it does not allow the essence of this outer world to enter our cognition..." When Goethean science is working properly its fundamental substance is the quality of the perception—the redness of the red and the blueness of the blue. Such things are absent from modern physics.

What Goethe saw as the basic principle is that these colors appear though the interaction of light and dark or, we might say, through the metamorphoses of light and dark. Goethe found that the contemplation of such phenomena led to the experience of connections between events in the natural world that seemed quite disparate to the orthodox mind. Like metamorphosis in the vegetable world, the interaction of light and dark needs no explanation. This being the case, Goethe regarded it as a primal phenomenon and valued the observation because it enabled him to gather together phenomena which could be understood as explaining each other.

The observation that when colors appear in the natural world it is through the interaction of light and dark has nothing to do with any mechanistic explanations about how the colors are produced, but the light and the dark do have to interact and not simply to be placed side by side. This is what happens with the sunset, the prism and the rainbow. The sky is blue because light and dark interact in the earth's atmosphere. If there were no atmosphere the sky would look black and the sun would always look white. Goethe agreed with the nineteenth century physicists that turbidity was an essential ingredient in the process and used this idea in his explanations of all his color manifestations, even those of the prism. It seems to me that in doing this he floundered a bit and came close to invoking turbidity as a mechanism. Goethe's work in optics has its problematical aspects even among anthroposophists, and Steiner stated explicitly that he had no desire to defend every detail of the *Farbenlehre*. It is therefore important to realize that Goethean science is not a collection of observations and theories but a disciplined way of seeing and understanding, developed by Steiner from his perception of Goethe's attitude to nature and his effort to raise the science of qualitative experience to the level of precision and clarity to which mathematical science aspires.

Unlike Bacon's proposed scientific method, Goethean science is not "barren of works", although its implications for our technological society still need a lot of exploring.

* * *

In his critique of Bacon, Steiner made only one explicit reference to Goethe, but I often have the feeling that Goethe is there in the background.

Part V

Steiner versus Bacon

"What good is a groping search for isolated phenomena and a derivation of general ideas from them, if these general ideas do not, like strokes of lightning, flash up out of the ground of being in the soul of man, rendering account of their truth through themselves."

(Rudolf Steiner, *The Riddles of Philosophy*)

(xxv)

Steiner on Bacon's Scientific Method

While Steiner's picture of Bacon incorporates both the Anglo-American view of the Chancellor as a failed innovator and the old European view of His Lordship as the inaugurator of All that is Bad in modern technological society, it is both wider and deeper than either of them. At the same time, anyone who is familiar with Bacon's writings will undoubtedly come up with some serious questions about Steiner's reporting of them. I must emphasize that I am not talking about nit-picking—combing through Steiner's words in the hope of finding a mistake here and there. It is more like being at a concert. You are not listening for mistakes, but when a musician plays a wrong or out of tune note, it hits you in the ear; and if the whole orchestra is out of tune, you may find yourself waiting for a convenient moment at which to leave the auditorium.

Here, from the *Riddles of Philosophy*, is Steiner's description of Bacon's scientific method.

"Bacon of Verulam demands that the investigation of world phenomena should begin with unbiased observation. One should then try to separate the essential from the nonessential in a phenomenon in order to arrive at a conception of whatever lies at the bottom of a thing or event. He is of the opinion that up to his time the fundamental thoughts, which were to explain the world phenomena, had been conceived first, and only thereafter were the descriptions of the individual things and events arranged to fit these thoughts. He presupposed that the thoughts had not been taken out of the things themselves. Bacon wanted to combat this (deductive) method with his (inductive) method. The concepts are to be formed in direct contact with the things. One sees, so Bacon reasons, how an object is consumed by fire; one observes how a second object behaves with relation to fire and then observes the same process with many objects. In this fashion one arrives eventually at a conception of how things behave with respect to fire. The fact that the investigation in former times had not proceeded in this way had, according to Bacon's opinion, caused human conception to be dominated by so many idols instead of the true ideas about the things."

There is, of course, no quarrel with the demand for "unbiased observation" and the effort to "separate the essential from the nonessential"; these are ideals of which Steiner was very much in favor, although the context and flavor of the quoted passage might lead one to suppose otherwise. Steiner states correctly that Bacon was deeply critical of earlier efforts to understand the world of nature and proposed a purely inductive method. However, it is not a trivial matter that Steiner fails to observe that the subject of Bacon's example of his method was *heat*, not *fire*. To anyone trying to be precise there is all the difference in the world, and it must be noted that most of Bacon's instances do not involve fire. Steiner describes only a table that bears a passing resemblance to Bacon's table of agreements, and doesn't mention that Bacon actually proceeds by comparing the contents of three tables—agreement, exclusion and degree. He also doesn't mention that, according to Bacon, this is only a preliminary survey, and he goes on to misstate Bacon's view of the origin of idols. When an over-arching principle is involved it often isn't necessary to go into the details, but any details given ought to be correct. It is also true that when one is preaching to the converted there is a considerable temptation to be somewhat arbitrary about the doings of the ungodly.

The key element in Bacon's thinking, not mentioned by Steiner, is that he believed that the truly fundamental thoughts of the world came from God the Creator, rather than from Aristotle and the Scholastics, and hoped that his method might to some extent reveal them.

Steiner goes on to quote Goethe:

"'Bacon is like a man who is well-aware of the irregularity, insufficiency and dilapidated condition of an old building, and knows how to make this clear to the inhabitants. He advises them to abandon it, to give up the land, the materials and all appurtenances, to look for another plot, and to erect a new building. He is an excellent and persuasive speaker. He shakes a few walls. They break down and some of the inhabitants are forced to move out. He points out new building grounds; people begin to level it off, and yet it is everywhere too narrow. He submits new plans; they are not clear, not inviting. Mainly, he speaks of new unknown materials and now the world seems to be well-served. The crowd disperses in all directions and brings back an infinite variety of single items while at home, new plans, new activities and settlements occupy the citizens and absorb their attention.

"'If through Verulam's method of dispersion, natural science seemed to be forever broken up into fragments, it was soon brought to unity again by Galileo. He led natural philosophy back into the human being. When he developed the law of the pendulum and of falling bodies from the observation of swinging church lamps, he showed even in his early youth that, for the genius, one case stands for a thousand cases. In science, everything depends on what is called an *aperçu*, that is, on the ability of becoming aware of what is really fundamental in the world of phenomena. The development of such an awareness is infinitely fruitful.'"

Galileo's "early youth" actually took place long before Bacon's scientific proposals were circulated, and the Italian's major works got him into so much trouble because they contradicted the Aristotelian world-view, favored by most of the participants in this story from al-Farabi and Averroes to Aquinas and Pope Leo XIII, and regarded as a great step in the flow of human evolution by Rudolf Steiner. Galileo has been criticized in anthroposophical circles for being so cold-blooded and detached that he could sit in church timing a pendulum with a constant pulse when he ought to have been deeply involved in the service—an example of the deplorable modern "observer consciousness." Furthermore, Galileo's pioneering work in the mechanics of moving bodies, which was completed twenty years before the publication of the *Novum Organum*, laid the groundwork for what some have called the Newtonian revolution and, therefore, for the emergence of our technological society. Rudolf Steiner makes his own view of Galileo perfectly clear a few paragraphs later, apparently without noticing that it is seriously at odds with Goethe's:

"Just compare the state of the form of thinking about nature as it develops in Copernicus, Galileo and Kepler with what has preceded them.

This natural scientific conception corresponds to the mood of the human soul at the beginning of the modern age in the sixteenth century. Nature is now looked at in such a way that the sense observation is to be the only witness of it. Bacon is one, Galileo another personality in whom this becomes apparent. The picture of nature is no longer drawn in a manner that allows thought to be felt in it as a power revealed by nature."

"Bacon does not understand that he is aiming at the same objective that has been reached by Plato and Aristotle, and that he must use different means for the same aim because the means of antiquity can no longer be those of the modern age.[136] He points to a method that might appear fruitful for the investigation in the field of external nature, but as Goethe shows in the case of Galileo, even in this field something more is necessary than what Bacon demands."

"The method of Bacon proves completely useless, however, when the soul searches not only for access to the investigation of individual facts, but also to a world conception. What good is a groping search for isolated phenomena and a derivation of general ideas from them, if these general ideas do not, like strokes of lightning, flash up out of the ground of being in the soul of man, rendering account of their truth through themselves. In antiquity, thought appeared like a perception to the soul. This mode of appearance has been dampened through the brightness of the new ego-consciousness. What can lead to thoughts capable of forming a world conception in the soul must be so formed as if it were the soul's own invention, and the soul must search for the possibility of justifying the validity of its own creation. Bacon has no feeling for all this."

To be strictly accurate, Bacon *did* have a feeling for this kind of soul activity; his feeling was that it had resulted in the stagnant pool of nonsense that he perceived in the science of his time.

Steiner gives only the sketchiest account of Bacon's method, and Goethe's report is not even a caricature, since the point of good caricature is to exaggerate something that is actually true; but they do align themselves with what was later identified as the "Anglo-American" view of Bacon as a champion of "what science has never been and will never be: a kind of knowledge obtained by observation, a process of accumulation of data, an illusory attempt to free the human mind from theories and presuppositions." Steiner's chief quarrel with Bacon, as far as method is concerned, is one already dealt with in this book, and echoes what William Whewell had written twenty years before Steiner was born: "At each step of the progress of science, are needed invention, sagacity, genius; elements which no [system] can give."

Bacon's way of eliminating preconceived ideas and hasty generalizations precludes the possibility not only of the kind of immediate insight (*aperçu*) to which Goethe refers—not, by the way, that Goethe's insights were always immediate; some of them took a very long time—but of any insight whatever.

Up to this point it may be said that in spite of problems in his exposition, Steiner has arrived at a tenable assessment. It is necessary to remark, however, that Steiner's reference to a "world conception" based on Bacon's scientific method is misleading. Bacon was approaching a picture of the world that would be the fruits of his whole endeavor, not only of his scientific work, so it is unfortunate that Steiner's view of Bacon is limited by his concentration on the Chancellor's scientific program and denial of its Christian context. Bacon's world conception may be deeply flawed, but its two branches are inextricably linked and the Christian one has the ultimate precedence. Unlike Steiner, Bacon had no expectation that his scientific study of nature would be aided by divine revelation; on the contrary, he hoped that his researches in the material world would *lead* to some inklings of God's intentions. Meanwhile, his Christian faith provided guidance for the general conduct of his life, including his scientific work.

Readers familiar with Steiner's view of Bacon's relationship to Christianity may have wondered why I quoted the Chancellor's Christian writings at such length before mentioning Steiner's dismissal of them. If this question were to arise, my response would be that it would be a good thing if people could receive Bacon's words in the context of his whole endeavor, not judgmentally but with an open mind. The student of anthroposophy who comes innocently to Steiner's comments is unlikely to pursue the matter any further, since Steiner states baldly that Bacon was only outwardly a Christian, giving no context for this assertion and no indication that he has made any significant study of Bacon's Christian writings.

"We see him working in the sphere of Christian civilisation. Yet there is no trace whatever of the Christian Impulse in his writings. Bacon of

Verulam might equally have arisen from some non-Christian civilisation. What he actually says about Christianity is extremely superficial compared with the real impulse that was within him." [137]

I have found that a prolonged study of Bacon, his writings and the historical context has led to exactly the opposite conclusion. To borrow another phrase from Steiner, anyone who finds Bacon's Christian writings superficial is "incapable of unprejudiced observation." In this regard the testimony of James Spedding, is worth noting.[138]

"Many years ago James Spedding, Bacon's greatest editor, briefly described Bacon's religious beliefs as embracing Christianity's moral and social emphases, accepting the authority and benevolence of God, and recognizing the life of Christ as the highest proof of divine care for man. But over and above these beliefs, Spedding felt, for Bacon 'the entire scheme of Christian theology—creation, temptation, fall, mediation, election, reprobation, redemption—is constantly in his thoughts; underlies everything; defines for him the limits of the province of human speculation.'"[139]

People who have been deeply influenced by negative interpretations of Bacon's life and work will, perhaps, recall Steiner's warning that the same words in different mouths may have very different meanings. There is no doubt about the wisdom of Steiner's *caveat*, but it has had the unfortunate effect of giving people an excuse, whenever it suits their purpose, to deny the validity of the words of people who are no longer here to defend themselves. Steiner's stated opinions make it easy and convenient for anthroposophical writers to dismiss Bacon's Christianity as "nominal" or even bogus, as Stewart C. Easton does in *And Another Strong Angel*[140]; but this is something that serious contemplation of the Chancellor's life and works makes impossible.

(xxvi)

"Words, Words, Words."

(Hamlet)

The word and nought else
in time endures.
Not you, long after,
perished and mute
will last, but the defter
viol and lute.

(Humbert Wolfe, 1885-1940)

You English words,
I know you.
You are light as dreams,
Tough as oak,
Precious as gold,
As poppies and corn,
Or an old cloak...

(Edward Thomas, 1878-1917: *Words*)

In *The Riddles of Philosophy*, Steiner presents Bacon as the wrongheaded creator of a hare-brained scheme for the advancement of science by the exclusion of insight; but now we come to a deeper issue, which Steiner draws out of the *Novum Organum* and presents in *The Riddle of Humanity*. This has to do with Bacon's doctrine of idols and his relationship to words. What were these idols and what were Bacon's opinions about words?

On the subject of words, Aphorism 14 of the *Novum Organum*, Book I, gives a good start.

The syllogism consists of propositions, propositions consist of words, words are symbols of notions. Therefore if the notions themselves (which is the root of the matter) are confused and overhastily abstracted from the facts, there can be no firmness in the superstructure. Our only hope therefore lies in a true induction.

The syllogism was humanity's main logical tool from the time of Aristotle until the nineteenth century, so at the risk of trying the reader's patience, I give the following brief explanation. Syllogisms come in many forms, the most well-known of which was immortalized by Tolstoy in his *Death of Ivan Ilych*. The idea can easily be understood from this classic example:

"All men are mortal; Caius is a man; therefore Caius is mortal."

The innocent bystander who raises the question, "But how do you *know* that all men are mortal?", will quickly be shushed and told that we are talking about logical structure, not mere observable facts. We can easily put things right by inserting a couple of "ifs":

"If all men are mortal, and if Caius is a man, then Caius is mortal."

To put this more generally:

"If we have a category of objects, each of which has a certain property; and if we find an object that belongs to the category; then this object must have the stated property."

To the modern mind, however, there is very little difference between a syllogism and a tautology.

"If we know that every object in a certain category has a certain property, then we know that any particular object belonging to that category has that property."

The practical questions are, "How do we *know* that every object in the category has that property?" and, "How can we tell if any particular object belongs to the category?"

This is all very well in a deductive discipline like traditional Euclidean geometry, where the categories are matters of definition,[141] but a syllogism that depends on an inductively derived proposition is not so reliable. In everyday life we use the syllogism all the time, but we know that it doesn't always work.

"All No. 79 buses go across town on 79th Street.

"This is a No. 79 bus.

"Therefore..."

Unfortunately the 79th Street transverse is flooded, so we go downtown, cross on 59th Street and end up two hours late for our appointment. As Newton pointed out long ago, induction can give us a good idea of the way things work, but it can never be logically conclusive. If you feed nonsense into the front end of the syllogism, you will get nonsense out of the back end; or as the computer experts say, "Garbage in—garbage out."

One good reason for Bacon's judgement that "syllogism is incompetent for sciences of nature" is that you can't construct a syllogism without a prior generalization, and he thought that generalizations should come at the end of a scientific process, not at the beginning. This is the justification for Aphorism 11:

Just as the sciences we now have are of no use in discovering works, so neither does the logic we now have help us in discovering new sciences.

The popular philosophy of Bacon's time is typified by the mock syllogism quoted in Section (iii); "Rhenyshe wine heateth, Malmesey heateth, Frenchewine heateth, neither is there any wyne that doth the contrary: Ergo all wine heateth"; but Bacon noted that even a properly constructed syllogism presents problems that go beyond those mentioned above. For Bacon, the fundamental difficulty is that the notions (ideas or concepts) to which the words refer are vague and unfocused. For Steiner, one would have expected that the real problem exposed by Aphorism 14 would lie in the assertion that "words are symbols of notions", that a word is not an entity that contains in itself some essence of the object to which it is related, but is merely a symbol, a name. It will become clear, however, that in this context, like Bacon, he is mainly concerned about the reality of the concepts to which the words refer.

In Aphorism 15, Bacon gives a list of the notions he has in mind and states his opinion of them: "*Substance, Quality, Action, Passion, Essence itself, are not sound notions; much less are Heavy, Light, Dense, Rare, Moist,*

Dry, Generation, Corruption, Attraction, Repulsion, Element, Matter, Form, and the like; but all are fantastical and ill defined."

Noting that *passion* is merely the opposite of *action*, we see that these "notions" are all connected with Bacon's scientific work. Part of the difficulty in achieving clarity was that in Bacon's time (and for at least another two centuries), the distinction between the inorganic and the organic had not been clearly made. "Corruption" was a fuzzy concept that might equally apply to the decay of fallen leaves, the rusting of iron[142] and the crumbling of tin organ pipes in unheated churches, caused by allotropic modification at low temperatures. In the nineteenth century, these were all seen to be radically different processes, one biological, one chemical and one physical; but, unlike other actions that fall under the umbrella of "corruption", such as bribery, they were all regarded as purely material and each was equipped with its own particular word. The distinctions between organic and inorganic, and between chemical and physical, achieved with great difficulty in the nineteenth century, have since been seen to be fuzzy, but that's part of a story that belongs elsewhere.

As Bacon says, "Some of the notions of less general species, as Man, Dog, Dove, and of the immediate perceptions of the sense, as Hot, Cold, Black, White, do not materially mislead us; yet even these are sometimes confused by the flux and alteration of matter and the mixing of one thing with another."

Thus we can safely use the words "hot" and "cold" as long as we have no difficulty in distinguishing hot objects from cold ones; but, as Bacon says, "even these [notions] are sometimes confused by the flux and alteration of matter." Our senses are easily confused and we find, for instance, that there are times when we need to use a thermometer—an option that Bacon didn't have.

Apart from these "less general" notions, Bacon continues, "All the others which men have hitherto adopted are but wanderings, not being abstracted and formed from things by proper methods."

To sum up very briefly: according to Bacon, as far as any form of precise communication is concerned, the real problem is that the notions to which our words refer are not clearly understood and defined. This lack of clarity is, as he says, "the root of the matter." Steiner's perception, although he doesn't mention it in this context, is that language has descended from a primal state in which words had inherent, archetypal meanings. That being the case, it may be presumed that words required no definitions. It is, indeed, hard to see how the concept of "definition" could have existed before the advent of the pre-Socratic philosophers.

At some point, however, we began to acquire the habit of conceptualizing things that don't exist or of which our knowledge is limited and imperfect. In the modern world this process is known as "reification", a classic case being the formation of the concept of intelligence as an entity susceptible to standardized testing. At one time, intelligence was a spiritual reality; now "intelligence" is the name of any one of a cluster of notions that have no clearly definable correspondence with any kind of reality.[143] The loss of the archetypal connection between thought and thing, between word and concept can be seen as an inevitable historical process; you can't have an archetypal connection with something that doesn't exist. This is really what Bacon was complaining about, although he expressed the problem differently. As we shall see shortly, however, Steiner asserts that Bacon was largely responsible for this loss of spiritually concrete meaning in language.

Meanwhile, it is a good idea to keep in mind that the *Novum Organum* is a plan for a new form of science, not a new form of everything. Nothing is said about the notions that have generally been the subjects of the most debate and the causes of the most confusion, such as love, hate, faith, honesty, loyalty, humility and beauty. Bacon may have thought that all words were merely symbols and that many of them referred to muddled or non-existent concepts, but he evidently felt no need for a new vocabulary and a new form of logic in order to express his religious thoughts clearly and fervently. Reading his *Confession of Faith*, for example, one has the impression that his words have not altogether lost their archetypal significance and that Bacon had no doubt about their ability to convey real meaning.

(xxvii)

The Doctrine of Idols

Steiner summarizes Bacon's intentions as follows:

"'In truth, it is necessary for you to free yourselves from the content of words, for words refer to idols.' Thus did Bacon introduce the misunderstanding of speech into our newly-arrived, fifth post-Atlantean epoch. Under the direction of the spiritual world, he began to drive out mankind's old feeling that language can contain the spirit. He referred to all substantial concepts and all universal concepts as idols."[144] [Note that the words presented as a quotation from Bacon are Steiner's, not Bacon's.]

Actually Bacon did nothing of the sort, as is clear from Aphorism 23, which differentiates between the imperfect fruits of human thinking and the divine thought inherent in nature.

23. *There is a great difference between the Idols of the human mind and the Ideas of the divine. That is to say, between certain empty dogmas, and the true signatures and marks set upon the works of creation as they are found in nature.*

According to Bacon, the problem is the presence of human fallibility, not the absence of divine ideas. He refers not to "all substantial concepts and all universal concepts", but to "certain empty dogmas", which have become so fixed in human consciousness that he will eventually conclude that the only remedy is to cut away the whole infected system, and, like any responsible surgeon, start with a sterile field. It's hard to imagine that any serious student of Rudolf Steiner would deny the existence of "empty dogmas"—Steiner thought that there were rather a lot of them. Bacon's proposed system of physical science may have been so sterile that it was very hard for any form of life to struggle into it, but he believed that it had the potential to reveal "the true signatures and marks set upon the works of creation as they are found in nature."

It will be seen later that Steiner is confused about Bacon's attitude to these idols, although the following aphorisms make it perfectly clear:

38. *The idols and false notions which are now in possession of the human understanding, and have taken deep root therein, not only so beset men's minds that truth can hardly find entrance, but even after entrance is obtained, they will again in the very instauration of the sciences meet and trouble us, unless men being forewarned of the danger fortify themselves as far as may be against their assaults.*

39. *There are four classes of Idols which beset men's minds. To these for distinction's sake I have assigned names, calling the first class* Idols of the Tribe; *the second,* Idols of the Cave; *the third,* Idols of the Market Place; *the fourth,* Idols of the Theater.

40. *The formation of ideas and axioms by true induction is no doubt the proper remedy to be applied for the keeping off and clearing away of idols. To point them out, however, is of great use; for the doctrine of Idols is to the interpretation of nature what the doctrine of the refutation of sophisms is to common logic.*[145]

In Aphorisms 41-44 Bacon characterizes the four kinds of idols. Steiner's method of dealing with them appears to be to take the aphorisms one by one, reporting what Bacon says, and commenting on it. If this is so, it has to be said that Steiner is not a very accurate reporter. It may be suggested that he was reporting what Bacon or his putative spiritual handlers really meant or intended, rather than what he actually said; but if that is the case, he ought to have said so. In making an appraisal of the man's life, work and influence, it's a good idea to be accurate about what he actually did and said. After that we can discuss the question of whether when he said *x* he really meant *y*. History may be, as Steiner and others have asserted, merely a *fable convenue*, or in Henry Ford's more picturesque version, "Bunk", but we actually do know exactly what Bacon said about a host of topics and we have a clearer picture of the course of his life than we have of the Vietnam War, to mention a notorious example.

In each case I give Steiner's paraphrase first, follow it with a brief comment and then give Bacon's actual words. This may be a counter-intuitive procedure, but after trying various other approaches, I have found it the most efficient.

Steiner paraphrases Aphorism 41 as follows:

"Firstly, Bacon said, there are certain words that have simply arisen out of people's need to live together. Men believe that these words designate something real. These words are idols of the clan, of the people, *idols of the tribe.*"

In this Aphorism, Bacon makes one of his most depressing assessments of human nature and understanding in general. We may disagree entirely, or feel that although there is a grain of truth here, Bacon's verdict is very one-sided; but we have to acknowledge that the aphorism is not about words but about the perceptions of the individual human being, and that there is nothing about "the need to live together." The tribe is the whole human race, not merely a clan. As members of the human race we share a common nature by which each one lives in his or her own "reality distortion field", to borrow a phrase from my good friend Linda Blanchard.[146]

41. *The Idols of the Tribe have their foundation in human nature itself, and in the very tribe or race of men. For it is a false assertion that the sense of man is the measure of things. On the contrary, all perceptions as well of the sense as of the mind are according to the measure of the individual and not according to the measure of the universe. And the human understanding is like a false mirror, which, receiving rays irregularly, distorts and discolors the nature of things by mingling its own nature with it.*

Steiner continues with a very inaccurate account of the content of Aphorism 42:

"Then, once men start to understand the world, they attempt to mix an erroneous spirituality into their way of seeing things. The knowledge mankind obtains arises as though in a cave; but to the extent that he hauls the external world into this cave, man creates words for what he would like to know. These words also refer to something unreal. They are the *idols of the cave*: idola specis."

The cave, according to Bacon, is in the mind of the individual—we each have one of our own. Subject to all kinds of influences and bombarded, as we would say these days, with sense impressions, individuals form their own mental environments. The serious student of Steiner's work can hardly fail to notice that Bacon's lament for the human condition is highly reminiscent of Steiner's description of Ahriman's plans for isolating each soul in its own little box.[147]

42. *The Idols of the Cave are the idols of the individual man. For everyone (besides the errors common to human nature in general) has a cave or den of his own, which refracts and discolors the light of nature, owing either to his own proper and peculiar nature; or to his education and conversation with others; or to the reading of books, and the authority of those whom he esteems and admires; or to the differences of impressions, accordingly as they take place in a mind preoccupied and predisposed or in a mind indifferent and settled; or the like. So that the spirit of man (according as it is meted out to different individuals) is in fact a thing variable and full of perturbation, and governed as it were by chance. Whence it was well observed by Heraclitus that men look for sciences in their own lesser worlds, and not in the greater or common world.*

It will be noticed that so far, in his description of the Idols, Bacon has said nothing about words.

Steiner continues with the idols described in Aphorism 43:

"There are still other kinds of idols — words, that is — that designate non-existent entities. These arise out of the fact that men are not just gathered together into races or peoples by virtue of their blood relationships, but because they also form associations in order to manage one thing and another… Bacon says that other unreal entities, along with the words that express them, have arisen because of this. These unreal entities stem from our living together in the market-place; they are the *idols of the market-place*: idola fori."

Bacon, in fact, expresses great concern over the corruption of language, but in this aphorism he does not refer to words themselves as idols. The real problem is that beliefs, observations, systems or philosophies are conveyed in ill-chosen words whose meanings have been corrupted.

43. *There are also Idols arising from the dealings and association of men with each other, which I call Idols of the Market Place, because of the commerce and consort of men there. For speech is the means of association among men; but words are employed according to the understanding of the vulgar. Consequently the ill and unfit choice of words obstructs the understanding to a remarkable extent. Nor do the definitions or explanations wherewith in some things learned men are wont to defend and validate their opinions, by any means set the matter right. But words plainly overrule the understanding, and throw all into confusion, and lead men away into numberless empty controversies and idle fancies.*

Steiner now comes to the fourth type of idol:

"Then, there are yet other idols which arise when science creates mere names. Naturally, there are frightfully many of this kind. For if you were to set all our lecture cycles before Bacon, with all they contain about spiritual matters, all the words referring to spiritual things would be idols of this kind. These are the idols that Bacon believes to be the most dangerous, for one feels especially protected by them, believing that they contain real knowledge: these are the *idola theatri*. [Note that in Aphorism 59, Bacon states that the most troublesome idols are those of the marketplace, the *idola fori*.] This theatre is an inner one where mankind creates a spectacle of concepts for itself. The concepts are no more real than are the characters on the stage of a theatre. All the idols expressed in words are of these four kinds."

(It is worth noting that at this point, Steiner refers to "idols expressed in words", whereas in the previous Steiner quotation the idols *are* words.)

Here is what Bacon actually said:

44. *Lastly, there are Idols which have crept into men's minds from the various dogmas of philosophies, and also from faulty methods of demonstration. These I call Idols of the Theater, because I regard all the philosophies that have been received or invented as so many stage plays, creating fictitious and*

imaginary worlds. Nor is it only of the systems now in vogue, or only of the ancient sects and philosophies, that I speak; for many more plays of the same kind may yet be composed and in like artificial manner set forth; since errors of the most diverse kind often have similar causes. Neither again do I mean this only of entire systems, but also of many principles and axioms in science, which have become established through tradition, credulity, and negligence.

Here the idols are not words but "fictitious and imaginary worlds." It will be seen that there is nothing in this aphorism to suggest an aversion to spiritual matters. Taking Bacon's writings as a whole, and not restricting ourselves to the scientific writings, we see him as a man who experienced no difficulty in expressing the most profound and deeply felt spiritual matters in words.

It should be noted that in his descriptions of idols (Aphorisms 41-44), Bacon is not *prescribing* anything but *describing* the state of knowledge and philosophy as he sees it. After explaining all the defects that he has observed, he then moves to the "modest proposal" of throwing out the whole of the current endeavor and replacing it with something that he believes to be new and capable of freeing us from the old misconceptions. When, in describing the third kind of idol, he deplores the ways in which words are used, he does not assert that *all* words and usages are the results of the abuses he describes, but that these abuses are prevalent and make serious scientific discourse difficult or, perhaps, impossible. *The problems are not innate to our words but to ourselves.* Our perceptions are distorted, our thinking is confused, and we have failed to perceive "the true signatures and marks set upon the works of [God's] creation as they are found in nature." Words "employed according to the understanding of the vulgar" are victims of our divagations, and, having been victimized, contribute further to the confusion.

Bacon has now finished introducing the four categories of idols. They arise, (a) from the failings that we have in common as human beings; (b) from our characteristics as individual human beings; (c) from confusions, linked to the misuse of words, that stem from our interactions; and (d) from the influence of erroneous philosophies and scientific methods. It would be hard to deny that there was, and is, a great deal of truth in Bacon's diagnosis. This is not the end of the matter, however. Before prescribing the treatment, Bacon feels it necessary to explain the diagnosis further.

In Aphorisms 45-48, Bacon mentions several human failings. These include our habit of projecting more order into the world than is justified by our observations, such as the assumed circularity of the planetary orbits. He also notes our tendency to shoot first and ask questions afterwards— in other words, to form our opinions first and then look for supporting evidence. Aphorism 48 brings an observation which, for the student of Steiner's scientific work, rings a very loud bell.

48. *The human understanding is unquiet; it cannot stop or rest, and still presses onward, but in vain. Thus it is that we cannot conceive of any end or limit to the world, but always as of necessity the thought arises in us that there is something beyond... A similar subtlety arises concerning the infinite divisibility of lines, from the same inability of thought to stop. But this inability interferes more mischievously in the discovery of causes; for although the most general principles in nature ought to be considered purely positive* [that is, not dependent on other things], *just as we have found them, and cannot with truth be referred to a cause, nevertheless the human understanding, being unable to rest, still seeks something prior in the order of nature. And then it is that in struggling toward that which is further off it falls back upon that which is nearer at hand, namely, on final causes, which have relation clearly to the nature of man rather than to the nature of the universe; and from this source have strangely defiled philosophy. But he is no less an unskilled and shallow philosopher who seeks causes of that which is most general, than he who in things dependent and particular omits to do so.*

To this can be added the final paragraph of Aphorism 66:

Nor again is it a lesser evil that in their philosophies and contemplations their labor is spent in investigating and handling the first principles of things and the highest generalities of nature; whereas everything of practical utility results entirely from things intermediate. Hence it is that men cease not from abstracting nature till they come to potential, formless matter, nor on the other hand from dissecting nature till they reach the atom; things which, even if true, can do little for the welfare of mankind.

These remarks are inescapably reminiscent of a well-known passage in Steiner's *The Boundaries of Natural Science.*

"What happens is that when I as a human being confront the world of nature, I use my concepts not only to create for myself a conceptual order within the realm of the senses but also to break through the boundary of sense and construct behind it atoms and the like. I cannot bring my lucid thinking to a halt within the realm of the senses. I take my lesson from inert matter, which continues to roll on even when the propulsive force has ceased. I have a certain inertia, and I roll with my concepts on beyond the realm of the senses to construct there a world the existence of which I can begin to doubt when I notice that my thinking has only been borne along by inertia. It is interesting to note that a great proportion of the philosophy that does not remain within phenomena is actually nothing other than just such an inert rolling-on beyond what really exists within the world. One simply cannot come to a halt. One wants to think ever farther and farther beyond and construct atoms and molecules—under certain circumstances other things as well that philosophers have assembled there. No wonder, then, that this web one has woven in a world created by the inertia of thinking must eventually unravel itself again."[148]

Bacon points to the inability of thought to stop and warns us against the error of seeking the causes of general principles, which corrupts philosophy and can result only in a purely subjective view of reality. Steiner speaks of the inertia of thought, its tendency to roll on "beyond the realm of the senses to construct there a world the existence of which I can begin to doubt when I notice that my thinking has only been borne along by inertia." Furthermore, Bacon gives us one of the basic ideas of Goethean science, namely that we experience general principles—in Goethe's case, those of metamorphosis and the primal phenomenon—as primary and not caused by anything beyond them. Steiner and Bacon agree that philosophy has been negatively affected by this inertial rolling on beyond the observed phenomena, which has generated, among other things, atomic theories of very dubious value.

At this point—if we have not done so already—we may begin to wonder whether Steiner's judgement has been somewhat influenced by the perception that Bacon has stolen some of his thunder.

In Aphorism 59, Bacon returns to his misgivings about the ways in which words are used and abused through the activities of the "vulgar" and the lack of "acuteness or a more diligent understanding."

59 But the Idols of the Market Place are the most troublesome of all — idols which have crept into the understanding through the alliances of words and names. For men believe that their reason governs words; but it is also true that words react on the understanding; and this it is that has rendered philosophy and the sciences sophistical and inactive. Now words, being commonly applied according to the capacity of the vulgar, follow those lines of division which are most obvious to the vulgar understanding. And whenever an understanding of greater acuteness or a more diligent observation would alter those lines to suit the true divisions of nature, words stand in the way and resist the change. Whence it comes to pass that the high and formal discussions of learned men end oftentimes in disputes about words and names; with which (according to the use and wisdom of the mathematicians) it would be more prudent to begin, and so by means of definitions reduce them to order. Yet even definitions cannot cure this evil in dealing with natural and material things, since the definitions themselves consist of words, and those words beget others. So that it is necessary to recur to individual instances, and those in due series and order, as I shall say presently when I come to the method and scheme for the formation of notions and axioms.

"The alliances of words and names" is an odd-sounding phrase, since names are, after all, words. It makes sense if we realize that the names in question are often those of entities which we could otherwise indicate only by pointing. As Bacon remarks, many of the names refer to entities that are abstract, poorly understood or non-existent, so that pointing is not an option.

Bacon was not to know that the "use and wisdom of the mathematicians" was insufficient and that, paradoxically enough, they would eventually find it necessary to start with undefined terms. This is a point to which I shall return eventually[149], but it is worth remarking that there is really nothing very mysterious about it. Every word in a dictionary has to be defined in terms of other words in the dictionary, so there is necessarily an inherent circularity in the system, even though, with tens of thousands of words, it may be difficult to pin down.

In Aphorism 60 Bacon gives a further explanation of the problem of words and names.

The idols imposed on the understanding by the misuse of words are of two kinds. They are either names of things which do not exist (for as there are things left unnamed through lack of observation, so likewise are there names which result from fantastic suppositions and to which nothing in reality corresponds), or they are names of things which exist, but yet confused and ill-defined, and hastily and irregularly derived from things.

If we are talking about an object of which we have no clear notion or which does not exist at all, all we have is a name. In the twentieth century, for instance, was it intelligence or "intelligence" that became an idol? I'm fairly sure that the question never arose in the minds of the idolaters. In any case, it is clear that the problem is the inadequacy of the notion.[150] Bacon continues with a list of such notions.

Of the former kind are Fortune, the Prime Mover, Planetary Orbs, the Element of Fire, and like fictions which owe their origin to false and idle theories. And this class of idols is more easily expelled, because to get rid of them it is only necessary that the theories should be steadily rejected and dismissed as obsolete.

Even if we had not been deeply concerned with Bacon's attitude towards words, he might still have incurred our opprobrium through his summary rejection of certain notions that are very dear to some of us. However, huge numbers of people have rejected these ideas without being identified as agents of destructive spiritual powers. It is only necessary to emphasize again that whether we are talking about the names of things that do not exist or of concepts that that are "confused and ill-defined", the root of the matter, as Bacon says, lies not the words themselves, but the inadequacy of the notions to which they are attached.[151]

In relation to this aphorism, it is worth noting that in other contexts Steiner complains rather frequently about such things as "lack of observation", "fantastic suppositions" and "false and idle theories." Steiner inveighed against a general lack of "unprejudiced observation" and, sounding remarkably like Bacon, felt "compelled to reject as impossible every theory of nature which, in principle, extends beyond the domain of the perceived world, and to seek in the sense-world the sole object of consideration for natural science."[152] His distress at the prevailing tendencies of philosophy and physiology led to a sweeping dismissal: "Those whose capacity for conceiving ideas has not been corrupted by Descartes, Locke, Kant and the modern physiologists will never comprehend how light, color, sound and heat can be considered only subjective states within the human organism and yet an objective world of processes outside this organism can be affirmed."[153] At a teachers' meeting at the original Waldorf School in 1919, he expressed himself even more strongly: "Modern philosophy is all nonsense. In much of what it brings, there is some truth, but there is so much nonsense connected with it that, in the end, only nonsense results."

Like Bacon, Steiner speaks as someone who has inherited a confused system based on faulty principles and feels that whole regions of discourse accepted by most of his contemporaries must be rejected and replaced with a new approach. I am not saying that Steiner was wrong, but it is clear that Bacon was right in much of his diagnosis and that many of the difficulties that we find today in human discourse and communication were already apparent in his lifetime.

*   *   *

Bacon's distress at the way in which words, "being commonly applied according to the capacity of the vulgar" are used has been echoed by many writers. Our language is littered with the corpses of words, such as "contemporary", "fortuitous", "exponential", "ultimate"[154] and "liberal", that we can no longer use because of the capacity not only of the vulgar, whoever they may be, but also of schoolteachers, college professors, television personalities, politicians and anthroposophists to corrupt them.

Consider the following announcement: "Shakespeare's *Macbeth* will be performed with contemporary music." Some people will go to the play expecting to hear music from Shakespeare's time; some will expect music from the present day; and others will know that there's no way of knowing what to expect.[155] The trouble with such verbal mishaps is that they reduce our ability to communicate intelligibly with one another. A similar problem exists in the case of *fortuitous*; fifty years ago, the word was not used very often, and when it was it was invariably with its proper meaning of "happening by chance." Now I can't use the word at all since, for many people, its meaning is indistinguishable from that of *fortunate*.[156] The mischief has even got into abbreviations. So many people now believe that "i. e." means "for example" that when I encounter the abbreviation I have to try to figure out the intention from the context.

Most of these acts of degradation happen through ignorance, but some are politically motivated. The use of *liberal* as a term of abuse is the result of a deliberate political campaign. Legislation that increases pollution can be made palatable by calling it a "Clean Air" act. There is nothing new about these processes; they are what Bacon was complaining about and they weren't new in his time either. What Steiner regarded as an attack on words, a fatal blow to the experience of language as a divine gift, may be seen rather as Bacon's response to the degradation that had already taken place.

I hope that it has become clear by now that one of the most difficult problems for the anthroposophist coming to Bacon's doctrine of Idols is that so much of what he says has also been said by Steiner. We *do* tend to live in our worlds of private fantasy. Language *has* been corrupted. Words *are* often used like weapons, just as they were in Shakespeare's time. As Benedick says about Beatrice, "She speaks poniards, and every word stabs."

As Steiner says, much of what is taught and believed in the modern world consists of *fables convenues*. We can't blame Bacon for this, since this was already true in his time. It is what he was complaining about; hence his warnings about idols. Language was one of the gifts of God, but like nature, it had fallen.

It seems to me that, like Bacon, Steiner is sometimes too wholesale. Bacon's behavior is like that of the British Government when an outbreak of foot and mouth disease is discovered. Not all of the cows have the disease, but the whole herd has to be destroyed. Steiner's position is like that of someone who sees the whole herd being destroyed and concludes that the Government officials must have thought that all the cows were infected. As far as the cows and, perhaps, the further history of agriculture, are concerned, the result is the same. But the mindsets and motivations of the officials have been misunderstood.

* * *

Steiner summarizes his view of Bacon's intentions as follows:

"And learning to see through these idols is to provide the salvation of human knowledge—this was inaugurated by Bacon of Verulam. The idols must be understood, their idol-like character, their character of unreality, must be recognised, so that we can at last turn our attention towards reality. But if all these species of idols are removed, nothing remains but the five senses. Everyone can prove this for themselves. Notice has thereby been served on humanity of the fifth post-Atlantean epoch: although we need the idols and the words that express them as a kind of common currency, they are only seen in the correct light when we recognise their character as idols, their unreal character. *We need them as currency for the tribe, or for individual knowledge, or the market-place we share. We even need them for scientific investigations, for the inner theatre.* But only that which the hands can grasp and the eyes can see is to be accepted as real—only what can be investigated in the chemical laboratory, in the experiments of the physicist, in the clinic. The important book which gave Bacon of Verulam's doctrine of the idols to the fifth post-Atlantean epoch inaugurated this way of looking at the world; it is the classic source. And such a book shows us how the very thing that, from a certain point of view, must be resisted, nevertheless can make its appearance in the world in accordance with the rightful cosmic plan. The fifth post-Atlantean epoch had to develop materialism. Therefore the programme for materialism had to be introduced from out of the spiritual world. And the first stage of the programme of materialism is contained in the doctrine of the idols, which did away with the old Aristotelian doctrine that words refer to categories which have real significance."[157] (My italics)

Contrary to what Steiner says, it was not Bacon's opinion that we need the idols; for any serious philosophical work, he made it plain that the idols had to be dismissed. "The formation of ideas and axioms by true induction is no doubt the proper remedy to be applied for the keeping off and clearing away of idols." (Aphorism 40) "This class of idols is more easily expelled, because to get rid of them it is only necessary that the theories should be steadily rejected and dismissed as obsolete." (Aphorism 60)

Steiner makes it sound as if Bacon was responsible for the death of language and would have liked to dance on its grave, whereas the Chancellor's own words constitute a lament for the loss of meaning and communication that had already taken place.

(xxviii)

The Whammy

Steiner's further characterization of Bacon's influence is as follows:

"Today, humanity is already very advanced along the course of regarding anything that is not perceivable by the senses as idols. Bacon is the great inaugurator of the science of idols. Why, then, should the spiritual world not employ the same head that was intended to draw mankind's attention to the idol-like character of speech, to introduce also the practical details of what more or less appears to be a materialistic paradise on earth? In any case, it was essential to present it in a light that would seem paradisiacal to the materialistic frame of mind that had to emerge in the fifth post-Atlantean epoch. This age needed some corresponding practical ideal. An age which had these views on language was bound to respond to the idea or applying its mechanics to neighbouring spheres of the heavens. Thus the ideals of the materialism of the fifth post-Atlantean epoch are born from the same head that gave us the doctrine of idols. One of the not-yet-fulfilled ideals that you can find in Bacon is the idea of artificially-created weather. But that will come! This ideal from Bacon's *Nova Atlantis* will also be fulfilled. In Bacon we encounter for the first time the idea of airships that can be guided, and the idea of boats that can submerge. This far we already have progressed in the intervening time. For Bacon, Bacon of Verulam, the great inaugurator, was also a practical materialist, capable of conceiving of these practical mechanisms that are appropriate to our fifth post-Atlantean period."

The reader will, no doubt, observe that Steiner continues to give a false impression of Bacon's view of idols and that he attaches far more importance to the *New Atlantis* than Bacon did or I do. What aroused the Chancellor's enthusiasm most strongly was the compilation of his natural history.

Steiner was also mistaken about airships and the submarine— Leonardo da Vinci had made detailed plans for an airplane more than a century earlier, and had also floated the idea of a submarine. William Bourne, a British mathematician, drew plans for a submarine in 1578, and in 1620, seven years before the publication of the *New Atlantis*, a Dutch inventor called Cornelius van Drebbel managed to build a primitive submarine that stayed submerged for three hours in the waters of the Thames. Note that the only reference to flight and submarines in the *New Atlantis* is as follows: "We imitate also flights of birds; we have some degrees of flying in the air. We have ships and boats for going under water." There is no indication that Bacon ever conceived any "practical mechanisms", or that he would have been technically capable of doing so.

It might have been possible to dismiss such details as merely incidental if Steiner had not made such a point of them, but could he really not have known about Leonardo's pioneering work? The more I continue to study Bacon and Steiner and to ponder their relationship, the more I am visited by the suspicion that there is something at work here that is not to be accounted for in elevated cosmic terms, but rather in terms of something simpler and more earthly; namely a personal dislike or animus, which could perhaps be described in a more high-flown way as a karmic knot. We are, at any rate, confronted by the beginnings of a multiple whammy; Bacon's proposed system is incapable of generating any kind of science and, at the same time, responsible for all the ills of modern technology.

Steiner continues:

"One can always discover impulses that are intruding, as though from the substrata of the world, when one is trying to strike the fundamental character of a particular period of time. Inventions for controlling the weather, for sailing in the air, for sailing under the sea, belong with those of the theory of idols. Those are ideas and ideals that belong together, and so it is that they appear in the fifth post-Atlantean epoch. These things must be judged objectively. One needs to see clearly that words can be employed differently without either viewing them as idols or by turning them into idols. There is a plan behind human evolution. Gradually, according to plan, various impulses appear in the course of evolution. Now that the theory of idols and all that is contained in *Nova Atlantis* has made its appearance, the last remnants of the great atavistic spiritual theories, views and experiences have been extinguished. So this ground must be recaptured by a newly-appearing spiritual science, proceeding now in the full light of consciousness. During the fourth Atlantean Epoch, someone formulated the ideas that introduced materialism into the ancient Atlantean period. This is described in my writings. Just as it was necessary, in the fourth epoch of Atlantis, for the materialism of Atlantis to be formulated in the head of an old Atlantean, so the fifth post-Atlantean epoch needed its *Nova Atlantis*, which has a similar function for this epoch. These things cannot be grasped unless they are considered in the light of spiritual science. A person who can observe the fine details of history will find these deeper connections. But today a foundation in spiritual science is necessary. For ordinary history is just a *fable convenue*; it only says what the various nations, races, peoples and citizens want to hear. Real history has to be obtained from the spiritual world.

"Personalities like Lord Bacon, Bacon of Verulam, more or less set the tone of an age. In the case of such persons, the biography is of much less importance than what is revealed by their place in the entire process of developing humanity."

Steiner does not recognize that the fruitful employment of words and the extinction of idols were actually among the intended benefits of Bacon's plan. Here, also, we have the continuation of the multiple whammy that I mentioned before; Steiner has now tied up the whole parcel by asserting that we should not worry if received history seems to contradict his account of events, since history is merely a *fable convenue*.

(xxix)

"Constrained and Vexed"
(A chapter not strictly necessary)

In his remarks about Bacon and the *Novum Organum,* Steiner scarcely touches on one of the most compelling reasons for a student of spiritual science to treat the Chancellor's work with great reserve, if not to reject it outright. As I remarked in Section (xxii), one of the reasons why there was so little progress in the physical sciences before 1600 and such a tremendous acceleration subsequently is that instead of seeing natural processes as expressions of something akin to human sympathies and antipathies, the scientists began to treat both mineral and organic matter as if it were lifeless and subject only to impersonal forces. If nature is inanimate we can do whatever we like to it (no need to say "her" any more) with no twinge of remorse or conscience. As Bacon put it:

"Now as to how my Natural History should be composed, I mean it to be a history not only of Nature free and untrammeled (that is, when she is left to her own course and does her work in her own way)... but much more of nature constrained and vexed; that is to say when by art and the hand of man she is forced out of her natural state and squeezed and moulded."

It is this attitude, among other things, that makes the *New Atlantis* so repulsive. The natural resources, including plants and animal, are there more for research than for wonder and beauty. We are not told what form this research might have taken, but we can't avoid the perception that the kind of constraint and vexation that Bacon had in mind was quite different from anything that happens in a Goethean scientific institution. Steiner remarks that "only that which the hands can grasp and the eyes can see is to be accepted as real—only what can be investigated in the chemical laboratory, in the experiments of the physicist, in the clinic." Goethean scientists have laboratories and anthroposophical doctors have clinics, but their relationship to what they are investigating is intended to be one of love and appreciation, rather constraint and vexation.

I have noted, however, that the attitude which Steiner ascribes to Bacon was on its way to becoming the norm before the *Novum Organum* and the *New Atlantis* were published. By about 1600, many of the characters who set the scene for modern developments in science and the humanities had appeared. The revival of the ancient atomic theory, rejected by Bacon, had begun, and the early stirrings of the industrial revolution would soon be felt. I'd like to put a little flesh on these historical bones by giving the example of Johann Baptista van Helmont, who was born in Brussels in 1579 and died there or thereabouts in 1644.

What, in addition to the change of attitude noted above, gave a new and powerful impetus to the development of modern chemistry and physics? Undoubtedly it was the development of techniques for accurately weighing and measuring the solids, liquids and gases taking part in chemical reactions. It took a long time for these techniques to reach the point where they could provide accurate information for the burgeoning atomic theory, but van Helmont made an excellent start.

Van Helmont did not find his true vocation until he was thirty years old. Having started as a student of the arts, he moved to a Jesuit school, which he in turn abandoned in favor of a study of the Christian mystics Thomas à Kempis and Johann Tauler. Becoming interested in medicine he studied Hippocrates, Galen and Avicenna, and many of his contemporaries. Eventually he came to the conclusion that his study of medicine had been fruitless and gave his books away, afterwards feeling that it would have been better if he had burnt them. In 1609 he took the degree of M. D. but he did not practise medicine. What happened next we can learn in his own words: "God has given me a pious and noble wife. I retired with her to Vilvorde and there for seven years [1609-1616] I dedicated myself to pyrotechny and to the relief of the poor." In this context, *Pyrotechny* is chemistry, not fireworks, and its derivation from the Greek word *pyr* emphasizes the major importance fire as the chemist's principle agent. Van Helmont referred to himself as *philosophus per ignem*, which we can translate as "a philosopher by way of fire" as long as we remember that philosophy at that time included what we now call "science."

Many of van Helmont's experiments were of a precise, quantitative nature and his use of the balance led him to the conclusion that matter is indestructible. What actually happens, for instance, when a metal is dissolved by an acid? Van Helmont emphasized that when metals dissolve in acids they are not destroyed but can be recovered from the solution. Silver dissolved in nitric acid can be restored to its original form by evaporating the solution and heating the resulting solid, or by adding a solution of common salt, filtering to obtain the precipitate of silver chloride, and heating. Van Helmont did many such experiments, using mercury and sulphuric acid, producing copper sulphate by throwing sulphur on molten copper and pouring rainwater over the result, and carefully distinguishing the chemical behavior of copper from that of iron. He knew how to prepare nitric acid from saltpetre, sulphuric acid from sulphur, and hydrochloric acid from salt. Many of these experiments involved weighing. Before observing the reaction of mercury with sulphuric acid, van Helmont weighed the mercury. The reaction produced a white powder resembling snow, which turned yellow when washed with water and, on reduction, yielded the original weight of mercury. This is the kind of result that led him to the belief that matter is indestructible, a principle without which the quantitative methods of the nineteenth century would have made no sense at all. His experiments led him also to the concept of *gas*.

After burning 62 lb. of oak charcoal he found that 1 lb. of ash remained, leading him to the conclusion that 61 lb. of *spiritus silvestre* – wild or woody spirit – had escaped with the flames. If the charcoal is heated in a closed vessel the wild spirit cannot escape and the weight of the vessel as a whole remains the same. "I call this spirit, unknown hitherto, by the new name of Gas, which can neither be contained by vessels, nor reduced into a visible body, unless the seed is first extinguished." Van Helmont gave the name *gas sylvestre* to the "untameable gas" that breaks all but the strongest vessels and escapes into the air. Describing an experiment in which nitric acid and sal ammoniac are mixed in a closed glass vessel, he says, "the vessel is filled with a plentiful exhalation, yet an invisible one, and although the vessel may be thought to be stronger than iron, yet it straightway dangerously leapeth asunder into broken pieces."

It may appear that van Helmont, whose chemical studies were completed four years before the publication of the *Novum Organum*, was into constraint and vexation to a remarkable degree; so it is well to remember that this kind of assault on natural materials had been part of the traditional stock-in-trade of the alchemist for a very long time. Van Helmont, in fact, still had one foot firmly embedded in the alchemical tradition. It was the quantitative, mathematical nature of his work that was new and pointed to the way in which science would develop.

The moral of this story is that constraint and vexation were not invented by Bacon and that the idea that they could be used to obtain the kind of quantitative results that would lead to a new science is absent from his writings. C. and V. certainly get results—but not when the system described in the *Novum Organum* is employed.

(xxx)

This is all very interesting but...

You may be feeling that while what I have had to say is of some interest, it misses the point. If Steiner's insights into Bacon's karma and his influence on the development of Western European culture came directly from realms to which most of us have little or no access, the real story is something else. According to Steiner, "ordinary history is just a *fable convenue*; it only says what the various nations, races, peoples and citizens want to hear. Real history has to be obtained from the spiritual world." In the case of such individuals as Francis Bacon, "the biography is of much less importance than what is revealed by their place in the entire process of developing humanity." If we were to take these statements at face value, it would mean that it is simply a waste of time to look among exoteric sources for corroboration of Steiner's narrative.

It is clear, however, that these strictures do not always apply and that there are many points at which exoteric history correlates admirably with Steiner's esoteric view of world evolution, including the beginning of Greek philosophy, as described earlier in this study. To put the matter as brutally as possible, Steiner accompanies his esoteric picture of the Bacon individuality with a deeply flawed view of Bacon's philosophy and influence, which he then shields from criticism by asserting that exoteric histories and biographies are of no evidential value.

In saying this, I don't intend to sound bitter or anti-Steiner, but it does make one realize the enormous difficulty faced by the individual in coming to any reasonable assessment of the accuracy of his perceptions and the truth of his conclusions. What he says about "ordinary" history may be true *de facto*, although not in principle, and it echoes what Bacon had been saying three hundred years previously. Nationalistic, ideological and theocratic histories continue to be propagated all over the world, but accurate exoteric history is a goal worth pursuing even though it may require extraordinary exertions. Such exertions have clearly shown the inadequacy and inaccuracy of nineteenth and early twentieth century European ideas about Bacon, which portrayed him as the founder of a system that dominated western science and led to all the evils of industrial and technological society. This is the picture of Bacon which Steiner grew up with and which is incorporated in his assessment of Bacon's historical influence. And it is clearly a *fable convenue*.

It is evident that, far as Steiner traveled in his search for the truth, he did not escape the influence of his local earthly origin—in other words, his Austro-German-ness and his nineteenth-century-ness. To acknowledge this is simply to state my conviction that belief in the reality of Steiner's access to occult spiritual history would not be incompatible with belief in the appropriateness of applying ordinary critical standards to his works. This attitude is, after all, very much in tune with that of Aquinas with regard to divine revelation and philosophy. With that in mind, I shall now take Steiner at his word and return to the questions of occult history that seemed most important to him.

Part VI

Karma Revisited

"As we look back, the question arises: Had not Bacon and Darwin passed through earlier lives on earth? They carried over from those earlier incarnations the traits and characteristics revealed in their later lives. When we understand them as *individuals,* then and only then do we understand their real place in history. For when the reality of karma is taken seriously, history resolves itself into deeds of men, into streams of human lives flowing from remote ages of the past into the present and thence into the future."

(Rudolf Steiner, *Cosmic Christianity*)

(xxxi)

"The Morbid Elimination of Old Spirituality"

In Chapter 10, Volume 1 of *Karmic Relationships* we find the following, which I quote in order to remind the reader of Steiner's view of Bacon's karmic ancestry:

"When with this knowledge of an historic karmic connection we turn to Bacon and his writings, we recognise why these writings have so little that is Christian about them and such a strong Arabic timbre. We discover the genuine Arabist trend in these writings of Lord Bacon. And many things too in regard to his character, which has been so often impugned, will be explicable when we see in him the reincarnated Harun al-Rashid. The life and culture pursued at the Court of Harun al-Rashid, and justly admired by Charles the Great himself, become the abstract science of which Lord Bacon was the bearer. But men bowed before Lord Bacon too. And whoever studies the attitude adopted by European civilisation in the 8th/9th centuries to Harun al-Rashid, and then the attitude of European learning to Lord Bacon, will have the impression: men have turned round, that is all! In the days of Harun al-Rashid they looked towards the East; then they turned round in Middle Europe and looked towards the West, to Lord Bacon."

There is no need for me to comment further on this view of Bacon's Christianity, which I believe to be deeply mistaken.

Steiner returns to the theme of Bacon's influence in Chapter 6 of the fourth volume of *Karmic Relationships*:

"I have already spoken of Lord Bacon of Verulam as the reincarnated Harun al-Rashid. We know how intense and determining an influence Bacon's conceptions had on the whole succeeding evolution of the spiritual life, notably in its finer impulses and movements. Now the remarkable thing is this, that in Lord Bacon himself something took place which we may describe as a morbid elimination of old spirituality. For such spirituality he had after all possessed when he was Harun al-Rashid.

"And thus we see, proceeding from the impulse of Lord Bacon, a whole world of daemonic beings. The world was literally filled supersensibly and sensibly with daemonic beings. (When I say "sensibly" I mean not of course, visibly, but within the world of sense.)"

When Steiner says, "We know", I am not always sure whether he means, "I know", "We in the anthroposophical movement know", or "Everyone knows." We (whoever we are) should remember that not everyone knows "how intense and determining an influence Bacon's conceptions had on the whole succeeding evolution of the spiritual life, notably in its finer impulses and movements", and that many would disagree. Steiner says that "personalities like Lord Bacon, Bacon of Verulam, more or less set the tone of an age. In the case of such persons, the biography is of much less importance than what is revealed by their place in the entire process of developing humanity." In response to this I have to say both "Yes" and "No". Yes; if we are to grasp Steiner's view of Bacon, we need to see him as part of a whole evolutionary picture; no, it *is* important to amend a manifestly incorrect and misleading biography.

To repeat Paolo Rossi's characterization of the old, discredited European view: "Bacon as... the symbol of what science has been up until now and should no longer be: the impious will to dominate nature and tyrannize mankind... it is the scientific and technological enthusiasm of the Lord Chancellor that leads to materialism, the mercantilization of culture, to modern industrial society, which is the realm of alienation and conformism, of the standardization and destruction of all human values."

This view is demonstrably incorrect, but its persistence, well into the second half of the twentieth century, shows the enormous durability of such ideas once they have become part of the group consciousness. The emotional power of the standard nineteenth century European model of Francis Bacon is illustrated by the experience of Loren Eiseley.

In 1961, the four hundredth anniversary of Bacon's birth, Eiseley, who held the Chair in Anthropology at the University of Pennsylvania and had recently been elected to the National Institute of Arts and Letters, gave several addresses on Bacon's life and scientific work. "I rapidly discovered", he writes in the preface to *The Man Who Saw Through Time*[158], "that I had unwittingly assumed the role of attorney for the defense against sometimes extremely self-righteous public prosecutors who had been unduly influenced by Macauley's[159] intemperate and acerbic treatment of Bacon in the nineteenth century, writings upon which many later treatments of Bacon were modeled. I found myself embroiled, in fact, in sufficient controversy to make me wonder whether it was I who was threatened with the Tower, and whether Parliament was in full cry upon my own derelictions." Having been amazed at the fury of the reactions stirred up by his efforts to "do honor to a great scholar and seer", Eiseley found that by the time he revised his papers for reprinting in 1972, much of what he had said had been accepted, and scholars who had actually studied Bacon's work had noted the successive vulgarizations of it by the puritans and the Victorians. Eiseley quotes the historian Margery Purver to the effect that "the Victorian image of Francis Bacon, distorted and inconsequential, continues to dominate historians." It did not dominate Loren Eiseley, but some aspects of it seem to have been uncritically accepted by Rudolf Steiner. It is worth noting, too, that changes in the way in which scholars perceived Bacon and his work took place at a time when reactions against the technological society had reached a new level of intensity, so they were plainly not caused by a mere whim of fashion.

To observe that the exoteric historical record does not support the contention that Bacon was responsible for the "whole succeeding evolution of the spiritual life" is not necessarily to dismiss Steiner's esoteric findings. While it is important to get the historical record right in order to avoid red herrings and simply because it is always better to get something right, it is also necessary to consider Steiner's contention that in relation to the whole karmic picture his actual deeds on earth were not of any great moment and that the spiritual powers, the daemons of materialism, would have used the individuality incarnated as Francis Bacon no matter what he did. As far as they were concerned, the opportunity to cherry-pick useable elements from his scientific method would just have been a bonus. We should therefore ponder the "morbid elimination of old spirituality", which, according to Steiner, is what let the daemons in.

It is observable that the elimination of older forms of spirituality had been going on among apparently healthy people for centuries or, if Steiner is correct, millennia: and, as shown in Part I, Section (i), its manifestations became increasingly violent in sixteenth century England. Is there some sense in which it was particularly morbid in the case of Francis Bacon?

*   *   *

While Bacon was working on his *Great Instauration*, science, like religion, was undergoing a radical transition—namely, the adoption of the kind of mathematical and quantitative methods that he eschewed. At the same time, efforts to penetrate to the divine world by means of natural magic and spiritual insight—in other words, genuine alchemy—did not vanish overnight. In the seventeenth century van Helmont, Boyle and Newton, among many others, were deeply influenced by the work of Paracelsus. Over the centuries, however, countless quacks and impostors had given alchemy a bad name and Paracelsus himself had been given a disreputable, fictionalized biography[160], with the result that later practitioners, including Newton, could keep their good, respectable names only by keeping their alchemical work *sub rosa*.

The *Novum Organum*, which eliminated the magic of nature and did not allow any kind of window for individual intuitive insight, could hardly have been more squarely antithetical to alchemy, which seems to have been a pursuit for the archetypal loner, not for a cog in a cognitive machine. Bacon's belief that the human mind needed the assistance of a quasi-mechanical system in order to encompass the subtlety and multiplicity of nature does not seem to have occurred to anyone else. Was this belief a product of "the morbid elimination" of spirituality? Was it a desperate clutching at straws, motivated by acute discouragement over the current state of science? Was it a genuine insight?

Taking the third question first, it can be seen that in Bacon's time, and for hundreds of years after his death, all the major advances in physical science were made by individuals whose achievements resulted from a complex interplay of intuition, technique and experimentation—Galileo, Snell, Huygens, Newton, Lavoisier, Faraday, Planck, Rutherford, Bohr, Heisenberg, to mention only a few. If this appears to contradict Bacon's notion of the inadequacy of the human mind, we should recognize that each of these workers achieved eminence by tackling closely defined problems one at a time. We may believe that all the disparate manifestations of the physical world are interrelated, but we realize that we can't tackle them all at once. The result of this is that we know a lot about how individual systems work when isolated, but we are not so good at understanding what happens when they are put back together.[161]

In fact, the steady increase in specialization and of specialties within specialties has been a tacit admission that there was some truth in Bacon's assessment of the capabilities of the human mind. The manifestations of the cosmos, as it appears to the modern scientific mind, really are too many, too varied and too complex to be encompassed by the individual. We have simply adopted a solution to the problem different from the one Bacon proposed. It is highly productive but not necessarily healthier.

As far as the second question is concerned, Bacon's despair and frustration are obvious. He wouldn't have liked the suggestion that he was clutching at straws, but if we try to imagine someone searching a haystack without having any previous concept of a needle, we can see that there is something apt about the metaphor—as long as we are prepared to ignore the fact that hay and straw are two quite different things.

The question of the morbid elimination of old spirituality is more difficult to deal with. Even if we were willing to accept this diagnosis simply on Steiner's authority, we should still have to try to understand what the phrase means.

Bacon made no scientific discoveries, and his proposed scientific method was unworkable. In spite of his considerable accomplishments it is arguable that he generally had too many irons in the fire and would have done better to have spent less time instructing others and more time putting his own advice into practice. He loved the pomp and circumstance[162] and the cut and thrust of Elizabethan and Jacobean court life. He loved to occupy his powerful mind with legal issues and to write edifying essays filled with good advice. He loved to live as a person of great wealth with carriages, fine clothes and servants galore, most of which he could not afford, and he projected his desires into his New Atlantis, where he would undoubtedly have been one of the Fathers, with all the luxuries his heart desired. But he also loved the philosophical life, the life of contemplation, the life of one who knew the past intimately, who could propel his thought into the future, and who suffered with all who bore the burden of the present; and so Bensalem, instead of becoming the New Jerusalem, became the fading memory of a self-indulgent dream. And in his old age, after his disgrace, he regretted the choices he had made, writing in a private and unpublished prayer, part of which I have already quoted:

"Oh Lord my strength! I have since my youth, met with Thee in all my ways; by Thy fatherly compassions; by Thy comfortable chastisements; by Thy visible providences. As Thy favours have increased upon me, so have Thy corrections. Thus Thou hast always been near me, oh Lord, and ever as my worldly blessings were exalted, so secret darts from Thee have pierced me; that when I have ascended before men, I have descended in humiliation before Thee.

And now, when I thought most of peace and honour, Thine hand is heavy upon me, and hath humbled me according to Thy former loving kindness; keeping me still in Thy school, not as an alien, but as a child. Just are Thy judgments upon me for my sins, which are more in number than the sands of the sea, but have no proportion to Thy mercies; or what are the sands of the sea? Earth, heavens, and all these, are nothing to Thy mercies! I confess before Thee, that I am debtor to Thee, for the precious talent of Thy gifts and graces, which I have neither put into a napkin, not put out as I ought, to exchangers, where it might have made best profit; but misspent it in things for which I was least fit; so I may truly say, my soul hath been a stranger in the house of her pilgrimage. Be merciful unto me, O Lord, for my Saviour's sake; and receive me into Thy bosom, or guide me in Thy way."

There was, and is, a sickness in the human soul that Christians in general ascribe to the work of the devil, and Steiner in particular to the activities of spiritual beings inimical our healthy evolution. Our chronic sickness, whatever the cause, is manifest throughout recorded history, and at no time and place is it more apparent than in fifteenth and sixteenth century Europe. This is a condition that everyone with any spiritual aspirations has in some way to deal with, and it is arguable that Bacon dealt with it better than most of his contemporaries. His highly individual Confession of Faith is clear and trenchant, and he was willing to go out on a limb in professing his convictions, both religious and scientific, in ways that few members of the English upper classes would have been willing to contemplate. Publically, he diagnosed an aspect of the sickness in European spiritual and intellectual life and proposed a cure; privately, he diagnosed the sickness in his own soul and asked for help. His diagnosis in the public sector was incomplete, and his proposed treatment ineffective, but his self-diagnosis was spot on, and his plea for help expresses what any human being might justly feel when nearing the end of this earthly life.

It is possible to relate the morbidity that for several centuries had increasingly afflicted Europeans to the loss of the ancient access to the divine and the struggle to find a relation to thinking, individuality and the physical world. According to Steiner, this is part of the divine plan, and we are still in the fairly early days of the transition, so while Bacon's soul may have been a mess, it would have been the kind of mess familiar to most of us if we are given to a little introspection. Steiner, however, asserted that while we may deplore the activities of certain spiritual powers in using the Chancellor as the pipeline through which the daemons of materialism invaded our civilization, we must recognize that this was really a good thing or, at worst, a necessary evil.[163] Was this a case of the good powers countenancing the evils of our materialistic society in order that good might eventually become? If this was the case, was Bacon intuitively aware of an incongruity between his karmically determined mission and his actual benevolent intentions and deeds on earth? Or was his painful consciousness of something amiss in his soul something that many of us share—the knowledge that we could have done much better, that "we have done those things which we ought not to have done and left undone those things which we ought to have done, and there is no health in us."[164] Bacon acknowledged that he had failed to fulfill his true purpose in life, that, like the Prodigal Son, he had "spent his substance in riotous living" when he ought to have devoted himself to the family farm—in other words to the cultivation of Christianity and philosophy.

Having said all this we come back to the fact, as I see it and Rudolf Steiner does not, that Bacon's Christianity was sincere and heartfelt; his concern for his fellow human beings was genuine and the goal of his proposals was to make their lives more tolerable.

Steiner asserts that we cannot expect to find confirmation of his view of Bacon in a study of the historical and biographical record, and this assertion is justified in terms of the actual results of such a study. We may decide to accept Steiner's esoterically based findings for other reasons, or purely on trust; or we may decide to do our best with exoteric sources, which will almost certainly result in the rejection of Steiner's view.

Part VII

An Interim Report

As the uses of light are infinite in enabling us to walk, to ply our arts, to read, to recognize one another — and nevertheless the very beholding of the light is itself a more excellent and a fairer thing than all the uses of it — so assuredly the very contemplation of things as they are, without superstition or imposture, error or confusion, is in itself more worthy than all the fruit of inventions.

(*Novum Organum*, Book I, Aphorism 129)

(xxxii)

Bacon's System and the Unicity Theory

One approach to the history of science is the "genius" or "great individual" theory, according to which science has progressed in a sequence of discontinuous leaps brought about by such as Galileo, Newton, Einstein, Bohr and Gell-Mann. Another is the evolutionary theory of a continuous advance through the systematic experimental verification of inductive generalizations, the creation of conceptual models and the verification, or otherwise, of predictions. That the former is the stuff of romanticized popular histories indicates only that it is the easier, more appealing approach, not that it is necessarily wrong. That the latter corresponds closely to the old-fashioned textbook description of scientific method is likewise not evidential. Most histories include elements of both approaches and may add contributions from Zeitgeists, paradigm shifts and pure fortuity. Bacon may have been the first author to try to write the history of science before it happened and possibly the only one to provide a detailed mechanism for it. Although his method suggests a large-scale fishing expedition rather than a steady progression, it contains elements of what is described under the evolutionary heading and casts considerable doubt on the need for the "genius" or "great individual." Bacon's scientist, unlike the Fathers of Bensalem, was "a man of peaceful and serene air, save that his face had become habituated to an expression of pity, [who] took his seat, not on a platform or pulpit, but on a level with the rest...."[165] "The perfection of the sciences is to be looked for not from the swiftness or ability of one inquirer, but from a succession" of them.[166] The scientific institution was to be hierarchical, insofar as the different services of artisans, writers and those skilled in inductive reasoning would be required; but the nature of the whole endeavor was such that strokes of individual genius would not be needed and might indeed be undesirable.

Bacon acknowledged the need for highly talented individuals, but, as he states in Aphorism 61 of the Novum Organum, the system was designed to be independent of individual gifts; "But the course I propose for the discovery of sciences is such as leaves but little to the acuteness and strength of wits, but places all wits and understandings nearly on a level." The "rude mechanicals" might seem intellectually inferior to the "inductors", but it would be a common duty to banish from consciousness anything remotely resembling an individual, intuitive idea.

In Bacon's system, therefore, the human intelligence works as a blank page on which nature is to be encouraged or persuaded to write her own script, just as, in Aristotle's *De Anima*[167], the potential intellect is overwritten by the external and universal active intellect. Aristotle speaks somewhat obscurely of the active, potential and passive intellects, and passes on without giving the impression that he has been dealing with a matter of great difficulty or importance. The operation of human intelligence became a matter of great moment for some of the Arabian philosophers because the universality of the active intellect and the mortality of the passive intellect made it very difficult to incorporate human individuality and personal immortality into a consistent philosophical system. Christian philosophers wrestled with related difficulties, and after the great Thomist synthesis had been attacked and its credibility somewhat damaged, scholastic philosophy drifted into vain imaginings and occupied itself more and more with futile speculation.

Bacon set out to replace these futilities with something new, vital and fruitful, but his system carries with it the imprint of the old unfathomed mystery of individuality, insofar as it treats the human mind largely as a passive receptor and assigns to nature the role previously thought to have been played by the divine active intellect. Patterns that exist in nature are simply to be allowed to impress themselves on the mind of the observer. As we have seen from the *Novum Organum*, this can work up to a point—it can take us a little way, but not very far. The real rewards of studying nature come only when the thought of the student actively encounters the thought inherent in nature. The outcome then depends on the kind of thought and the kind of observation. What Goethean science and mainstream science have in common is that the knowledge of nature is developed in active, individual intellects, whereas, in Bacon's system, individual intellects are to function largely as conduits in a cognitive assembly line.

If Bacon's inductive engine had worked exactly as stated in the *Novum Organum*, the result would have been a body of knowledge which was exactly the same for all concerned with it. Exactly the same set of thoughts and concepts would have been available for all scientific workers, and these thoughts and concepts would have come from somewhere outside the individual mind. It is tempting to say, "Aha! Here we have a reincarnation of the old unicity theory"; but we mustn't go too fast.

I think it is fair to say that for the past several centuries the ideal of deriving from nature a universally accepted body of impersonal knowledge has been held by almost all scientists, in spite of the fact that they have not worked in Baconian institutions or used Bacon's methods. It is largely an unconscious ideal, rarely thought or spoken about, because it has been taken so much for granted that the scientists are investigating an inanimate physical world that exists independently of their efforts to understand it. The ideal embraces the concept of objectivity, which is essential since science would be impossible if different observers obtained different results.

Or would it?

At this point in my cogitations a plaintive little voice said, "But surely, the whole point of science *is* that it's exactly the same for everyone. It must be, if it's true. In fact, everything that's true must be the same for everyone. All that Bacon did was to propose an excessively restrictive, cumbersome and unpractical way of finding it out."

It struck me that I had always unconsciously accepted this overwhelmingly simple proposition, and that, like many obvious propositions, it needed careful examination. There might well be landmines concealed beneath its smooth surface. So I replied, "Science has done this by restricting its enquiries to the portion of experience in which a particular kind of truth is obtainable, a truth that really is the same for everybody and can be communicated exactly. Some have taken this further by asserting that the whole of experience is expressible in terms of this kind of truth, or even that this is the only kind of truth available to the human being."[168]

If this sounds too easy, the fact is that it is. The problem lies in the Pilatesque difficulty of explaining what we mean by "true", a problem that I'm not prepared, in any sense of the word "prepared", to tackle.[169] At a very rough guess I would say that about fifty percent of the time, when we use the word "true", we have a good practical idea of what we mean, even though we might not be able to put it into words. It's true, we may say, that there's a refrigerator in the kitchen, that ducks waddle and that Winston Churchill smoked cigars. The concept becomes much more doubtful when we talk about the "true path of evolution" or "truly human behavior." In practice, these are statements of value or approval rather than of actuality, and although it may be important to understand what lies behind them, they do not belong in this particular paragraph. A few percentage points that do belong here have to do with the realization among Goethean scientists that the most saturated and vividly experienced form of knowledge arises when the barrier between the observer and the observed is dissolved, a condition which, together with the realization among mainstream physicists that the observer is part of the experiment, casts doubt on the old notion of objectivity. To the Goethean, nature is alive and can talk to us if we'll listen. Mainstream scientists may still believe that physical processes continue under their own steam as long as no one tries to find out what's happening, or they may believe that such statements are meaningless; but the fact is that the process of investigation changes whatever it is that we are investigating, even if we're only taking the temperature of a beaker of water.

Truth is not "relative" in the sloppy old sense of the expression, but it is a precise statement of interaction, and the closer we come to the spiritual world, the more it becomes an individual matter.[170] As Steiner said about one of Kant's remarks about the human relationship to knowledge, "That may be true for him but it isn't true for me." What is true of my interactions may not be true of yours. Wallace and Thatcher[171] observed that "religion is not a branch of knowledge to be reduced to propositions and systems of dogma, *but a personal and inward power, an individual truth* which stands distinct from, but not contradictory to, the universalities of scientific law." [My italics]

The word "religion" is loaded with irrelevancies and the "universalities of scientific law" might mean different things to different people; but it is our experience of the spirit that gives us a dynamic relationship to reality, incorporating the kind of truth that outlasts galaxies.

* * *

In view of the millions of words that have been uttered in the attempt to explain what truth is, without producing much that is useful for the art of daily living, I must confess to a feeling of embarrassment on rereading this resounding conclusion to a discussion that has taken place on the scale of a church porch leaflet. From the pre-Socratics ("Nothing is stronger than what is true.") to the modern age in which we have truth tables and "truth" sometimes means nothing stronger than "absence of error and inconsistency", many people have worried about what it means to know something. Others have followed the example of "The more ancient of the Greeks", who, as Bacon put it, "took up with better judgment a position between these two extremes — between the presumption of pronouncing on everything, and the despair of comprehending anything; and though frequently and bitterly complaining of the difficulty of inquiry and the obscurity of things, and like impatient horses champing at the bit, they did not the less follow up their object and engage with nature, thinking (it seems) that this very question — viz., whether or not anything can be known — was to be settled not by arguing, but by trying."

Bacon commended the "more ancient Greeks", meaning the pre-Socratics, but "They too, trusting entirely to the force of their understanding, applied no rule, but made everything turn upon hard thinking and perpetual working and exercise of the mind." In the modern world, people who have trusted to the force of their understanding have found that they have had great difficulty in certifying the consistency of their abstract logical structures, let alone saying something true about the perceived world. We can't even agree about the meaning of "the perceived world", which we often refer to as "the external world", as if the phrase had an obvious meaning that everyone understood.

Perhaps, however, the fact that the millions of words mentioned earlier have produced very little of any benefit to the human race can be seen as encouraging. After all, the bullseye occupies only a small fraction of the target area. So, bearing in mind that your experience of the spirit may be different from mine, and both may differ from Rudolf Steiner's, I'll stick to my conclusion and move along before I get into any further trouble.

(xxxiii)

Fragments and Correlations

In Section (xi) I noted that, in terms of Steiner's view of history, Bacon appears to have been part of an evolutionary stream that resisted the transition into the consciousness soul age, and this appearance seems consistent with the actual nature of his scientific program, which denies the possibility of inner vision and individual insight. I also noted that, in spite of this appearance, Steiner associated Bacon with the impulse of Gundi-Shapur to encourage an intellectual brilliance that would bring about the development of the consciousness soul before the human race was ready for it. In my view there is nothing brilliant about the *Novum Organum* when it is considered purely as scientific method, although there are elements of brilliance in the exposition. The move into a new kind of science and a new relationship to the material world was in the air, and had made its presence felt long before Bacon published any of his scientific work. It seems to me that if the daemons of materialism really chose Bacon to usher in a new and brilliant age of materialism, they made a serious mistake.

* * *

Under Elizabeth I, religious observance was compulsory and its form strictly defined by the Act of Uniformity. Everyone's religious experience was to be imposed by a higher authority and to be exactly the same. The Queen's religious system was thus in some ways analogous to Bacon's scientific system, although it would be top-down rather than bottom-up. Bacon, at some risk to himself, counseled a greater degree of tolerance for individual worship and tried to achieve his goal by reason rather than legislation. There is a breath of freedom and individuality about Bacon's relationship to Christianity that has a very different flavor from anything to be found in his scientific work.

* * *

It has been suggested that after Bacon's design for a scientific community had all but vanished from human consciousness for a couple of centuries, it reappeared in the form of the assembly line, made famous by Henry Ford when he adapted it to the manufacture of automobiles. We must be careful not to assume that Henry Ford was altogether a bad guy. He did, after all, shock his fellow industrialists by paying his workers way above average wages and instituting a profit-sharing scheme which distributed $30 million a year among them. Some of Bacon's ideas may have foreshadowed the appearance of industrial communities in which workers are treated like indistinguishable, expendable units, but it would be much too simple-minded to hold Bacon personally responsible for the evils of industrial society, against which he uttered some very severe warnings.

Steiner spoke of the danger of entrapment in the material world and of the aspiration to raise matter to the spirit. In that respect, as long as we are awake we still have a choice, of which one aspect is the wish to balance the ideal of individuality and the ideal of community. Great numbers of people, as far as their daily lives were concerned, have had no choice, having been trapped in one age of the world in the feudal system, and in another in the industrial machine, and having endured terrible privations in order to obtain less than the barest necessities of life. Something akin to this has been true throughout history, even before the feudal system and the machine existed, and it is a terrible irony that the modern versions of these sufferings are attributed to a man who dedicated a great part of his life's work to improving the conditions, both material and spiritual, of human life.

To be safe, well-fed, housed and able to afford a few luxuries places one in a small minority of the earth's population. The sacrifice of the majority, in terms of physical misery and death, soul agony and despair, is incalculable, but even out of these abysses of inhumanity some elements of transformation and redemption emerge. There is no image that is more moving and apt than that of Welsh miners ascending from the coal-black depths of the earth and filling the air with glorious song. The great choral societies and religious and educational movements created in large industrial cities in the nineteenth century form one side of the picture. The other is the formation, against heavy odds, of Trade Unions, and the emergence of socialism and communism. Out of the frying pan into the fire, one might think, but if the loss of individuality is to be accepted, at least it may be turned to economic advantage. People are extraordinarily resilient, and while devoting so much time and thought to great individuals like Aristotle, Averroes, Aquinas and Bacon, it is a good idea to remember the continuation of the exhortation, "Let us now praise famous men", in Ecclesiasticus.

"And some there be that have no memorial, and are perished as though they had never been. But these were merciful men, whose righteousness hath not been forgotten. Their bodies are buried in peace, but their name liveth for evermore."

One does not have to be an anthroposophist to acknowledge the influences that flow, for good or ill, into everyone in the whole mass of mankind who is at all susceptible to intimations of the divine.

* * *

For someone who had grave doubts about the powers of human intelligence Bacon took a surprisingly optimistic view of the future: "Only let the human race recover that right over nature which belongs to it by divine bequest, and let power be given it; the exercise thereof will be governed by sound reason and true religion." Bacon's enthusiasm for radical intervention in the processes of nature was greatly magnified by his hopes for the elevation of the human race and the amelioration of all forms of suffering, but his faith in the efficacy of "sound reason and true religion" seems tragically misplaced in the light of four centuries of hindsight.

It must be remembered that in Bacon's time modern forms of democracy were still a long way off, and that it was taken for granted that the great mass of the people should be ruled by a small elite.[172] His contribution was the idea that the elite should base their rulership on religious and scientific principles and that the new form of science should be employed for the benefit of people in general. What he did not foresee was that many of the scientists and technologists, whatever their own ambitions might be, would become the tools of those who desire to rule mankind for their own purposes—the religious fanatics and the power-mongers of politics and commerce, who are ignorant of science and opposed to anything that might bring peace and harmony into the world. The author of the *Instauratio Magna* would have been astounded that such consequences should be attributed to the thoughts which he brought into the world, and the same might well be said of the Arabian philosophers. Whatever uses the divine powers have found for these individuals, one cannot doubt the sincerity of their efforts to understand and integrate their experiences.

We should certainly avoid the frame of mind in which we blame the Arabians of the Dark and Middle Ages for the problems of modern Western Civilization. Whatever their sins may have been, it is hard to imagine that they were any worse than ours.

* * *

Stripped of its Christian guardianship, of its insistence on humility, love and charity, and of its elaborate and inconvenient system of checks and balances, there is nothing left of Bacon's philosophy but the germ of a soulless experimental science. Looking at the individuals who, over the years, have made science what it is today, we see many who have been deeply religious, many who have been moral and humane, and many whose honesty and integrity are not to be doubted; but even the works of the most devout have flowed into the rising tide of materialism. Bacon's hope that the study of God's works might reveal something of His will and militate against atheism has been replaced by a strong presumption that science will be able to explain away that weird human property previously known as the soul, including its capacity for imagining transcendent being. All this is possible, and happens, in the name of scientific truth. Whether the spectacle of these goings on is more or less bleak than the picture of what is done by those who use science and scientists in the service of egoism, pride, hate, greed and the lust for power is a question hardly worth debating. In our time it is generally believed that when people fall into such a morass of sin it is the result of human frailty rather than demonic influence, but it is noticeable that frailty does not seem to be a characteristic of the commercial and societal systems that arise out of these sins. Sometimes the combination of greed and stupidity results in the collapse of part of the evil empire and the jailing of a few executives, but the strength, dominance and enormity of evil in that empire indicate that vast spiritual energies and impulses are at work, with intentions that are anything but healthy for humanity.

* * *

One thing still being debated is the modern form of the question of faith and reason. A stream of books with dualistic titles confirms this: *Physics and Philosophy*; *Man or Matter*; *Science and Mind*; *Mind or Matter*. The struggle is now to maintain some consciousness of the objective existence and nature of the human soul, and through it to keep open the path to the spirit. If we have been thrown out of the nest by the spiritual powers, we shall have to learn to fly on our own. It seems much safer and more inviting to stay on the ground and to forget or even to deny the existence of the upper air. Flying requires much more energy than walking or hopping. But we do not wish to let our wings fall into disuse; birds that have done this, we are told, are apt to bury their heads in the sand. I am not denying that there are many interesting things to be found in the sand, but birds that can still fly know that there is much more to life than sand, or even grass, trees and mountains, and that the view from above makes a lot more sense of what is below.

* * *

As a man, Bacon honored truth and let it dictate the course of his actions in a way which aroused the contempt of those who placed personal relations ahead of honesty. Humanity and compassion were the wellsprings of his efforts to bring salvation and the necessities of human life to his fellow men.

Catherine Drinker Bowen writes in her fine biography:

"But has any man in history been so variously bespoken, so loved and hated, admired and despised, venerated and damned? Ben Jonson, who knew him, said that he loved Francis Bacon not only for his eloquence but for his virtue—and said it when the Lord Chancellor was in disgrace with all his world. ...Alexander Pope referred to Bacon... as 'the wisest, brightest, meanest of mankind.' Lord Macauley condemned Bacon out of hand as treacherous to his friends, a time server, magnificent of intellect, cold of heart. Whereas Shelley the poet said flatly that he would rather be damned with Plato and Lord Bacon than go to heaven with Paley and Malthus. Let me confess I am on Shelley's side, and heartily..." [173]

It's possible that Bacon was a man whom one could have liked; the breadth and depth of his learning and the penetration of his intelligence may have been intimidating, but there is something very appealing about his sense of humor, his enthusiasm and his passionate commitment to bettering the lot of his fellow human beings. It also must be observed that his self-confidence was apt to be overwhelming and that clearly no one had a higher opinion of his abilities that he had himself. Even his deepest humilities were apt to be laced with a tincture of arrogance. The oddest thing, in view of Steiner's strictures, is that his greatest gift lay in the apt and persuasive use of words, without which *The Advancement of Learning* and the *Novum Organum* might have been very dull and plodding documents.

I can see Shelley's point but, frankly, I'd prefer not to be damned with anyone.

(xxxiv)

The Great Divide

"Looked at from the spiritual world, people have lost a great deal precisely because in the course of their evolution they have had to be led towards freedom. What has been lost, however, must be regained, in the way that Anthroposophy, for example, would show. And now is the historical point of time when a striving to regain what has been lost must begin."

(Rudolf Steiner, *The Evolution of Consciousness*, Penmaenmawr, 1923.)

In Section (xi), I spoke of a persistent notion that Bacon shared with the true alchemists, and with Newton and Goethe, that his scientific work might lead to the perception of the divine. As a pre-teen, I was overwhelmed by the majesty and mystery of the Periodic Table. In his memoir *Uncle Tungsten*, Oliver Sacks describes a similar experience.

"To have perceived an *overall* organization, a superarching principle uniting and relating *all* the elements, had a quality of the miraculous, of genius. And this gave me, for the first time, a sense of the transcendent power of the human mind, and the fact that it might be equipped to discover or decipher the deepest secrets of nature, to read the mind of God."

While the boy's opinion of the human mind was evidently much higher than Bacon's, he aspired to the same ideal as the Lord Chancellor. But what exactly is meant by "reading the mind of God" or, as Bacon put it, penetrating to "the ideas of the divine mind... the creator's true stamp on created things, printed and defined on matter by true and precise lines"? Isaac Newton put the matter as follows:

"And if natural Philosophy... shall at length be perfected, the Bounds of Moral Philosophy will also be enlarged. For so far as we can know by natural Philosophy what is the first Cause, what Power he has over us, and what Benefits we receive from him, so far our Duty towards him, as well as that towards one another, will appear to us by the Light of Nature."[174]

Bacon gives no impression that he thinks of God or any divine spirit as being active in the natural, material world. Following *Genesis*, he believed that God had done the work of creation and then placed the whole project in the hands of human beings, with certain provisos that we promptly ignored. There is, however, in his view of the human condition, a partial parallel with Steiner's story of the separation of divine thought from the objects in which it had originally inhered.

When, as Steiner tells it, the Exousiai took the first step in the release of the divine intelligence, it was evidently with the expectation that 2,000 years later people would begin the process of re-coupling thought and perception in such a way as to bring the spiritual world to human waking consciousness. Bacon's ideal also was a recoupling; to establish "forever a true and lawful marriage between the empirical and the rational faculty [i.e. between the sense world and the thought world], the unkind and ill-starred divorce of which has thrown into confusion all the affairs of the human family."

But illuminations of the kind that Bacon hoped to find and that Oliver Sacks experienced are in a different category from those that Steiner or the Exousiai expected us to seek. The periodic table, the earliest intimations of which appeared in the work of Goethe's chemistry teacher, Johann Wolfgang Dobereiner[175] (1780-1849), is a miracle of phenomenological synthesis, but it is the result neither of a Baconian nor of a Goethean process. We may feel that in summarizing and illuminating our knowledge of substance, it reveals the stamp of the divine mind, but that divinity is no longer there, "constrained and vexed" and driven out by the extreme treatment of natural substances; but was it really driven out, or did it leave of its own accord? Or could it be that it is still there, but we have either decided to ignore it or lost the capacity to perceive it? Or all or some of the above?

In the *Letters to Members*[176], written in the last year of his life, Steiner speaks at length of the role of the archangel Michael[177] at the present stage of human evolution. It must be borne in mind that these letters were written to people whose lives were devoted to anthroposophical work, and that without the context of anthroposophy they may be largely opaque; but at least one thing is made unequivocally clear. In Letter 7 he describes the perception of the divine working in nature as an illusion.

"For anyone who has imbued his whole mind, in all sincerity of feeling, with the inner conception of Michael's being, and Michael's acts, there will come also a right understanding of how Man must treat a world, which is neither one of divine being, nor revelation, nor workings, but is the wrought work of the gods. *To look at this world with knowledge, is to have before one forms, formations, which everywhere tell with a plain voice of the divine, but in which divine being in its own self-existence is not to be found, if one be led away by no illusions.* Nor must one look only at the knowable aspect of the world. True, this reveals most plainly the configuration of the world which surrounds Man to-day. But of more essential importance for everyday life is the feeling, willing and working in a world *which may be felt in its formation to be divine, but in which no divine life can actually be experienced.*" [My italics.]

Questions continue to pile up: does the thought or intention that Aristotle, Aquinas and Goethe perceived in the workings of nature count as divine life? If so, does Steiner mean that it is no longer there? Must we conclude that Goethe was deluded when he saw the development of a plant as an advancing on a spiritual ladder? It would have been more understandable if Steiner had said that the Hierarchies have finished their work of Earth evolution and left the processes of our planet to carry on under the influence of lesser spiritual forces which we may actually experience, but his message is perfectly clear; we are living in a world *which may be felt in its formation to be divine, but in which no divine life can actually be experienced.* When we feel that we experience divine life in nature, we must take Steiner's word for it that we are deluded, and must conclude that the Goddess Natura, whose work Steiner eloquently describes in his lecture on Brunetto Latini[178] and in Karmic Relations[179], has withdrawn. Speaking of the Middle Ages, when descendants of the ancient mystery schools were still active, Steiner tells us:

"Natura was the metamorphosis of Proserpine of antiquity. She was the ever-creating Goddess with whom he who would seek for knowledge must in a certain way unite himself. She appeared to him — appeared to him from every mineral, from every plant, from every creeping beast, from the clouds, the mountains, the river-springs. Of this Goddess who alternately in winter and in summer creates above the earth and beneath, — of this Goddess they felt: She is the hand-maid of that Divinity of whom the Gospels tell. She it is who fulfils the divine behests.

"And when the seeker after knowledge had been sufficiently instructed by the Goddess about the mineral and plant and animal natures, when he was introduced into the living forces, then he learned to know from her the nature of the four elements — earth, water, air and fire. He learned to know the waving and weaving within the mineral and animal and plant kingdoms of the four elements which pour themselves in all reality throughout the world. He felt himself with his etheric body interwoven with the life of the Earth in its gravity, water in its life-giving power, air in its power to awaken sentient consciousness, fire in its power to kindle the flame of the I. In all this he felt his human being interwoven, and he felt: This was the gift of instruction from the Goddess Natura — the successor, the metamorphosis of Proserpine. The teachers saw to it that their disciples should gain a feeling, an idea of this living intercourse with Nature — *Nature filled with divine forces, filled with divine substance.* They saw to it that their pupils should penetrate to the living and weaving of the Elements."

Has the world of nature changed so much since the Middle Ages that divinity is now completely absent from it? Are those of us who vividly experience the almost tangible presence of spirit in nature really deluded? Is there some kind of spiritual presence that does not count as divinity?[180] These questions may seem vitally important, but Steiner's main point can be stated without answering any of them; we have come to the stage of the great evolutionary plan in which we must form our social and ethical life without any aid from the spiritual powers who have brought us so far.

"To bring real ethical life into such a world as this, requires those ethical impulses of which I gave an indication in my *Philosophy of Freedom.* Amidst this world of past works, for the man of genuine feeling, Michael's being and Michael's present world of action may shed a shining light. Michael does not enter the physical world in a visible appearance. He remains with all his doings in a supersensible region, but one which is just on the borders of the physical world in the present evolutionary phase of the worlds. Thus no possibility can ever occur, that any impressions made on men by Michael's actual being, should lead their views of Nature into fantastic realms, or tempt them to build their practical social and ethical life — within a God-wrought, but not God-actuated world — on the pretense that any other impulses could be at work there, save those of which Man himself must be the ethical and spiritual agent." (Letter 7.)

It is not my business—even if I were able—to summarize, paraphrase or elucidate Letter 7, but only to compare two views of the human situation.

Steiner's picture of the world of nature—God-wrought but not God-actuated—is in one respect very close to Bacon's: "The ideas of the divine mind... are the creator's true stamp upon created things, printed and defined on matter by true and precise lines—the true signatures and marks set upon the works of creation as they are found in nature."

However, Steiner's view of the human relationship to ethical and spiritual impulses is in extreme opposition to Bacon's.

Steiner: Thus no possibility can ever occur, that any impressions made on men by Michael's actual being, should lead their views of Nature into fantastic realms, or tempt them to build their practical social and ethical life — within a God-wrought, but not God-actuated world — on the pretence that any other impulses could be at work there, *save those of which Man himself must be the ethical and spiritual agent.*

Bacon: That man made a total defection from God, presuming to imagine that the commandments and prohibitions of God were not the rules of Good and Evil, but that Good and Evil had their own principles and beginnings: and lusted after the knowledge of those imagined beginnings, to the end *to depend no more upon God's will revealed, but upon himself and his own light as a God: than which there could not be a sin more opposite to the whole law of God...*

The ideal of ethical individualism, embraced in Steiner's *Philosophy of Freedom*, had become an important element in the 19th century philosophical atmosphere, notably in the thinking of Soren Kierkegaard (1813-1855) and Friedrich Nietzsche (1844-1900). Later it blossomed into 20th century existentialism. Ethical individualism is very appealing to people who have no religious affiliations and wish to take moral responsibility for the ways in which they conduct their lives; but even if the principle is accepted, the evidence is overwhelmingly against its viability, since it demands a quality of selflessness rarely to be found. I part company with Steiner on a number of issues, but it would be hard to quarrel with the following remarks from 1904:

"The attainment of selflessness alone will enable humanity to be kept from the brink of destruction. The downfall of our present epoch will be caused by lack of morality... Our epoch and its civilisation will be destroyed by the War of All against All, by evil. Human beings will destroy each other in mutual strife. And the terrible thing — more desperately tragic than other catastrophes — will be that the blame will lie with human beings themselves."[181]

Bacon's view of the future was cautiously optimistic

"And this I also humbly ask, that things human may not run counter to things divine, and that from the opening of the paths of the sense-world and the increase of natural light there will arise no unbelief or darkness in our minds towards the divine mysteries; but rather that the understanding thereby being purified and purged of fancies and vanity, yet nonetheless obedient and wholly submissive to the divine oracles, we may give to faith that which is faith's. Lastly that with knowledge rid of the poison instilled by the serpent, whereby the human mind becomes swollen and puffed up, we may not be wise above measure and sobriety, but may seek the truth in Christian love."

In spite of Steiner's strong warnings against egotism, and his insistence on selflessness and humility, it is highly probable that Bacon would have found in the pursuit of anthroposophical spiritual science a tendency for the human mind to become "swollen and puffed up."

"For it was not that pure and uncorrupted natural knowledge whereby Adam gave names to the creatures according to their kind, which brought about the fall. It was the ambitious and proud desire of moral knowledge to judge of good and evil, to the end that man might revolt from God and give laws to himself..."[182]

It would be easy, and even plausible, to suggest that this view of the human relationship to moral knowledge, which is antithetical to the notion of ethical individualism and cuts deep into the roots of the anthroposophical endeavor, was in Steiner's eyes Bacon's fundamental error. However, there is no indication that Steiner had ever read the *Confession of Faith* or the introductory notes to the *Great Instauration*. As has been seen repeatedly, anything that seems easy is almost certainly a half-truth at best.

Of course, this is not the end[183]—just a place to stop and contemplate. I only add that it is possible to appreciate many aspects of Bacon's life and work while being severely critical of his scientific program, whereas all the threads of Steiner's massive output are so interwoven that any such dichotomy is impossible. History has consigned the *Novum Organum* to its waste paper basket, while treating Bacon's writings on religious, moral and social issues with a certain degree of respect and even approval. No such division is possible in Steiner's world, since anthroposophical spiritual science provides the basis and texture of all his initiatives, whether scientific, religious, artistic, social, or educational. Some of my friends believe that everything Steiner ever said was rooted in esoteric knowledge, and maintain that if they found just one error at any point in his work, it would destroy their faith in his whole endeavor. This view is rarely stated explicitly, but the great difficulty often encountered in getting an anthroposophist to give serious consideration to the suggestion that Steiner may have been mistaken about any particular point indicates that it is usually there, just below the surface. No one will actually assert that Steiner was infallible, but if he appears to be mistaken about something, we are likely to be told that we must withhold judgement until, with better understanding, we see that he was really right. If, as has been supposed, Steiner has a trans-human role in the spiritual leadership of humanity, belief in his infallibility may be understandable, although actual experience speaks loudly in the opposite direction. Seen in the light of common day, he appears as a human being having unusual insights and abilities, and suffering, like the rest of us, from the effects of the Fall.

To doubt the validity of Steiner's anthroposophical world view does not imply a lapse into materialism or, indeed, a lapse of any kind. Processes of physical, psychological and spiritual evolution have clearly been at work that go far beyond anything to be found in Darwinian or neo-Darwinian theories.

Appendices

(1)

On Freedom

From an address by Pope John II

"St. Paul writes in the Letter to the Galatians: 'For you were called to freedom, brethren; only do not use your freedom as an opportunity for the flesh, but through love be servants of one another. For the whole law is fulfilled in one word: You shall love your neighbor as yourself.' It might seem that Paul was only contrasting freedom with the law and the law with freedom. However, a deeper analysis of the text shows that in Galatians St. Paul emphasizes above all *the ethical subordination of freedom to that element in which the whole law is fulfilled, that is, to love,* which is the content of the greatest commandment of the Gospel. Christ set us free in order that we might remain free, precisely in the sense that he manifested to us the ethical subordination of freedom to charity, and that he linked freedom with the commandment of love. To understand the vocation to freedom in this way ("You were called to freedom, brethren": Gal 5:13) means giving a form to the ethos in which life according to the Spirit is realized.

(2)

Eddington and Steiner

Sir Arthur Eddington (1882-1944), who was a deeply committed member of the Society of Friends, is most famous for what must be regarded as one of his lesser achievements, the verification of Einstein's prediction of the bending of light rays as they pass close to the sun. His work on the internal constitution of stars placed him in the highest rank of astrophysicists and his quick and comprehensive understanding of Einstein's General Theory of Relativity gave him a very special place among the educators of his time.

Stated as briefly as possible, Eddington's proposition was that the universe described by physical science is a fundamentally different entity from the "objective" world of everyday experience. This is not to say that people have their own individual versions of physical science, but that the structure and content of physical science are dictated by the selective nature of its admission process. "The selection is subjective because it depends on the sensory and intellectual equipment which is our means of acquiring observational knowledge. It is to such subjectively-selected knowledge, and to the universe which it is formulated to describe, that the generalizations of physics – the so-called laws of nature – apply."[184] This subjectivism is largely collective rather than individual, since what we allow into science is filtered by processes that we all have in common, but there is also an element of subjectivism brought about by individual decisions on the admissibility and interpretation of observational data. There is always the hope, of course, that all the different choices and interpretations will lead to a common truth, but the fulfillment of that hope remains a very long way off.

In the 1890's and early 1900's, the numerical values of what were known as the "constants of nature" – such things as the mass of an electron, its electrical charge and the ratio of its mass to that of the proton – were treated as if they were brute facts calculated from experimental results and there was no particular reason why they shouldn't have had different values. What Eddington did that seems to have upset people even more than the idea that the cherished laws of physics were somehow subjective, was to suggest that these values could be calculated without doing any experiments at all, just by considering the type of input and the method of calculation – in a word, epistemologically. In 1934 he made his views available to the general public in his *New Pathways in Science*, which included a calculation of the proton-electron mass ratio. This, according to him, was the ratio of the roots of a very straightforward quadratic equation obtained by considering the nature of the experimental measurements and their application – but without actually doing the experiment. By 1939 he had developed his ideas to the point of opening Chapter XI of *The Philosophy of Physical Science* as follows:

"I believe there are 15,747,724,136,275,002,577,605,653,961,181,555, 468,044, 717,914, 527,116,709,366,231,425,076,185,631,031,296 protons in the universe and the same number of electrons."

Eddington went on to say that he hadn't actually counted them and that if he had thought that anyone would ever count them he wouldn't have published his calculation. (Eddington's sense of humor helped to make his books very readable, even for people with very little scientific background, and also provided a supply of banana skins for his opponents to slip on.) An electron has no exact location and, furthermore, electrons are indistinguishable from one another, so, as he said, they don't make "very promising material for counting." He thought that the number was inherent in the structure of quantum physics rather than in some objective "actual physical" universe.

As far as Newton was concerned, when God created the universe he could have made whatever number and variety of "hard, massy particles" he thought appropriate. Eddington, however, wasn't talking about what God created but what it was possible for a modern physicist to *think*. But he was, at the same time, a committed Quaker who experienced the validity of intelligent mysticism. The world of physical science was not the great objective, all-embracing edifice that we had once taken it to be. "The purely objective sources of the objective element in our observational knowledge have already been named", he says emphatically in *The Philosophy of Physical Science*. "They are *life, consciousness, spirit.*"

It was not only that the scientific community and the philosophers on its fringes found Eddington's ideas outrageous. What may have worried them the most was that he had a gift for communication unparalleled among writers of popular scientific literature, so that his apparently subversive ideas could be communicated to the tens of thousands of people who read his books. It is unfortunate that the controversy obscured his magnificent achievements as, by general consent, the first astrophysicist and the leading authority in the English-speaking world on Einstein's General Theory of Relativity. By the time I went to Cambridge as an undergraduate in 1953, nine years after Eddington's death, most people remembered very little about him and if his name was mentioned the usual response was, "Eddington? Wasn't he the chap who said that there were 10^{79} electrons in the universe? Ha, ha, ha!"

Was Eddington's approach valid? Well, no and yes. The answers that he obtained for such physical constants as the proton-electron mass ratio and the fine structure constant were very close but not quite close enough – at least according to the generally accepted values – and quantum physics was still in its fairly early stages when he was working out the epistemology described in *The Philosophy of Physical Science* (1939). As he remarks on page 51, "The terminology of quantum theory is now in such utter confusion that it is well-nigh impossible to make clear statements in it." His attempt at a unified theory was unfinished at the time of his death in 1944 and even the most sympathetic readers have found it problematical. And yet there are still people, myself included, who find his work inspirational and feel that he was on the right track. In one very important respect he has been thoroughly vindicated; one of the major preoccupations of present-day physicists is the search for a theory that will account not only for the masses, charges and other characteristics of the proton, electron and all the other particles that have been either discovered or predicted, but also for the laws governing their interactions, including gravitation. No one believes that these items are brute facts – as Parmenides would have said, "Nothing can be which cannot be thought" – so there must be a fundamental, rationally expressible framework into which they all fit. This is the "theory of everything" that continues to elude physicists and the continued search for it indicates the strength of their urge to find a thought structure that generates the structures of their physical world and, unwittingly, to shed a new light on Steiner's contention that thought and atom are made of the same thing.

I say "their" physical world because as Steiner and Eddington pointed out in their different ways, the world of physical science differs radically from the world of everyday experience. Once again, here is Steiner speaking in January 1923:

"We have to become clear about what we actually do when, in our thinking, we cast inwardly experienced mechanics and physics into external space. That is what we are doing when we say: *The nature of what is out there in space is of no concern to me; I observe only what can be measured and expressed in mechanical formulas, and I leave aside everything that is not mechanical."*

And here is Eddington, "speaking as anyone might do who depends not on specialized knowledge but on that which is the common inheritance of human thought."

"We recognize that the type of knowledge after which physics is striving is much too narrow and specialized to constitute a complete understanding of the environment of the human spirit. A great many aspects of our ordinary life take us outside the outlook of physics… Any discussion as to whether they are compatible with the truth revealed by physics is purely academic; for whatever the outcome of the discussion, we are not likely to sacrifice them, knowing as we do from the outset that that the nature of Man would be incomplete without such outlets…"

What distinguishes us most clearly from the rest of creation and unites our religious, artistic and scientific faculties is the impulse to attain "something after which the human spirit is bound to strive", namely truth.

Clearly there is "something to which the truth matters" and it belongs "in our own nature, or through the contact of our consciousness with a nature transcending ours, [with] other things that claim the same kind of recognition – a sense of beauty, of morality, and finally at the root of all existence an experience which we describe as the presence of God."

Steiner and Eddington, out of very different life experiences, agree in asserting that physical science seeks a kind of truth that excludes all the *human* qualities that are most precious to those whose devotion to the truth embraces beauty and goodness. In *New Pathways*, Eddington illustrates this with a reference to Dante Gabriel Rossetti's Blessed Damozel, who looks down from the "gold bar of Heaven" and sees the earth spinning "like a fretful midge."[185]

"Looking from the abode of truth, perfect truth alone can enter her mind. She must see the earth as it really is – like whirling insect. But now let us try her with something fairly modern. In Einstein's theory, the earth is a curvature of space-time… What is the Blessed Damozel to make of that?" If, like Einstein, she sees the earth as a curvature in space-time with a spin that is the ratio of two components of curvature, "she will be seeing truly – I can feel little doubt of that – but *she will be missing the point*. It is as though we took her to an art gallery, and she saw ten square yards of yellow paint, five of crimson, and so on."

There have been many physicists with deeply spiritual aspirations but, in my experience, Eddington is by far the most helpful in providing a tenable view of physical science that illuminates its specialized relationship to the whole human being.

(3)

Ultimate Nominalism

"Mathematics may be defined as the subject in which we never know what we are talking about, nor whether what we are saying is true." (Bertrand Russell.)[186]

"The logical [as distinguished from the experimental] starting point of physical science is knowledge of the group-structure of a set of sensations in a consciousness." (Sir Arthur Eddington.)[187]

The need for a new form of communication was widely recognized in the seventeenth century. As George Steiner[188] (no relation) says: "The decline of Latin from general currency had created important gaps in mutual comprehension. These deepened with the rise of linguistic nationalism… Intellectual and economic relations were developing on a scale that required ease and exactitude of communication." Science needed "a clearly articulated vocabulary and grammar." According to Steiner (George) the requirements were an international language to replace Latin, and a rigorous symbolic language for the expression of all actual and possible knowledge, "a true universal semantic [which] would prove to be an instrument of discovery and verification." These goals, he says, were implicit in Bacon's plea, in *The Advancement of Learning*, (from which Rudolf Steiner does not quote), for the establishment of a hierarchy of 'real characters' capable of giving precise expression to fundamental 'things and notions'." Later, as we have seen, Bacon made it clear that the real problem was not with the "characters", but with the notions

It is of great, although possibly parenthetic, interest to find that immediately after referring to Bacon's plea in *The Advancement of Learning*, Steiner (G.) speaks of Descartes, who welcomed the suggestion but thought that the time was not yet ripe for it, and then of Amos Comenius, who looked for the creation of an "ideal philosophical language with a universal concordance between words and things, a language in which nothing false can be expressed and whose syntax will, necessarily, induce new knowledge." The beauty of the English language arises in great part from its potentialities for ambiguity and fine shades of meaning that depend on context and emphasis. Poetry, indeed any kind of imaginative writing, would be impossible in the kind of one-to-one language proposed by Comenius. Steiner (G.) gives an amusing and enlightening account of efforts to achieve a sanitized international language and a perfect scientific terminology, the results of which would have provided the perfect justification for Rudolf Steiner's lament for the loss of the spiritual dimension in language. The process reached its logical terminus in the nineteenth and early twentieth centuries with the development of symbolic logic, the dismissal of the ancient idea that mathematics has an inherent relationship to the physical world, and the creation of a new form of physical science, the language of which goes far beyond nominalism and removes not only the spiritual but also the physical. This language concerns itself only with *structure*, a concept that is not quite as easy to grasp as it sounds.

Anyone who studies the mathematics and physics of the nineteenth and twentieth centuries soon realizes that content – the nature, quiddity or "thingness" of actual things, such as the steeliness of steel, the woodiness of wood and the pointiness of points – becomes less and less important, and that the real concern is not with things but with relationships. This sounds quite reasonable; relationships are very popular these days. The relationships that mathematicians talk about, however, are not between people or even between things that we recognize from our experience, but between objects that we know nothing about. Unless we are mathematicians we probably think that we know exactly what a point, a line or a plane is, but when we try to define these terms we find the task unexpectedly difficult. If we allow our naïve, intuitive notions into our mathematics we may end up with contradictions.

So about 1900 we decided in our mathematical wisdom that it is not only very hard to explain what a point, a line or a plane is, but also inadvisable and unnecessary. We have sets of postulates and operating rules governing the relationships between these entities and with these we are content, allowing the terms to remain undefined. Having set up our abstract geometry we may then slyly apply it to the physical world, identifying our abstract points, lines and planes with those that we see with our physical eyes in the corner of every rectangular room; but in so doing we are going beyond the terms of reference of pure mathematics.

Mathematicians started this process, more because the nature of the discipline demanded it than because they wanted to, and later the physicists joined in rather reluctantly. If you ask a physicist what an electron is he[189] won't tell you what it is made of or what color and shape it is, but he will give you a set of rules for its transformations. The more we know about electrons, the more we realize that everyday ideas of size, shape, color and trajectory do not apply to them.

The fact is that modern particle physics is not about particles but about *events*, transitions between related states, although to hear the way physicists talk you would never think so. When they talk about photons, electrons and quarks, they sound as if they are speaking of actual perceptible objects, whereas Eddington and Steiner thought of such things as "entities disporting themselves in some metaphysical realm", and as I have said elsewhere[190], our notions of the electron are almost as metaphysical as our notions of God. The real difference between an electron and a baseball is that the properties of an electron are expressible only as a set of quantum transitions, whereas a baseball has form, texture, elasticity and internal structure as well as momentum and energy. This is not a criticism of the electron, a concept which serves its purpose admirably. If it had anything beyond mathematical rules for its transitions attached to it, it would not be a fundamental particle. The only time we can be aware of an electron is when it does something or has something done to it, and by the time we have become aware of it, it's utterly elsewhere doing something else; whereas a baseball can be observed sitting serenely in a box with a bunch of other baseballs or being caught by a fan in the bleachers.

When we talk about "transformations" we mean changing from one set of quantum numbers to another. The quantum numbers form a pattern or *structure*, which is not to be confused with the older notion of atomic structure such as we find in the Bohr atom with its nice concrete picture of electrons orbiting round a nucleus. This new kind of structure is typified by the set of relationships between the ways in which an electron can pass from one state to another.

"Physical science consists of purely structural knowledge", wrote Sir Arthur Eddington in 1939[191], "so that we know only the *structure* of the universe which it describes. This is not a conjecture as to the nature of physical knowledge; it is precisely what physical knowledge as formulated in present-day theory states itself to be. The fact that structural knowledge can be detached from knowledge of the entities forming the structure gets over the difficulty of understanding how it is possible to conceive a knowledge of anything which is not part of our minds."

More modern physicists don't tell the public much about structure in this sense, possibly because it is too hard to explain to people who suffer from math anxiety, but the front-line theories all depend on the application of group theory, which deals with structure in the purest possible way. One of the fathers of the Grand Unified Theories of particle physics, Howard M. Georgi of Harvard University, quotes Eddington with approval:[192]

"We need a super-mathematics in which the operations are as unknown as the quantities they operate on, and a super-mathematician who does not know what he is doing when he performs these operations. Such a super-mathematics is the Theory of Groups."

From which we see that not only the objects are unknown but also the relationships between them, and what the group theorist deals with is relations between relations. This sounds like the beginning of a family feud so we had better move on.

The startling thing is that out of such an assembly of unknowns certain kinds of concrete, practical predictions of the nature of things are possible. But, to cut a long story very short, predictions of this kind are necessarily generic in character. The theory of the Big Bang depends on the most modern particle theory, which, in turn, depends on Group Theory. It is possible to work out the consequences of the Big Bang and predict the nature of the resulting universe. If we were really super-mathematical super-scientists we might even predict the eventual emergence of intelligent life. What we would never be able to predict is individuality. We might be able to predict suns, but not our particular Sun. We would, in fact, never reach the stage before individuality. We might predict life, but not daffodils, oaks, hyenas and cats. As far as individual human beings go the best comment is a New York City "*Fuh*geddabouditt!"

This is not a criticism of modern physics. You can't blame a discipline for not doing what it doesn't set out to do. It also makes no attempt to predict or explain our individual sense impressions. The inner workings of the eye are far more complex than people used to imagine, but even if we understood them perfectly we should still be as far as ever from explaining—or even describing—the actual experience of color. Something similar applies to the even more mysterious sensations of sound.

As Rudolf Steiner expressed the situation long before group theory was applied to electrons and quarks: "The mathematical treatment of nature helps to give us a feeling of unity with an outer world that otherwise seems foreign. But the picture we have created no longer contains the reality which presented itself to us originally." The abundance of sense impressions – colors, sounds, smells, tastes, textures – is lost, and nothing in the world of mathematical representation can replace it.

* * *

The steps by which modern logic and mathematics reached their present states were not taken arbitrarily. Inconsistencies can be tolerated and sometimes welcomed in the process of living, but in these abstract disciplines they are insupportable. In the physical sciences the situation is different but the end result is the same; inconsistencies are valuable propellants that have to be dealt with and reconciled. Logicians and mathematicians who worked on the problem of consistency in the early twentieth century concluded, like Bacon, that the only safe way of proceeding was to remove all preconceived notions and intuitive ideas; but their method of going about things was diametrically opposed to the Chancellor's. Bacon went out into nature for his material, but the moderns retreated into the world of logical relationships. We think that we know what *points*, *lines* and *planes* are, since we see them all around us, but if, like Euclid, we allow this knowledge into geometry, we run the risk of infecting the system with unconscious, unexamined assumptions. Now these terms are left undefined—in other words, there is no *thought* in them—and we deal only with relations between them.

The situation is quite similar with the electron. We can't talk about its being, but we can talk about its state by giving it a set of quantum numbers. If a problem arises we may be able to solve it by discovering or inventing a new quantum number, as was the case in 1925 when "under the compulsion of experiment", to use Max Born's memorable phrase, the so-called spin quantum number was introduced to account for the splitting of lines in the spectra of the alkali metals. The result of this is that when people think about electrons (if they ever do) they have a mental image of particle spinning like a baseball while it performs an elliptical orbit round the nucleus. Some of the physicists in the 1920's asserted that such images are boloney and that the equations are all that matters. They are justified by the fact that the picture of such a spinning particle leads to a contradiction to which Born referred as "a most interesting result which shows the hopelessness of trying to account for the properties of elementary particles by simple mechanical models."[193]

Although physicists are not preoccupied with the problem of consistency to the extent that some logicians and mathematicians are, they have still found it very important to drain their concepts of all the attributes of sense perception. There are at least two problems with this recipe for consistency; one is that there is very little left to be consistent about and the other is that, as Kurt Gödel showed in the case of arithmetic, it may not work.[194]

If extreme nominalism is right, language, logic and knowledge correspond to the structure of the mind, not that of a physical world outside the mind. But total nominalism is virtually impossible to maintain, even for the most determinedly atheistic philosophers, and the conceptual, mathematical structure which the physicists have created accounts for only a part of human experience, a part in which, as Eddington maintains, there must be a strong element of the subjective. The objective elements of experience, he said, are already well known—they are consciousness, life and spirit.

Eddington thought that the structural approach is a good way—possibly the only way—of doing fundamental physical science; but he considered it a bad way to approach life as a whole. Steiner (R.) and Eddington emphasized the importance of recognizing that the mathematical science of the physical world makes no attempt to convey the actual experience of being alive amid this profusion of hills, dales, birds, beasts, trees, flowers, streams and songs—not to mention our fellow human beings. Some scientists of the present time, however, believe that the structural approach is the only possible one, and that it has the potential to account for all phenomena, including those of consciousness, without remainder. Many others, including those who write popular books in which the word "structure" appears only in its more common usage—as in "atomic structure"—simply go on with the job without thinking about such problems. What Steiner (G.) describes as an attempt to pioneer the kind of language necessary for unambiguous communication was a step in the process of creating a system devoid of soul and spiritual experience and a fore-runner of the structural approach.

Modern physics and mathematics, however, have their own kinds of austere beauty, and they are the offspring of the human mind, which, no matter how far it falls, still carries the imprint of its celestial origin.

Notes

1   CUP, 1934; Ann Arbor, 1959.

2   One day during my sojourn at Sidney Sussex College, Cambridge, I found myself in the room that had been occupied by Oliver Cromwell while James I was still on the throne. I thought that the strong smell of stale cheese was quite appropriate.

3   This was the occasion of Palmerston's famous *Civis Romanus Sum* speech.

4   For an enlightening view from a different angle, see Jared Diamond, *Guns, Germs and Steel*: Norton, New York, 1999.

5   As of this writing, the world-wide membership is under 48,000.

6   Unless otherwise specified, quotations from the *Novum Organum* and Bacon's other Latin works are based on the nineteenth century translation by James Spedding *et al.*

7   Old music hall song.

8   See Section (xiii).

9   Lollards believed that the clergy should be poor, that people should read and interpret the Bible for themselves, that the transubstantiation was false, and that priestly and monastic celibacy was unnatural.

10   Including the Spanish Armada.

11   This was a political post, not a zoological one.

12   *The Cambridge Dictionary of Philosophy*, Ed. Robert Audi, CUP, 1999.

13   I am using these words in their modern senses. The use of the word "philosophy" to include what we now think of as science died out very gradually, and was still to be encountered in the older universities in the twentieth century.

14   There was nothing unusual about such a marriage.

15   *Confessions*: VIII, 7. Sometimes quoted as, "Oh God, make me good, but not yet." Of course, he wasn't thinking of cell phones at the time…

16   Bacon's *Confession of Faith* was unusual in being a highly personal statement rather than an official document intended for public consumption.

17   This idea, which seems to have vanished from human consciousness, deserves some concentrated thought.

18   Graham Reese in *The Cambridge Companion to Bacon* (known in the Francis household as *Eggs*), C.U.P. 1996.

19   Bacon's use of the word "axiom" is a little confusing. Here he is referring to propositions or generalizations derived from observation, whereas traditionally an axiom is a statement of self-evident truth, not subject to any kind of proof. To the modern mathematician or logician, "axiom" simply means a proposition adopted because it is useful, convenient and consistent with other such propositions.

20   And have been! See Note 43.

21   Open Court, Chicago and La Salle, Illinois, 1994.

22   *The Advancement of Learning.*

23   Cambridge University Press, 1961.

24   Abbott of Monte Cassino from 1022 A. D. to1035 A. D.

25   In the *Exeter Book*, *Codex Exoniensis*, a tenth century compilation of Anglo-Saxon poetry, given to the library of Exeter Cathedral by Leofric, the first bishop of Exeter.

26   *The Advancement of Learning.*

27   (Literal-minded readers, please note that I sometimes have difficulty in getting my tongue out of my cheek.) Several key elements in the following discussion, are drawn from *Early Greek Philosophy*, Penguin 1987, translated, edited and introduced by Jonathan Barnes.

28   In other words, *cosmetic.*

29   *The Great Instauration*; Plan of the Work.

30   See A. G. van Melsen, *From Atomos to Atom*, Harper, New York, 1960.

31   See Averroes: *On the Harmony of Religion and Philosophy*. Tr. and ed. G. F. Hourani; Luzac, London 1976.

32   The idea of the atom goes back at least 2,500 years. It seems to have made its initial appearance in fifth century BC Greece and to have appeared in Indian and Chinese culture shortly thereafter. The story of the early days of the concept and the controversies that swirled around it among the early Greek philosophers is told at some length in my books *From Abdera to Copenhagen* and *Rudolf Steiner and the Atom*, from which I quote here liberally.

33   See A. G. van Melsen, *Op. cit.*

34   Simplicius (sixth century AD) was a neoplatonist philosopher from Cilicia (modern Turkey). His writings include quotations from, and commentaries on, many ancient sources that are now lost. He was one of the philosophers banished from Athens by Justinian in 529 AD.

35   J. B. S. Haldane (1892-1964) was an eminent evolutionary geneticist who fought in the Great War and in 1923 proposed a system of hydrogen-generating windmills, the first proposal for a hydrogen-based renewable energy economy. He was a pioneer of the use of quantitative methods in biology and one of

the founders of the mathematical theory of population genetics. His book, *The Causes of Evolution*, 1932, played a major part in re-establishing natural selection as the main mechanism of evolution by explaining it in terms of the mathematical consequences of Mendelian genetics.

36   Steiner, *Goethe the Scientist*, Tr. Olin D. Wannamaker, Anthroposophical Press, New York, 1950, p. 205.

37   *Ibid.* p. 245.

38   Not to be confused with "Tinker to Evers to Chance." The Cubs' famous double play combination was in its prime when Steiner was founding the Anthroposophical Society.

39   The reference to realism and nominalism will be discussed at a later stage.

40   Now available in paperback from the Anthroposophic Press.

41   That is to say, for the reader to become confused.

42   Rudolf Steiner; *The Riddles of Philosophy* (1914), Anthroposophic Press, Spring Valley, NY, 1973; p.64.

43   Sir Thomas Browne, 1605-1682. His best known works are *Religio Medici* and *Urn Burial*, both of which I thoroughly recommend for contemplative reading. As far as this study is concerned, the most apposite is his *Vulgar Errors* (1646), in the first part of which he attributes the huge volume of mistaken popular beliefs to our inclination to error, false deductions, credulity, adherence to authority, and the work of the devil. The rest of the book is a vast repository of quaint beliefs.

44   Quoted by C. S. Lewis in *The Discarded Image*, C.U.P., 1964.

45   Its exit was facilitated by a letter of 1997 from the General Secretary to the members of the Anthroposophical Society in North America, encouraging them to look up specific references to Bacon in the Karma Lectures.

46   See Rudolf Steiner, *Occult History—an Outline*, Rudolf Steiner Press, London, 1963.

47   This is the system described in the fifth century by the individual known to scholars as Pseudo-Dionysius, and repeated by St. Thomas Aquinas in the thirteenth. According to Steiner, this knowledge came originally from St. Paul, who gave it directly to Dionysius the Areopagite. It was passed on to the successors of Dionysius until it was eventually written down in the fourth or fifth century.

48   From Lecture 3 of the 1923 cycle, *The Driving Force of Spiritual Powers in World History* (Steiner Book Centre, North Vancouver, 1972).

49   Steiner speaks frequently and at great length about the activities of Ahriman, the prime spirit of materialism. Ahriman's origin in Zoroastrianism is well known, but how and where Ahriman first appeared in human evolution as reported by Steiner remains obscure to me.

50   Jonathan Barnes, *Early Greek Philosophy*: Penguin Classics, 1987.

51 Steiner, *Riddles of Philosophy*.

52 Except where Steiner is specifically mentioned, the material of this section and the following one is derived from exoteric sources, which include but are not limited to: *A History of Mediaeval Philosophy*, F. C. Copleston, Harper and Row, New York, 1972; *The Cambridge Dictionary of Philosophy*, Ed. Robert Audi, CUP, 1999; the *Cambridge Companion to Arabic Philosophy*, Ed. Peter Adamson and Richard C. Taylor, CUP, 2005; *The Cambridge History of Later Mediaeval Philosophy*, ed. Norman Kretzmann *et al*, CUP 1982; and the article, *Arabian Philosophy* by William Wallace and the Rev. G. W. Thatcher, Enc. Brit., 1940. This edition of the Enc. Brit. is full of immensely authoritative and scholarly articles which make no concessions to the casual reader. After reading the article on radioactivity, for example, I was delighted to find that the author's initials are E. Ru.—Ernest Rutherford himself. A little later I discovered that the article on the conduction of electricity had been written by J. J. Th(omson), and the one on Atomic Physics by N. B.—Niels Bohr. This is like finding an article on Elizabethan drama signed by W. Sh. and one on spiritual science signed by R. St.

53 This is the spelling I originally encountered in my research; the preferred spelling now seems to be *duophysite*. MS Word's spell check doesn't recognize either spelling.

54 Several different spellings of this name appear in English translations of Steiner's works. Since they are all easily recognizable, I have left them as I found them.

55 Aristotle: *De Anima*, Tr. R.D.Hicks, ed. Michael Durrant. Routledge, London, 1993.

56 This is the "orthodox" interpretation of Aristotle's statements about individuation. For alternatives, see www.heptapolis.com/aristotles-principle-of-individuation/ According to a reference that I am no longer able to find, it appears that Steiner may have believed that Aristotle had been misinterpreted. For the present purpose, the point is that mediaeval philosophers accepted the principle.

57 Quotations from the *Cambridge Dictionary of Philosophy*.

58 The age of the *consciousness soul*, as Steiner describes it, began early in the fifteenth century and is the period in which we have the potential to begin the process of working back into full and conscious communion with the spiritual world. As free human beings we experience our individuality and separateness, so that we are in danger of being overwhelmed by a feeling of isolation from both the spiritual and the physical world. To be at the same time both separate and involved – in other words, to interact without losing one's individuality—is an ideal that exists and challenges us independently of anything Steiner ever said.

59 Rudolf Steiner: *Materialism and the Task of Anthroposophy*, Tr. Maria St. Goar, Lecture 17, Dornach, June 5th, 1921; Anthroposophic Press, Hudson NY, 1987.

60 F. C Copleston, *A History of Mediaeval Philosophy*, Harper and Row, 1972.

61 The idea that God creates the world by knowing it, whether as a finished product or an ongoing process, is a recurrent theme in religious history, and is responsible for the only occasion on which Bacon stated explicitly that knowledge is power.

62 "That is to say, there is no room for the claim that, everything else being the same, a man could have acted differently from the way in which he did act. If by freedom, we simply mean acting consciously and deliberately, freedom in this sense is not incompatible with Avicenna's premises." (Copleston's footnote.)

63 From the Introduction to George F. Hourani's *Averroes on the Harmony of Religion and Philosophy*, London, 1961.

64 Since I have heard one of my anthroposophical friends speak as though this were a pejorative, I must emphasize that it was actually a term of great esteem, also applied to Thomas Aquinas.

65 Ibid.

66 "One can observe... in the pre-Socratic thinkers the prelude; in Socrates, Plato and Aristotle the culmination; after them a decline and a kind of dissolution of thought life.... Greek thought life has an element that makes it appear "perfect" in the best sense of the word. It is as if the energy of thought in the Greek thinkers had worked out everything that it contains within itself.... Later world conceptions have produced accomplishments through other forces of the soul. Of the later thoughts, as such, it can be shown that with respect to their real thought content they can always be found in some earlier Greek thinker." (Steiner, *Riddles of Philosophy*)

67 Perhaps the same should be said about the "big bang"; see Stephen Hawking, *A Brief History of Time*, on the grave difficulty of attaching any meaning to the notion of a time before creation.

68 *Commentarium Magnum*; "Great" is not a value judgement, merely an identifier. Averroes wrote three sets of commentaries—small, middle and large.

69 "Spiritual soul" is an alternative term for "consciousness soul."

70 Rudolf Steiner, *Karmic Relationships: Esoteric Studies*, Volume III.

71 See Note 53.

72 I assume that when Steiner refers to the "Gods", he means the members of the hierarchies.

73 *Letters to Members*, translated by Ethel Bowen-Wedgwood, revised by George Adams (1956). Now published as *The Michael Mystery*.

74 John Amos Comenius, 1592-1670, Moravian priest. He advocated a universal systematization of knowledge and education, using the vernacular instead of Latin and giving opportunities to women.

75 Rudolf Steiner, *Cosmic Christianity*, Torquay and London, 1924—Lecture II.

76 It is worth mentioning that Bacon had a very low opinion of Islam, as the following passage in *The Advancement of Learning* shows. "The use of reason in spiritual things, and the latitude thereof, is very great and general: for it is not for

nothing that the apostle [Paul] calleth religion 'our reasonable service of God', insomuch as the very ceremonies and figures of the old law were full of reason and signification, much more than the ceremonies of idolatry and magic, that are full of non-significants and surd [irrational] characters. But most specially the Christian faith, as in all things so in this, deserveth to be highly magnified; holding and preserving the golden mean in this point between the law of the heathen and the law of Mahomet, which have embraced the two extremes. For the religion of the heathen had no constant belief or confession, but left all to the liberty of agent; and the religion of Mahomet on the other side interdicteth argument altogether: the one having the very face of error, and the other of imposture; whereas the Faith doth both admit and reject disputation with difference."

77 The history of scholasticism is so tangled that one authority was moved to declare that "strictly speaking, there is no such thing as scholasticism", by which he meant to assert that, contrary to the usual explanations, no clearly identifiable philosophy was taught in the universities of Europe in the later Middle Ages. (Calvin G. Normore, in *The Cambridge Dictionary of Philosophy*.)

78 *Miracles*; MacMillan, New York, 1947. Subsequently revised and available in many different editions.

79 *The Reason for God*, Dutton, New York, 2008.

80 In one of Chesterton's Father Brown stories, the villain disguises himself as a Roman priest, and gives himself away by making a remark about the unreliability of thinking.

81 Averroes' Great Commentary on the *De Anima* was translated into Latin by Michael Scot in about 1235 A. D., but news traveled very slowly in those days. Translations of the short and middle commentaries had appeared much earlier.

82 This is an important qualification, since it is not altogether clear what the Averroists actually believed and they were apt to change their opinions in the face of criticism.

83 It seems that I made this word up. I like it.

84 Problems arising from the naming of categories are still with us. The question of whether a set of objects is itself an object is at the heart of an important logical paradox described by Bertrand Russell.

85 Rudolf Steiner, *Letters to Members*.

86 *Realism* has several meanings, of which the one we are concerned with seems to be of the least importance to modern philosophers. *Nominalist* and *nominalism* have not made it into the Microsoft "spellcheck" and have no separate entry in the *Cambridge Dictionary of Philosophy*. It is, however, of some interest to note that one of the greatest mathematicians of the twentieth century, Kurt Gödel, created a great deal of puzzlement among his colleagues by taking a Platonic view of numbers.

[87]   *The Advancement of Learning*, Oxford Authors, O. U. P., 1996, p.140. In this context, "matter" means "subject matter." In the unpublished tract *Cogitata et Visa* (c.1608) Bacon compares deductive logic as used by the scholastics to a spider's web, which is drawn out of its own entrails, whereas the bee is introduced as an image of inductive science. Like a bee, the empiricist collects real substance and transforms it into knowledge in order to produce honey, which is useful for healthy nutrition. The title can be translated as *Things Thought and Things Seen*.

[88]   *The Great Instauration*, Preface.

[89]   Anicius Manlius Severinus Boethius (c.480-525 AD), Roman philosopher. His Aristotelian translations and commentaries profoundly influenced the history of mediaeval philosophy. His most famous work, *The Consolations of Philosophy*, composed while awaiting execution on charges of treason, is a reflection on human happiness, evil, providence, fate, chance and the incompatibility of human free choice and divine foreknowledge.

[90]   Note that, as Lewis points out, the nomenclature was later reversed by Coleridge. In the following paragraphs I continue to use "reason" in the sense indicated by Aquinas.

[91]   The title, *Novum Organum*, has been interpreted as a dig at Aristotle, whose *Organon*, or instrument of reason, Bacon hoped his method would replace.

[92]   See Note 19.

[93]   "The term *ipsissimus*, much used in scholastic terminology, recurs in other passages of the *Novum Organum* with a precise technical meaning. The translation, 'truth and utility are the very same things,' broadly diffused among English and American scholars, is undoubtedly wrong…" (Paolo Rossi, in *The Cambridge Companion to Bacon*.) In all fairness I must point out that Rossi fails to mention that Spedding footnoted his apparently incorrect translation with the comment, "*Ipsissimae res*: I think this must have been Bacon's meaning, though not a meaning which the word can properly bear."

[94]   For an illustration of the ease with which Bacon's intentions can be misrepresented, see Owen Barfield; *Saving the Appearances*; HBJ, New York, 1965, p. 55. The use of the word "power", undefined but in a vaguely threatening context, the distorted and fragmentary presentation of a basic epistemological principle, and the facile equation of Bacon's vision of science with Barfield's view of technology give a disturbing impression of Barfield as a persuasive writer whose even tone cannot mask his polemical aim.

[95]   As before, the reader should recognize that Bacon's use of the word "axiom" is more or less the opposite of Euclid's and quite different from that of the modern mathematician.

[96]   It may have occurred to the attentive reader that Bacon's idea of form is a materialized version of Aristotle's.

[97]   Kepler had the same question and spent a long time trying to answer it.

98 *Novum Organum*, Aphorism 66.

99 The common forms of refrigeration were developed independently of any particular theory of heat. The only well-known example of a "designer" cooling effect is the "Porous Plug Experiment" or Joule-Kelvin effect. For the connoisseur there are also such things as adiabatic demagnetization.

100 William Whewell (1794–1866) was one of the most important and influential figures in nineteenth-century Britain. Whewell wrote extensively on numerous subjects, including mechanics, mineralogy, geology, astronomy, political economy, theology, educational reform, international law, and architecture, as well as the works that remain the most well-known today in philosophy of science, history of science, and moral philosophy. He was one of the founding members and a president of the British Association for the Advancement of Science, a fellow of the Royal Society, president of the Geological Society, and longtime Master of Trinity College, Cambridge. In his own time his influence was acknowledged by the major scientists of the day, such as John Herschel, Charles Darwin, Charles Lyell and Michael Faraday, who frequently turned to Whewell for philosophical and scientific advice, and, interestingly, for terminological assistance. Whewell invented the terms "anode," "cathode," and "ion" for Faraday. In response to a challenge by the poet S.T. Coleridge in 1833, Whewell invented the English word "scientist;" before this time the only terms in use were "natural philosopher" and "man of science". Whewell is most known today for his massive works on the history and philosophy of science. His philosophy of science was attacked by John Stuart Mill in his *System of Logic*, causing an interesting and fruitful debate between them over the nature of inductive reasoning in science, moral philosophy, and political economy. Whewell's philosophy was rediscovered in the 20th century by critics of logical positivism. It is generally considered that the most important philosophical aspects of Whewell's works were his philosophy of science, including his views of induction, confirmation, and necessary truth; his view of the relation between scientific practice, history of science, and philosophy of science; and his moral philosophy. Perhaps the most interesting is his view of induction, which is also the most misinterpreted. (*Stanford Encyclopedia*)

101 "Art" here is intended in the sense of "system" or "prescribed method."

102 Kepler's nested planetary system.

103 See Rudolf Steiner, *Building Stones for an Understanding of the Mystery of Golgotha*, March 27, 1917, Lecture 1. Steiner refers to the Eighth Ecumenical Council of 869 AD.

104 Advertisement, Columbia Business School, *New York Times*, September 4, 1997.

105 In *Meditationes Sacrae* (Holy Meditations), 1597. *Scientia* means "knowledge", not "science" in its modern sense.

106 In *The Cambridge Companion to Bacon*.

[107] A letter from the General Secretary to the members of the Anthroposophical Society suggested that *The New Atlantis* gives a picture of a secret scientific society trying to rule the world from a hidden island. This is nonsense—the purpose of the clandestine expeditions from Bensalem was to gather knowledge, not to exercise influence. The island remained secret in the interests of safety and purity.

[108] This is not a covert reference to Gracie Mansion.

[109] Paolo Rossi, *Bacon's Idea of Science*, in *The Cambridge Companion to Bacon*.

[110] It would be interesting, for example, to compare the percentage of people who know who said, "I think, therefore I am", with the percentage who understood what he meant when he said it.

[111] E. A. Karl Stockmeyer, *Rudolf Steiner's Curriculum for Waldorf Schools*: Steiner Schools Fellowship, 1969.

[112] Rudolf Steiner, *Practical Course*, 1919. An English translation of this course had existed for a long time but copies of it were almost as rare as the philosopher's stone.

[113] Rudolf Steiner, *The Boundaries of Natural Science*, Dornach, 1920; Anthroposophic Press, Spring Valley, NY, 1982.

[114] This and the quotations that follow are drawn from Rudolf Steiner, *Anthroposophy and Science*, Stuttgart 1921; Mercury Press, Spring Valley, NY, 1991.

[115] Steiner, *The Origins of Natural Science*, Lecture II, Dornach, Christmas Eve, 1922. Anthroposophic Press, Spring Valley, NY, 1985.

[116] Steiner, *The Boundaries of Natural Science*.

[117] In *The Discarded* Image, C. S. Lewis gives a marvelous survey of the creatures described by mediaeval writers and still appearing in the late renaissance. From Reginald Scot (1584), for instance, we have "bull-beggars, spirits, witches, urchins, elves, hags, fairies, satyrs, pans, faunes, sylens, tritons, centaurs, dwarfs, giants, nymphes, Incubus, Robin Goodfellow, the spoom, the man in the Oke, the fire-drake, the puckle, Tom Thombe, Tom tumbler boneless, and such other bugs." Apparently Scot didn't expect his list to be taken very seriously—these were the bugbears invoked by "our mothers' maids" to frighten children.

[118] Chaucer: *Hous of Fame*; quoted by C.S.Lewis in *The Discarded Image*, C. U. P., 1961. Lewis was quite sure that although mediaeval thinkers attributed life and intelligence to stars and planets, they did not believe "that what we now call inanimate objects were sentient and purposive." My reference is, however, to put it crudely, to what people thought when they weren't thinking—their intuitive grasp of reality before it became "sicklied o'er with the pale cast of thought." They did not have to believe that the apple deliberately falls to the ground; only that the operation of the whole universe is maintained by the unimaginable hand and mind of God.

[119] A more recent edition is available from Steiner Books.

[120] Steiner, *Goethe the Scientist*, Tr. Olin D. Wannamaker, Anthroposophical Press, New York, 1950, p. 205.

[121] Quoted by Steiner, *Ibid*, from remarks by Wilhelm Ostwald. Ostwald was one of the sceptics.

[122] *Ibid*. p. 245.

[123] Steiner, *The Philosophy of Freedom*, translated by Michael Wilson, Rudolf Steiner Press, London, 1964.

[124] Printed in John Tyndall, *New Fragments*, D. Appleton and Co. New York, 1896. Tyndall (1820-1893) succeeded Michael Faraday as Superintendent of the Royal Institution in 1860, and became his great friend. Although he was a very distinguished scientist in his own right, Tyndall is probably best known for his memoir, *Faraday as a Discoverer.*

[125] Henry Thomas Buckle (1821-1862) was the author of an unfinished *History of Civilization*. His delicate health prevented him from obtaining much formal training but he received a high degree of education privately. After his father's death in 1840, he directed all his reading to the preparation of a great historical work. Over the next seventeen years, he is said to have spent ten hours a day on it. The first volume, which appeared in June 1857, made its author a literary and social celebrity.

[126] Steiner: *Goethe the Scientist*, Section VIII.

[127] *Ibid*. Section II

[128] This interpretation of Goethe's archetypal plant seems to imply that it acts as a Platonic archetype, which I don't believe to be the case. You can add this to the list of unanswered questions.

[129] *Goethe the Scientist*, Section IV

[130] *Ibid.*

[131] Far-reaching conclusions about the functioning of heat engines can be drawn from the laws of thermodynamics, without any mention of atoms, molecules, quanta etc.

[132] To get the full benefit of Newton's spectrum I always used a hollow glass prism filled with carbon disulphide, a liquid with great dispersive power. CS_2 has such a disgusting smell that if you drop your prism you will probably have to evacuate the building.

[133] Ernst Lehrs, *Man or Matter*: Rudolf Steiner Press, London, 1985.

[134] Ibid. p.313

[135] Best known for his work in the discovery of the inert gases.

[136] This appears to contradict a statement in Section (vi): "Rudolf Steiner points out that Bacon did not realize that different soul energies are predominantly active in different ages, *but that he did feel, correctly, that the methods of Aristotle could no longer be used*." Careful reading of *The Riddles of Philosophy*, p.66, shows that the inconsistency is Steiner's, not mine.

[137] Steiner, *Cosmic Christianity*.

[138] James Spedding (1808-1881), editor of Bacon's complete works, 14 vol., London, 1857-1874.

[139] Brian Vickers, *Francis Bacon*, Oxford Authors, OUP 1996

[140] Rudolf Steiner Institute, USA, 1979.

[141] It has been argued that all geometrical theorems are therefore tautologies.

[142] When I was a boy, the stains left on clothing by rusty iron were known as "iron mould."

[143] See Stephen Jay Gould, *The Mismeasure of Man*; Norton, New York, 1981.

[144] This and the succeeding quotations are from *The Riddle of Humanity*, Lecture 15, September 1916.

[145] Note the parallel with Steiner's assertion that even if one does not actively follow the path of spiritual science, the knowledge of its truths is beneficial. The reference to Aristotle's attempt (*Sophistical Refutations*) to deal with the logical snafus of his time shows that Bacon retained some respect for his illustrious predecessor.

[146] Linda is the Choral Director at St. Andrew's Church in Newcastle, Maine.

[147] *Work of the Angels in Man's Astral Body*, Zurich, 1918

[148] Steiner, *The Boundaries of Natural Science*.

[149] See Appendix (3).

[150] The confusion that sometimes arises from the failure to distinguish between the name of an object and the object itself may be of great consequence in mathematics, as is shown by J. R. Newman and Ernest Nagel in their *Gödel's Proof* (NYU Press. 1958). As they point out: 'Chicago' is tri-syllabic; Chicago is a populous city.

[151] Bacon gives the following example of the second class of idol: *But the other class, which springs out of a faulty and unskillful abstraction, is intricate and deeply rooted. Let us take for example such a word as humid and see how far the several things which the word is used to signify agree with each other, and we shall find the word humid to be nothing else than a mark loosely and confusedly applied to denote a variety of actions which will not bear to be reduced to any constant meaning. For it both signifies that which easily spreads itself round any other body; and that which in itself is indeterminate and cannot solidify; and that which readily yields in every direction; and that which easily divides and scatters itself; and that which easily unites and collects itself; and that which readily flows and is put in motion; and that which readily clings to another body and wets it; and that which is easily reduced to a liquid, or being solid easily melts. Accordingly, when you come to apply the word, if you take it in one sense, flame is humid; if in another, air is not humid; if in another, fine dust is humid; if in another, glass is humid. So that it is easy to see that the notion is taken by abstraction only from water and common and ordinary liquids, without any due verification.*

152 Steiner, *Goethe the Scientist*.

153 *Ibid.* p. 254.

154 In a recent issue of *BBC Music*, Jonas Kaufmann was described as "the ultimate tenor." Not so very long ago this would have meant that we should not expect there to be any more tenors.

155 My introduction to the misuse of "contemporary" came in about 1948 from a young lady in an interior decorating store on Westgate Street in Gloucester, who was trying to sell my father some very odd-looking wallpaper. "It's contemp'ry", she explained.

156 *Fortunate* and *lucky* imply an element of chance, but they are invariably used in the context of a happy outcome. A *fortuitous* event may have a very bad outcome. Words sometimes make unexpected recoveries; when I was a boy, people who had heard their doctors speaking of chronic illnesses often thought that "chronic" simply meant "very bad." When people didn't like the music that was being played on the radio, they would say, "Isn't it chronic?" Now I often hear it used in its proper sense.

157 Steiner: *The Riddle of Humanity*.

158 MacMillan, New York, 1972.

159 Thomas Babbington Macauley (1800-1859)—English historian, M. P. and Secretary of War.

160 See Charles Webster, *From Paracelsus to Newton*, CUP, 1982.

161 Readers will recognize this as a mild reference to a huge problem.

162 Othello: "The pomp and circumstance of glorious war."

163 See Section (xxviii) "There is a plan behind human evolution. Gradually, according to plan, various impulses appear in the course of evolution. Now that the theory of idols and all that is contained in *Nova Atlantis* has made its appearance, the last remnants of the great atavistic spiritual theories, views and experiences have been extinguished. So this ground must be recaptured by a newly-appearing spiritual science, proceeding now in the full light of consciousness. During the fourth Atlantean Epoch, someone formulated the ideas that introduced materialism into the ancient Atlantean period. This is described in my writings. Just as it was necessary, in the fourth epoch of Atlantis, for the materialism of Atlantis to be formulated in the head of an old Atlantean, so the fifth post-Atlantean epoch needed its *Nova Atlantis*, which has a similar function for this epoch."

164 Anglican Book of Common Prayer.

165 Bacon, *Redargutio Philosophiarum*, (1608), tr. Farrington, 1964.

166 Quoted by Rose-Mary Sargent in *The Cambridge Companion*.

167 "...the intellect is in a manner potentially all objects of thought, but is actually nothing until it thinks: in the same way as in the case of a tablet which has

nothing actually written on it, yet the writing exists potentially. This is exactly the case with the intellect." Aristotle, *De Anima*.

168 For some comments on this kind of truth, see Appendix (3).

169 Bacon's famous essay, *Of Truth*, begins with a reference to Pontius Pilate: "'What is truth?' said jesting Pilate, and would not stay for an answer." Bacon doesn't answer the question, but goes into the matter of why people seem to prefer and obtain comfort from lies.

170 See Michael Polanyi, *Personal Knowledge,* for a profound treatment of these ideas.

171 See Note 53.

172 Athenian democracy depended on the existence of a large slave population. Democracy in the modern world is a very tender flower; without the exercise of "eternal vigilance", human societies at all levels gravitate to dictatorship or oligarchy, punctuated by periods of anarchy—witness the grave difficulty experienced by Waldorf Schools in trying to maintain Steiner's vision of a faculty-run school. ("The condition upon which God hath given liberty to man is eternal vigilance; which condition, if he break, servitude is at once the consequence of his crime and the punishment of his guilt." John Philpot Curran, 1790.)

173 Catherine Drinker Bowen: *Francis Bacon; The Temper of a Man: Fordham University Press*, 1963/1993.

174 Isaac Newton; *Opticks*, Edition of 1730, Dover, New York, 1952; Question 31, p.400.

175 Dobereiner noticed certain groups of three elements, such as chlorine, bromine and iodine, which have similar chemical properties and in which the atomic weight of the middle one is approximately the average of those of the other two.

176 *Letters to Members*, translated by Ethel Bowen-Wedgwood, revised by George Adams (1956). Now published as *The Michael Mystery*

177 See Section (viii).

178 Dornach, 1915. A notary by profession, Brunetto shared in the revolution of 1250, by which the Ghibelline power in Florence was overthrown, and a Guelph democratic government established. He held various offices, including that of secretary to the Commune, took an active part in Florentine politics, and was influential in the counsels of the Republic. A man of great eloquence, he introduced the art of oratory and the systematic study of political science into Florentine public life. Among the individuals who came under his influence was the young Dante Alighieri. In the "Inferno" (Canto XV) Dante finds Brunetto, who had taught him "how man makes himself eternal", among the sodomites.

179 Volume III, Lecture 6.

180 Note Steiner's repeated use of the word "divinity" rather than "spirit." Does absence of divinity mean complete absence of absence of spiritual beings, or only the absence of the beings who had overseen the evolution of human consciousness?

181 Rudolf Steiner: *The Work of Secret Societies in the World—The Atom as Coagulated Electricity*; Berlin, Dec. 23 1904.

182 The Great Instauration.

183 "This story has no moral;/ This story has no end;/ This story only goes to show/ That there ain't no good in men." *(Ballad of Frankie and Johnny.)*

184 Sir Arthur Eddington: *The Philosophy of Physical Science*, C. U. P., 1939, Ann Arbor, 1959.

185 D. G. Rossetti (1828-1882), an English poet and painter, was a founding member of the Pre-Raphaelite Brotherhood, formed in protest against the materialism of industrialized England. Like Maeterlinck, he owes part of his fame to Debussy, who set *The Blessed Damozel* (*La Damoiselle Elue*) for chorus and orchestra in 1893, the year in which he started work on *Pelléas et Mélisande*.

186 Bertrand Russell (1872-1970) was a British philosopher, logician, mathematician, historian, writer, social critic, anti-war activist, and Nobel laureate. At various times, Russell considered himself a liberal, a socialist and a pacifist, but he admitted that he had "never been any of these things, in any profound sense." With A. N. Whitehead he wrote *Principia Mathematica*, an attempt to create a logical basis for mathematics. His work has had a considerable influence on mathematics, logic, set theory, linguistics, artificial intelligence, cognitive science, computer science and philosophy.

187 Sir Arthur Eddington; *The Philosophy of Physical Science*: CUP, 1939; University of Michigan Press, 1958.

188 George Steiner; *After Babel*: OUP, Third Edition, 1998.

189 I apologize if this gives the impression that I think women have less potential than men as physicists or members of any other profession that requires mental or physical agility. I am so old that I can remember the time when, as my English master used to say, "man" embraced "woman." I usually manage to handle such literary dilemmas without excessive numbers of he-or-she's or confusing plurals, but this time I can't.

190 See Keith Francis, *The Education of a Waldorf Teacher*, Iuniverse, 2004.

191 In *The Philosophy of Physical Science*.

192 In *The New Physics*, Cambridge, 1992.

193 Max Born, *Atomic Physics*, trans. John Dougall; Dover reprint of final 1969 edition, Blackie and Son, Glasgow.

194 See Newman and Nagel, *Gödel's Proof*; New York University, 1958—revised edition, ed. Douglas Hofstadter, 2001

Printed in the United States
By Bookmasters